Realism versus Realism

CHHANDA GUPTA

ROWMAN & LITTLEFIELD PUBLISHERS, INC.
Lanham • Boulder • New York • Oxford

This book was originally published as *Realism versus Realism* in 1995 by Allied Publishers Limited, in collaboration with Jadavpur University, Calcutta, India.

ROWMAN & LITTLEFIELD PUBLISHERS, INC.

Published in the United States of America
by Rowman & Littlefield Publishers, Inc.
A Member of the Rowman & Littlefield Publishing Group
4720 Boston Way, Lanham, Maryland 20706
www.rowmanlittlefield.com

12 Hid's Copse Road
Cumnor Hill, Oxford OX2 9JJ, England

British Library Cataloguing in Publication Information Available

Library of Congress Control Number: 2002110795

ISBN 0-7425-1386-6 (cloth : alk. paper)
ISBN 0-7425-1387-4 (pbk. : alk. paper)

Printed in the United States of America

♾™ The paper used in this publication meets the minimum requirements of American National Standard for Information Sciences—Permanence of Paper for Printed Library Materials, ANSI/NISO Z39.48-1992.

In memory of my father

Samirendra Nath Chaudhuri

Contents

Foreword

The book the reader is about to have the pleasure of perusing is a remarkable achievement; it is at once clear enough to introduce a reader who has not previously studied this area of philosophy to a rich and hotly contested area of contemporary—and not only contemporary—metaphysics, and profound enough so that the specialist will come instructed and challenged.

In this brilliant essay, Chhanda Gupta not only develops and defends her own reconciliatory version of realism, but presents and incisively discusses an amazing amount of the contemporary literature concerning realism and anti-realism (and this involves discussing the writing of some of the most celebrated contemporary analytical philosophers). She manages to do all this without ever being pedantic or losing sight of the essential issues. One of the reasons that she is able to accomplish this *tour de force* is her deep appreciation of the fact that these are, in fact, not just contemporary issues; by treating Kant (and even the ancient skeptics) as important participants in the debate, she is able to shed new light on such heavily discussed texts as the writings of W. V. Quine, Donald Davidson, Sir Karl Popper and myself. In addition, she rightly sees the importance of Peirce's contribution for understanding the kind of present-day "internal realism" that she favors. The result is an important and highly readable contribution to the discussion, and one which will not soon become dated.

Hilary Putnam

Preface

"Reality" and "appearance," "objective" and "subjective," "absolute" and "relative" are terms of seemingly irreconcilable contrasts which tend to polarize philosophical viewpoints. The conflict between realism and various forms of anti-realism typically illustrates such polarization. Curiously however, the contrasts which these paired terms express do not divide realists and anti-realists only; they divide realists themselves, entangling them in a civil war. The adversaries locked in fighting both the wars, global and civil respectively, seem to be asking: which of the two terms in each pair is to be given predominance? My main concern in this book is to loosen the grip of these dichotomies and advance a point of view which seeks to resolve the conflict, especially the one I call a civil war: "Realism versus Realism." Hilary Putnam's "internal realism" breaks away from the dichotomies around which the conflict revolves. I shall defend Putnam's immanent realist approach and try to show how this can be applied to resolve the issue between old-style transcendent realists and relativist/subjectivist anti-realists, and also between realists themselves who take opposed stances.

Old-style realism takes a transcendent metaphysical stance, focusing on reality, on what there is in itself independently of what we know or say about it.

Opposed to this are "realisms" that take an immanent stance insisting on the need of linking the question, "what there is?" with the question, "what do we conceive, know and say about it?"

A few points may be noted to make the contrast between these two views leap to vision. They also highlight the main strands of the type of realism I have tried to defend following Putnam's lead.

1. Things exist independently and must be described too in terms that have nothing to do with us, according to transcendent realists. Things have features intrinsically, non-relationally, and not as objects of anyone's belief, thought, experience and knowledge. This is the requirement of absoluteness.

xi

1'. Things and their features do exist independently and are not our own making, the internal realists maintain like all realists. These are not projections and reifications of our own conceptual and cognitive nature, and are in this sense nonepistemic. But internal realism maintains additionally that such realities can be intelligibly talked about only when construed as thinkable, knowable and describable. No meaningful discourse is possible about anything, including its most fundamental features, unless it is an object, at least a putative object of some belief, conception or knowledge. To stress the relativity of things and their features to thought in this way however, is not to deny that things exist whether or not we know or say anything about them. Relativity here means that things which we may or may not know, are not transcendent, that is, they are not trans-conceptual, trans-cognitive and trans-phenomenal.

2. Things and their features according to transcendent realists are radically nonepistemic in the sense of being entirely independent of all beliefs and conceptions. This is another way of saying that all our beliefs and conceptions may remain just as they are and yet reality and truth about reality may be entirely different from what we believe and conceive.

2'. Things and their features according to internal realists on the contrary are nonepistemic *simpliciter*, not radically nonepistemic. They are so in the sense that they are not our own making. The features are real, not projected on to something which does not have them. Nevertheless they are what we conceive and believe them to be (in numerous cases).

3. Transcendent realism perpetuates the reality/appearance divide.

3'. Internal realism rejects the dichotomy. The ways things appear are the ways they really are.

4. Transcendent realists regard the world in itself and things that have intrinsic features by themselves as real. This tempts one to label appearances as unreal. There is no knowing, according to them, whether what appears is really what a thing is by itself. This suits the skeptic's game plan.

4'. Internal realists believe that things really do have the features, even the most fundamental features, which our best available theories conceive and believe them to have. But how can this claim to truth staked on behalf of our best available theories be defended? The very claim that the ways things appear are the ways that they are is suspect. Not all appearances are real. Characteristic statements intended to foil the skeptical game plan include the following:

(i) The internal realists do not put all appearances on a par. Like any other fallibilist, they admit the possibility of error. One conception may be revised by another until through long-drawn investigation the best theories become entrenched. It may still be argued that even erroneous conceptions get entrenched. The answer is Putnam's anti-skeptical argument. Not all appearances are real; but not all are unreal projections either. To make fallibility a plea for saying that all our conceptions are false is to give in to total skepticism which cannot be coherently articulated.

(ii) Some of our beliefs, it follows, must be claimed to be true. But to justify the claim it is not enough to show that skepticism is self-refuting. Something more positive is provided by the kind of transcendental argument which Putnam and Davidson offer. The point of the argument is to show that many of the beliefs held even by proponents of different theories must be assumed to be true. Despite difference, these theorists communicate. Without communication they would not know in what respects they differ. Communication presupposes common shared or coherent beliefs. But coherence itself has to be explained. To explain it, most of our beliefs in a coherent set of beliefs must be assumed to be true. Coherence is due to the fact that things and events about which we have these beliefs are really what we believe them to be.

(iii) This may be supplemented by another "explanationist" argument. The shared and coherent beliefs which are assumed to be true get settled gradually, especially when the truth-seeking investigators experience exactly what they expect and predict on numerous occasions on the basis of such beliefs. These beliefs should be taken as justified true beliefs, for as the explanationist argument seeks to show, this is the best explanation of the successful predictions made on the basis of such beliefs. Hence the declaration for which Putnam has been hailed for inaugurating a new era of interest in realism: realism is the only philosophy that does not make the success of science a miracle.

(iv) This declaration is a development of a view that dates back to Peirce. A provisionally accepted belief fixed by investigators through a long-drawn process is to be regarded as knowledge. For that is the best explanation of the success we do have when we experience the effects which we expect and predict on the basis of such a belief. Putnam however eschews Peirce's utopian idea of "the final opinion" which the investigators are supposed to achieve at the ultimate stage of inquiry. For that comes dangerously close to the notion of "God's eyeview" which he is anxious to avoid.

(v) Truth which is claimed for most of our coherent stable beliefs is not to be reduced to justification. Truth is not justified or warranted assertability per se; it is idealized rational acceptability. But the line between justification and truth that is drawn by bringing in the notion of idealization need not invoke the fantasy of "God's eyeview"! If a statement can withstand all the criticism that is appropriate given its context then that is truth enough. Success in withstanding criticism is what is needed for establishing truth. Critics will persist in accusing the internal realist for making truth depend on success and workability. The answer Putnam gives is: usefulness of true ideas is the result of their agreement with reality. Workability and usefulness do not determine and constitute truth. On the contrary, it is agreement of ideas with reality which explains workability. That an idea agrees with fact is shown when it leads us to what it purports.

Acknowledgments

I am indebted to many, more than I am able to acknowledge, but most of all to my teachers.

I became interested in the theme of this book decades ago while doing doctoral research under Professor D. P. Chattopadhyaya. The thesis, a defense of Karl Popper's realistic cosmology, was a legacy from my teacher, a student of Sir Karl himself. I am indebted to Professor Chattopadhyaya for the help and guidance I have received from him in this project as in every other project I have undertaken so far.

As debating voices of realists and relativists were heard in the years that followed, the influence of Popper's metaphysical realism waned. My views concerning the debate were largely shaped by Professor Pranab Kumar Sen, my teacher and supervisor of post-doctoral research at Jadavpur. I recall with gratitude the numerous discussions we had from which this work has benefited immensely.

Caught up in the cross current of the realist-relativist controversy, I went to Harvard to work under Professor Hilary Putnam. He gave me the access to a new vista which sees realism as a thesis that is compatible with relativism. Showing the way of resolving the conflict, he brought me to a turning point in my intellectual journey making possible the writing of this book. Words seem inadequate for expressing my gratitude for his constant support, extensive suggestions and concern.

A few years after the book was first published, I had the opportunity of auditing a lecture delivered by Professor Michael Krausz at Jadavpur. This was the beginning of a sustained interchange and understanding of each other's ideas. I was delighted to find that he too was moving in the direction I had been following, in search of a reconciliatory ontology that seeks to syncretize opposed perspectives. I am deeply indebted to Professor Krausz for the interest he had taken in my work, and especially for the entire manuscript, he had sent, of his excellent book: *Limits of Rightness*. The book provides a rich, absorbing and informative overview of several irenic ontologies which are resonant with "internal realist" ideas. This instilled in me a desire to reach out to the Western authors who were advancing such reconciliatory views and participate in their conversation. Hence the endeavor to publish the second edition of my book for Western readers, a project for which I have received constant encouragement from Professor Krausz.

I am also grateful to all my colleagues at the Department of Philosophy, Jadavpur University, particularly to Kalyan Sen Gupta, Pradyot Kumar Mukhopadhyay, Tushar Kanti Sarkar, Hiranmoy Banerjee, Amita Chatterjee and my teacher Arun Kumar Mookerjea for helpful comments. I thank especially my friend and colleague Tirtha Nath Bandopadhyay for his involvement with the work from its inception to completion, and for helping me in preparing the index.

Some portions of some chapters overlap the text of a few papers written when the work was in progress. Part of chapter 1 under the title "Has Putnam Turned Renegade?" has been published in *Realism: Responses and Reactions*, edited by D. P. Chattopadhyaya, Sandhya Basu, Madhabendra Nath Mitra and Ranjan Mukhopadhyay (New Delhi: Indian Council of Philosophical Research, 2000). A shorter version of chapter 6 titled "Putnam's Resolution of the Popper-Kuhn Controversy" was published in *The Philosophical Quarterly*, 43, No.172 (July 1993).

Two research grants, a General Fellowship of the Indian Council of Philosophical Research, New Delhi, and a Fulbright Fellowship of the Council for International Exchange of Scholars, Washington, D.C., in 1985-86 supported research which enabled me to begin work for writing this book. I gratefully acknowledge this support. I also acknowledge the support I have received from Jadavpur University for publishing the first edition of this book in collaboration with Allied Publishers. I am grateful to Rajat Bandopadhyay, the Registrar of Jadavpur University, Calcutta, for granting me permission to republish the book in its present expanded form.

My debt to my family is more than words can express. I am grateful to my mother, husband, daughter and son for their enduring love and support. I owe a special debt to my husband, Mukul Gupta. But for his unfailing support at home I would not have been able to move beyond its walls.

Chapter 1

Realism versus Realism: Transcendent and Immanent

Philosophers often get embroiled in global warfare. They are not interested in carving out zones of influence that can peacefully co-exist. For the war they wage is fought with the intent of bringing one contending creed under the hegemony of another. The conflict between realism and its opponents typically illustrates such polarization. I wish to move beyond this polarization.

What lies at the heart of the conflict perhaps, is a firm conviction about the way the world is, independently of the way we take it to be. The conviction stems from the deeply entrenched dichotomy between the notion of "the world as it is in itself " and the notion of "the world as it appears to us." "Reality" and "appearance," or to vary the paired concepts, "world" and "the mind to which it appears," "objective" and "subjective," "absolute" and "relative" are terms of seemingly irreconcilable contrasts. Indeed the deep divide these paired terms suggest, draws the boundary between the polarized zones of influence, and makes it look as though philosophical thinking is bound to move between what apparently are the only viable alternatives: realism and various forms of anti-realism; objectivism and subjectivism; absolutism and relativism; and other similar contrasts.

My concern is to loosen the grip of these dichotomies and advance a point of view that hopes to resolve the conflict. Realism of a particular type, that takes an immanent stance, may help in carving out zones of influence for the contending parties and thereby bring about peace. I will defend this immanent realist approach, particularly that of "internal realism" as authored by Hilary Putnam.

The Way the World Is Independently and the Way We Take It to Be

It is hard to achieve even a cease-fire, it may be said, let alone peaceful co-existence of opposed zones of influence. The effort to reconcile conflicting views, and draw up the terms of a treaty by combining what is right about each, seems pointless according to many. The contrastive positions mentioned above simply will not come to terms.

However, consider whether there really is a clear dividing line between the first members of the three pairs mentioned on the one hand, and the rest on the other, i.e., between realism, objectivism and absolutism on one side, and anti-realism (of various forms), subjectivism and relativism on the other. The line tends to get blurred. In fact, the terms of contrast are not intended to suggest that a realist has to be an objectivist, if for instance, the objectivist is said to be one who disputes the reality of the mind and subjective mental states. For a realist need not be a materialist. On the contrary she can, and does, acknowledge the reality of mental states notwithstanding their dependence on the mind, which shows that the usual characterization of the realist's position in terms of the belief in mind-independent reality is not so clear as it seems to be. Needless to add that the line between objectivism and subjectivism too is not sharp, for inter-subjectivity is a bona fide candidate for objectivity in some sense, though not for "objectivity" in the sense contrasted with subjectivity of both sorts: subjectivity per se and inter-subjectivity. Moreover, relativism as a thesis concerning plurality of conceptual schemes, though usually flaunted as constructivist anti-realism is not incompatible with the type of immanent/internal realism which I wish to defend here. Again absolutism has found vigorous supporters in metaphysical/objective idealism (Hegel) and also transcendental idealism (Kant), and there is no reason to suppose that an absolutist has to be a realist.

Yet, those who are skeptical about the prospect of a cease-fire may point out that the line gets blurred only in case it is drawn between realism, objectivism and absolutism taken conjointly, and similarly anti-realism, subjectivism and relativism together. The sharp divide suggested by the terms of contrast, they might say, is not between one group of "allied forces" in the battle array, and another. Rather consider each pair separately and the contrast will leap to the eye. In each case the adversaries seem to be asking: which of the two terms of contrast in the different pairs is to be given predominance, "world" or "mind," "objective" or "subjective," "reality," or "appearance?"

(i) Are we to focus on the "world," on "what where is" and not on the "mind" in the sense that whatever there is, is what it is by itself irrespective of how and whether it is known by the mind?

(ii) Again, do we not exalt the "objective" as something starkly opposed to the "subjective" because (a) ontologically "objective" is the contrast-term of both "subjective" and "inter-subjective" insofar as these expressions pertain to the mind or anything dependent on it?[1] (b) Moreover, is not the "objective" also exalted because it signifies something that is not constituted, affected and in any way distorted by us, the human subjects?

(iii) Finally, from the fact that "reality" exists independently of us human beings, must we not conclude that it should be *described* too in terms that have nothing to do with humans? An independently existing reality should surely be described in terms of properties which it possesses independently or intrinsically, irrespective of how they appear to us? And only that account of reality should be deemed correct perhaps, which describes it in its own terms, revealing it in just the way it is in itself? Some philosophers call the requirement of giving such an account the "requirement of absoluteness." This demands that one must eschew reference to all subject-related properties, i.e., properties which things possess not by themselves, but only as they appear to experiencing subjects.[2]

Many philosophers however, including realists themselves may hesitate to demand fulfilment of the rigorous "requirement of absoluteness." For the dominant mood of an influential group of realists is fallibilist. Still, even when the aim of *attaining* an absolute, uniquely true description of reality in itself is renounced, the idea that there *is* such an independent reality, intrinsically structured, is not given up. Nor is the possibility of there being such a uniquely true account denied. So fallibilistic realism does not intend after all to loosen the grip of the old idea that there is a deep cut between the "in-itself" and "for us," between "reality" and "appearance."

It is this "cut," and the consequent conviction about the way the world is independently of the way we take it to be, that embroil philosophers in the global war. And although the issues involved in the conflict are too complex to be articulated simply in terms of the contrasts mentioned, the divide which they signify does figure centrally in the massive literature that has grown around the subject. Curiously the "cut" divides not only realists and anti-realists of different stripes. It divides the realists themselves.

As a result a civil war seems imminent. Whether there will be a civil war within the empire of realism however, can be answered only when we answer what it means to call anyone a realist. Old style realists will not consider this to be a civil war. The war is to be fought not within but beyond the frontiers of the empire, they will urge, for the "internal realists" against whom it is waged are anti-realists in disguise. My intention, on the contrary, is to show that Putnam who authors "internal realism" has not turned renegade by becoming anti-realist.

Realisms

In the conflict precipitated by the conviction about the way the world is independently of the way we take it, however, it is old style realism that seems to emerge with the charisma of a superpower. And if there is anything to which it owes its charisma, then it is to be found in its simple conviction that there is a world out there which exists independently of us, and it is this world which we wish to discover, as it is, by itself. There really are things existing independently in it like hills and dales and rivers and seas, whether or not they appear to any mind. The old style realist comes forward as a champion in the homeland of these plain and obvious truths, saving its natives from the xenophobia of fearsome anti-realists who preach the bizarre thesis that there really are not things like hills and dales existing independently of us, and there really are only minds, or even mere ideas, impressions, sensa or whatever.

If "internal realism" strays away from these plain and obvious truths about the absolute independence of things as they are by themselves, then any effort to bring it under the banner of "realism" will meet stiff resistance. It may be accused of inverting standard definitions of "realism." Is the "internal realist" then, an ally of the fearsome enemy, the anti-realist?

It is hard to give a yes or no answer, especially in view of the variety of positions that are given the common label "realism" leaving one wondering: "is there really a single perennial dispute or do we really have several radically different disputes misleadingly appropriating the same name? Philosophical notions, particularly 'isms' often function more rhetorically than cognitively. . . . This seems especially true of 'realism.' . . . One is struck by the chameleon-like character of the notion of realism."[3] Current research on the subject is replete with instances of similar observations: "several distinct and independent positions have at various times been identified with realism, and the debate is marked by confusion, equivocation and arguments at cross-purposes to one another."[4] Notwithstanding these remarks, and variations in approach, it will be misleading however, to hold that the thesis can be fragmented into totally disparate independent positions. There may be types and sub-types; but the minimal common denominator is that one must believe in realities, which are not our own making. Even if one stresses conceptual relativity, one cannot say that the real is our own making or construction, in the way the subjective idealist, and also the transcendental idealist would say they are.

Realists may be concerned with a variety of subject-matters, and so the single thesis "realism" may be unscrambled into a number of "realisms" about a number of different subject-matters, namely universals, physical objects, mental states, theoretical entities postulated by science, mathematics, the past and the future and so on. And realism about some of these subject-matters need not entail realism about the rest. A scientific realist, for example has been likened to an "imperialist" who is trying to colonize the realm of theoretical entities like "mesons," "quarks," etc. in addition to the already existing domain of ordinary observable objects like monkeys and meatballs whose reality few would dispute. She is therefore, sponsoring a thesis of "global realism" so to say. But a realist may steadfastly hold on to realism about observable objects without being a realist about "quarks," "mesons" or "muons." That is to say, an anti-realist about theoretical entities may nevertheless be a realist about meatballs and monkeys. She is a "local realist."[5] Does this indicate a "chameleon-like" character of "realism" that fragments it into "realisms" which represent "distinct and independent positions" as stated above? It does not, for all that it means is that according to some thinkers "global realism" has to give way to "local realism." The relation between "global" and "local" realism is construed here as a whole-part relationship which has got nothing to do with changing or inverting standard definitions of "realism." So although the "global realist" might be compared to an "imperialist," she is not allowing the "local realist" to instigate a civil war within the empire of "realism" itself. Once again the question arises: what is it to be a realist?

Two Realisms: Transcendent and Immanent

A cluster of views standardly accepted as "realism" may be given a common name "transcendent realism" (TR for short). The demand they regard as typically realist is that the two notions of "the way the world is independently" and "the way we take it" must be kept strictly apart. The way things are independently may be said to be transcendent in different senses:

(a) They transcend our concept-forming powers totally. (TR believing in such things may be dubbed trans-conceptual realism.)[6]

(b) They are unknown and unknowable, though thinkable. (TR here may be characterized as trans-cognitive realism.)

(c) They have intrinsic features by themselves, not by virtue of being related in any way to experiencing subjects to whom they may or may not appear. (This variant of TR may be called trans-phenomenal realism.)[7]

"Internal realism" (IR for short) which takes an immanent stance, opposes each of these and the effort to delink the two notions of "the way things are" and "the way we take them to be." The questions "what there is?" and "what do we conceive and say about it?" are indissolubly linked, it urges. And one cannot meaningfully discourse about things which are "transcendent" in any of the senses noted above in (a), (b) and (c). The things we can talk about, and consider ontologically admissible are, according to it, phenomenal, but not unreal on that score, i.e., not unreal for being phenomenal. Even in the case of things with so-called intrinsic features which trans-phenomenal realism talks about, if we take away the reference to how we and our theories or conceptual schemes take them to be, then, we will be left with a bare thought of a noumenal reality it seems, and no vocabulary, no concept to describe such a reality. In other words, taking a transcendent stance threatens to make version (c) i.e., trans-phenomenal realism collapse into version (b) namely, trans-cognitive realism. TR, however, will stick to the claim of delinking the notions of "how things are" and "what we take them as" because linking them up threatens to turn something real and independent into something we *construct* and *project*. If IR switches conceptual constructions in place of independent realities, it must not even masquerade as some form of realism.

　　Will it be proper in that case to describe the feud between two realisms âs a civil war? To say "yes" or "no" one must answer the question: what is it to be a realist? To assess the conflicting claims of TR and IR, I want to ask the question specifically, with reference to some specific subject-matter, say, entities of certain kinds.

Entity Realism

Consider "theoretical entities" like electrons, mesons, quarks for example. One may take very different stances towards them:

　　One may be a realist about the theory of quarks, holding that it is true, or has a claim to truth, inasmuch as the phenomenal laws falling within it are borne out by observed facts. Apparently a theory-realist of this sort will also subscribe to entity realism. For "if you believe a theory is true, then you automatically believe that the entities of the theory exist. . . . What is it to think that a theory about quarks is true, and yet deny that there are quarks?"[8] Still, the same person who believes in the truth of theories can be an anti-realist about theoretical entities, like quarks. For unobservable entities like these can simply be treated as "logical constructions," and the term "quark" as a short via logic for a complex expression referring only to observed phenomena. These observed phenomena alone can be said to exist while the unobserved entities are not believed to exist; they are only posited as "instruments" for predicting some phenomena on the basis of some others. This, needless to add, is anti-realism about entities. Different positions, realist and anti-realist about entities may be listed as follows:

　　(1) Just as one can be an anti-realist about entities without being an anti-realist about theories (understood phenomenalistically), similarly one can be an anti-realist about theories without being an anti-realist about entities. In other words, one can believe in entities without believing in any particular theory in which they are embedded. Entity realism of this kind would simply assert the existence of entities, denying that there is any deep theory giving us true information about what they are like. From the fact that some entity seems to "intervene" in an experimental situation, it may be inferred, at most, that the thing in question is causally effective. But this hardly adds to the meager knowledge of existence *simpliciter*. Strictly speaking, though we know that there must *be* a cause, we do not know *what* it is like. In fact the entity realist is not interested in knowing the nature of the inner constitution of entities, and even maintains, to repeat: "no general deep theory about the entities could possibly be

true for there is no such truth."[9] Entity realism of this shade seems to take a transcendent stance, at least with respect to the question concerning the *nature* of entities. It is reminiscent of what Locke had said about "real essences" which, in the absence of sufficient insight, are "we know not what," and also of Hume's "secret cause" regarding the nature of which we do not have any clear conception. Since the nature of entities is unknown and perhaps even unknowable, in the absence of a "deep theory" about the same, entity realism of this variety may be brought under version (b) of TR, i.e., under trans-cognitive realism.

(2) Some realists however, not only claim that there really are entities like quarks, but also believe that it is possible to discover their intrinsic nature and constitution a posteriori. Can this variety of entity realism be labelled "transcendent" too? Prima facie it cannot. For the entities are not said to elude our concept-forming power; nor are they unknown and unknowable. On the contrary, their nature is supposed to be discoverable a posteriori. Nevertheless it seems to merit the characterization "transcendent." For in trans-phenomenal realism (version (c) of TR) a thing is considered "transcendent" by having whatever nature it has by itself, not by virtue of being taken as something by us and our theories. Moreover, even if we are said to *discover* its nature and not merely *take it* as something, these are matters pertaining to *knowing*; while having an intrinsic nature is a matter pertaining to *being*. This way of delinking being and believing/knowing is just what is demanded by sense (c) of the term "transcendent" in trans-phenomenal realism.

(3) IR by contrast insists on the need of bridging the gulf between being on the one hand and believing/knowing/saying and conceiving on the other. Talk about entities, theoretical or of some other sort must be relativized to what we believe, think and say. Otherwise it will not be meaningful. This calls for an explanation of what is considered "meaningful" in this context.

Realism versus Realism about Entities

When we merely assert the existence of quarks, electrons, etc., denying that there is any theory giving us information about what they are like (as in type (1) of entity-realism above) we are certainly not saying something incoherent. On the contrary, the talk about entities in this case may even be said to be "empirically meaningful" (not just logically coherent). For it is on the basis of experimental inputs that we are talking of a felt or inferred presence of something that "intervenes" in an experimental situation and causes certain effects.

But what exactly is the duty performed here by the description "causes such and such" for shedding light on what is meant by "quark," "electron," etc.? The duty performed is that of *referring*, and that also in a typical way. All that we do with the help of this description is refer to something, to whatever is the cause of such and such, though we do not know *which* entity that is. The use of the description can be characterized as a typical "attributive" use, recalling Donnellan's distinction between the (purely) "referential" and "attributive" uses of a definite description.[10] Notice that both the uses are *referential*, though of different kinds. In the "purely referential" use it does not matter if the description is inappropriate. The speaker has in mind who or what she is referring to, and succeeds in referring even if she chooses an inappropriate description, which therefore is *inessential* for the purpose. In the "attributive" use the speaker does not have in mind objects or individuals she has antecedently identified. Nothing is known about the referent except what the description says, which therefore is *essential*. The entity realist, for instance, knows nothing about the identity of quarks or electrons. There is no deep theory which enables her to identify the entities antecedently. So, although she might be referring to the cause of such and such depending entirely on the knowledge provided by this description, yet the reference she makes, is "blind" not "sighted," as it were, for the speaker does not know *which* entity this cause is.[11] If this is all the information at hand, can entity realism of type(1) be credited with the ability of carrying on a rich and adequate empirically meaningful discourse about quarks, electrons etc.? Is not there much more to meaning than reference? In fact we do not even know whether the description fits the intended referent and therefore whether it is appropriate. As it has been aptly observed: "the very question of appropriateness does not arise here: it arises only when there is an antecedently identified individual which is the intended object of reference, for it is only then that we can ask whether or not the description fits this object."[12]

Can version (2) of entity realism, which applied the general thesis of trans-phenomenal realism to a specific case, fare better in giving a more adequate empirically meaningful account of entities? The main contention of trans-phenomenal realism is that things have built-in features by themselves and not by virtue of being related in any way to experiencing subjects to whom they may or may not appear.

Once again IR will not dispute intelligibility per se of the idea of things with absolute and intrinsic features. Yet the following points may be raised:

(i) Grant that the idea of things-in-themselves possessing features by themselves is intelligible or *thinkable* because it is not incoherent. But what exactly are we able to think of with the help of pure unschematized categories of understanding? Absence of contradiction enables us to think of logically possible thoughts, the logically possible *concept* of a noumenal object, but not of the *object* itself. The real possibility of an object can be thought with the help of categories only in case the object is given in experience. This calls for schematized categories for they alone can apply to things given in experience. Needless to add that the object given in experience, though with the help of schematized categories is not noumenon, the intelligible object of a pure unschematized category.[13] So if trans-phenomenal realism insists that things-in-themselves with built-in noumenal features can be meaningfully talked about, and that meaningfulness derives from being conceived by understanding with pure unschematized categories, then all that it can talk about are bare *ideas*, not *existing objects*. Alternatively, if it does want to talk about "existence" then the object can no more be noumenal, the kind of thing which trans-phenomenal realism is interested in. It would be phenomenal, if of course, "existence" has meaning, as is being urged here, in relation to some empirical context.

(ii) It may be said, however, that we should give up this empiricist bias and admit *non-empirical* meaningfulness. Kant himself seems to have operated with a double sense of meaning. In one sense "meaning can only emerge in the context of possible experience. . . .," in which case "one cannot speak of 'existence' unless the conditions of experience are allowed for." On this score IR may hold that we cannot meaningfully discourse about entities possessing features by themselves without being related in any way to experience. But, as we have seen, there is a second non-empirical sense of meaning, in which "one is free to speak (or 'think') of noumenal existence. . . ." arguably of course, as long as the concept is not self contradictory.[14] However, we have also seen what the intelligibility of the object of an unschematized category has amounted to. "Being completely outside the sphere of those objects which can be given to us. . . ." it cannot be thought through any determinate predicate save what follows analytically from the pure concept itself. If "noumenon" means anything then, it is "the unamplifiable logical possibility that there should be atemporal data. . . ." But this is a far cry from absolutely objective existing transcendent "things as they are in themselves," i.e., the kind of things which trans-phenomenal realism posits.[15]

(iii) It may be pointed out that once we have eschewed the empiricist bias, we need not be put off by the fact that we cannot discourse meaningfully about the real possibility of existing things in the empirical sense of the term "meaning." An entity realist of type (1) taking a transcendent stance may contend, that it does not matter if the intrinsic nature of entities is not given to us in experience. It is enough that its effects are given. And so, without being driven to a bare "unamplifiable logical possibility" of a concept which is not self-contradictory, we can meaningfully talk about an entity, which is "the cause of such and such." But as we have seen, the reference made with the help of this description used "attributively" is "blind," and since we cannot antecedently identify the entity we intend to refer to, we cannot say whether the description, "causes such and such" fits it. In the absence of a fit we can only assert its existence. Can an idea so jejune of just the existence of an object enable us to talk about it meaningfully? Even if we cast aside epistemic considerations and stop demanding that the intrinsic features of the thing be given in experience, can we construe its identity conditions so that it can be considered ontologically admissible? Being unsure of the appropriateness of the only description at hand, how can we identify and reidentify it, and also distinguish it from other entities? At most we can think of an entity that has an identity determined by some inner constitution, which, however, we do not grasp.

(iv) Suppose, however, that the notion of a thing with some inherent constitution which we fail to grasp is not so vacuous as it sounds. In fact, it is such an inherent constitution which determines the identity of the thing in question, enabling us to identify and reidentify it and also distinguish it from other objects. This will be evident if, in lieu of theoretical entities, we consider some other objects, human beings and other natural-kind objects. Suppose, recalling Kripke's example, a baby is born and is baptized "Elizabeth." She is identified as being born of her parents at a particular time with whatever cells and tissues she had then as her constitution. Once the identity of what the term "Elizabeth" refers to is fixed this way, causally by the body itself with the constitution it had at that point of origin, the term will identify and reidentify her in all possible situations including counterfactual. It will distinguish her from another Elizabeth in a counter-factual "twin earth" even if the second Elizabeth had the same life history. This would be the case because she is born of *different* parents and is built of *different* body tissues, cells, etc. "Constitution at the point of origin" in each case settles the matter about identity, and is therefore a perfectly intelligible notion of the sort we had been looking for, in order to pick out things and talk about them meaningfully. Extending the same insight to a natural-kind object, one can say, if gold did actually have the composition it is said to have, namely, atomic number 79, then any other metal in a counter-factual situation having exactly similar phenomenal properties but a *different composition*, cannot be said to be gold just as Elizabeth's double being born of different parents with different tissues and cells cannot be said to be the original Elizabeth.[16]

Why then should IR have qualms about the notion of things with features and constitution they possess intrinsically, and not by virtue of being viewed by us in a certain way? Indeed, Putnam himself had co-sponsored the theory of direct reference with Kripke and Donnellan refusing to assign any role to ways of viewing, concepts and mental representations in fixing reference. We pick out a sample of a certain substance, say gold, he suggested, and annex to it a natural-kind term which is like a name given to it for the first time. From this initial baptism onwards, the term causally linked to the sample will continue to refer to it, and to other similar samples if they have the *same constitution*, because that is what determines their identity. Surely, if gold does have atomic number 79 as its constitution, then the identity statement "gold is that which has atomic number 79" is true. And if a statement of identity is true, then it is true necessarily, as Kripke says. This means "gold" designates or refers to the stuff having this constitution in all possible situations.

However, all this seems to depend on whether the assertion of identity is true. But how the truth of the identification "gold is that which has atomic number 79" is to be established, may raise questions. Saying that this is not an epistemic matter will not be satisfying. Of course I am not disputing Kripke's basic contention that the identification, if true is *necessarily* so, and necessity is metaphysical, not epistemic. But the question is what additional information do we have here for carrying on a meaningful discourse about something which we did not get in the accounts of things with intrinsic features given in (i), (ii) and (iii) above? I am not controverting, as I have just stated, that a purely metaphysical account can legitimately hold, whether anyone knows or not that something made out of something cannot be made out of something else, or something having one constitution cannot have another constitution. But if this be all that we have in our baggage of meaningful talk about entities with built-in features, then we have not gone further than where entity realism of type (1), and attempts to talk about such things sketched in (i), (ii) and (iii) had left us. In fact entity realism of type (2) wanted more; it wanted that the intrinsic constitution be made available to knowledge. That is why possibly Kripke too, felt the need of going beyond Locke's "real essences," of which, Locke himself said we have no clear idea.[17] To discourse meaningfully in an adequate manner we need to be told that things with intrinsic constitution are discoverable a posteriori. This is what Kripke wanted. But if it is hard to establish the truth of the identity-statement, and if it does not matter if it cannot be established, then, one has to go back to Locke it seems, and to his "real essences" which are "we know not what."

The points discussed in (i), (ii), (iii) and (iv) seem to saddle us with a dilemma:

(A) We may opt for TR and maintain that whatever our thoughts and descriptions are to be latched on to in the world outside, must be absolutely independent of us and our ways of describing. But then, as a price of absolute independence we are left with a purely metaphysical image of a thing with *some* constitution of its own—*whatever* that be. This sounds vacuous.

(B) Or, if we want to flesh out this truncated image and want more, a reference to our ways of taking and describing things seems imperative. Perhaps this will be favored by IR?

(B) links up the two questions: "what there is" and "what we take it as." By doing so it seems to reduce the relation of language to reality, namely reference, to a relation of something we have in our mind or "head" to reality. Indeed, if reference to something outside is determined by something "inside," which this reduction suggests, and if this is what the thesis of conceptual relativity of IR demands, then, IR will certainly come under the shadow of a serious doubt as to whether it should be called "realism" at all.

However, does (B) raise this question at all of reducing the reference-relation to a relation in which something "inside" the mind or head determines reference to something "outside"? If it does, Putnam's answer to it is a resounding "no." And obviously IR will not favor (B). The strength of his answer comes from what we have been considering, the theory that reference is fixed directly by a causal relation of the appropriate kind. But if this theory itself is renounced by Putnam, then it might appear that he is defenseless before a view like (B) against which the theory he had hitherto defended was a mounting challenge. This precisely is what prompts his critics to say that he has turned "renegade" after being "at the vanguard of Realism" for years.[18]

My claim on the contrary is that:

(1) Giving up a particular theory of reference, namely, the direct theory of reference, does not imply giving in to a view which this theory challenged, namely,

(B). Saying that reference is not fixed uniquely and solely by a stuff, independently of what we believe, think and say about it, does not mean that it has to be fixed by something in the mind. The latter view remains suspect and Putnam's "no" to it still resounds.

(2) Giving up the old account of reference being fixed causally by the stuff alone to which the word refers, is not tantamount to giving up the notion of reference itself. Putnam gives a new account of language-reality relation.

(3) Even if the new account emphasizes conceptual relativity, this does not turn him into a renegade by ushering in constructivist anti-realism.

Has Putnam Turned Renegade?

The view against which Putnam mounted a challenge has three main planks:

(i) When we understand a word, we associate it with a "concept," which is something we "have in the mind." We associate it with what may be called a "mental representation."

(ii) Two words have the same meaning just in case they are associated with the same mental representation by speakers using those words. "When we say that two words do or do not have the same meaning, what we are saying is that they are or are not associated with the same mental representation."

(iii) The mental representation determines what the word refers to.[19]

The slogan of the challenge against each of these is: "Meanings just ain't in the head." What this conveys is so well-known that it hardly needs restatement. I will briefly recollect some examples to show what absurdities the view "Meanings are in the head" leads to.

Vis-a-vis (i), Putnam does not suggest that there is nothing "in the head" or in the mind when words are used. The use may involve many psychological states. But this must not oblige one to assume, like the view being challenged, that knowing the meaning of a term is just a matter of being in a certain psychological state. It is absurd to equate meaning with psychic states (having images, thoughts in the mind or in the head). Not only do we have images and thoughts, when using the word, say, "tree," but also "the brains in a vat" (BIV for short) in Putnam's science fiction example can have a rich and similar set of proto-thoughts while making verbal responses containing the word "tree" to electronic impulses from a super-computer to which they are imagined to be switched. Similarly, some humans in a different planet who have never seen or even imagined trees may have images qualitatively identical with our mental images of a tree. They have those when, as an accidental result of some spilled paints, for instance, a picture looking like a tree is produced and dropped on their planet. But can we say that by having those mental representations accompanying word-use, the BIV and the humans in the other planet have understood the meaning of the word? If they did, simply by having these images, then surely they would have been able to use the words in the right context and answer questions about what they thought when they uttered the words.[20]

The absurdity involved in equating meaning with something "in the head" as stated in (i) brings out the absurdity of the claim voiced in (ii). Two words, in this case not two words but utterances of the same word are supposed to have the *same meaning* if they happen to be associated with the same mental representations. One has to say that what we mean by the word "tree" is what a BIV or a human of the other planet mean by it. But to say that they can understand what we mean by "tree," is to say something like: an ant which has never seen Churchill, or a picture of Churchill, has depicted Churchill just because by pure chance it has traced lines which look like a picture of Churchill. Saying that this line itself, produced by accidental crawling, represents Churchill is as absurd as saying that the picture resembling tree produced by accidental spilling of paints represents the tree, which is what we mean by the word "tree."[21]

This exposes the absurdity of the third contention of the view against which Putnam's slogan is raised. There is nothing "in my head" or in that of the human in the distant planet, or in the BIV, which can be said to represent intrinsically what it is about, just as there is nothing in the line itself drawn by the crawling ant which can be said to represent Churchill's face. Therefore a mental representation accompanying word-use cannot by itself determine what the word refers to. Obviously Putnam does not give in to this absurd contention.

If "image"/thought, i.e., mental representation of some sort cannot by itself refer to what it is about, then can it borrow its referring ability from something outside? How on earth can something "in the mind or head," an image, reach out and "grasp" an external object of which it is an image? The answer given is a recurrent theme in Putnam's works.[22] What the image of a thing has to borrow from something beyond itself, in order to be an image of the thing, is a causal relation of the appropriate kind to that thing itself. To make something "in the head" latch on to something outside, extra-cranial links to things outside are required. Suppose Oscar on Earth and Twin Oscar on Twin Earth, use the word "water" to refer to water on Earth and twin water on Twin Earth respectively. But if reference is determined solely by something "in the head," as the view which Putnam rejects demands, then Oscar and Twin Oscar must be said to have narrow psychological states, i.e., inner states which they have by themselves, not in virtue of a relation to some external environmental cause. Otherwise how can I say that reference is determined solely by something in the head? And if these states are similar, we will have to say they are referring to the same liquid. But this is not the case. Oscar's word "water"refers to water on Earth, Twin Oscar's to twin water. In fact not only do they refer to two different external objects, but they also have two different intentional contents. And the difference is explained by things external to the mind. Oscar's intentional content is obtained through causal interaction with water, Twin Oscar's through causal interaction with twin water.[23]

Causal connection then, is the very foundation of Putnam's polemic against the view that "meanings inside the head" determine reference. When he gives up the theory that reference is determined just by the stuff itself with which the speaker causally interacts, he strikes at that foundation.[24] Does this stage a comeback for the view which the polemic intends to destroy? The answer "no" still resounds, because Putnam holds: reference is fixed in a different way, and that different way is not to be traced to something "in the head."

Realism without the Causal Theory of Reference

When it is shown that something "in the head" does not have a magical intrinsic power to refer, by virtue of which it gets glued to a stuff outside, one feels tempted to look for the glue in the stuff itself. Perhaps the stuff has the magical power to get stuck to the word. If for instance, I have causally interacted with, say, horses, then these horses themselves give my word "horse" some kind of a lasso with which I manage to pick out these creatures. But then, how can the word lasso the horses I have not causally interacted with? The answer is what has been considered earlier: the word will get glued not only to horses I have causally interacted with, but also to ones I have not interacted with, for the latter are of the *same kind*, or have the *same constitution* as the former.[25] However, the ability to refer successfully to all the creatures falling within the extension of the word "horse" by virtue of their having the same constitution will depend on whether we are able to establish the truth of the identity statement "horse is the creature which has such and such constitution." Since the indentity statement, if true is necessarily true, and since necessity is metaphysical, not epistemic, it really does not matter for the causal theorist, as we have seen, if we fail to establish the truth of the statement in question. But then, will this constitution, which turns out to be something we know not what, enable us to refer successfully, by identifying all the creatures which are supposed to have it? In point of fact it will not be we who identify these creatures in that case, having no knowledge whatsoever about their inner constitution. Reference success, if there is any, will be due to some kind of a magical power which the creatures with their hidden inner constitution allegedly possess. Can we make reference depend on magic?

If there is no magic from either side, word/ thought/ image on the one hand, and stuff on the other, to bring them together, then what is it that can reinstate the world language link? Many things, according to IR, including image and stuff. There is the stuff or substance which partly fixes reference, as shown by the example of water or twin water. Putnam calls this the "contribution of the environment,"[26] or elsewhere, an "experimental input" which is an objective constraint on our thoughts.[27] But he differs from the hard-core realists who subscribe to TR, and to the causal theory of reference, for he takes a new look at the stuffs itself, and also at the manner in which the stuff can be said to contribute in reference fixation. He takes a new look at images too, or the data provided by "experiential inputs."

In the new account which Putnam gives, the stuff is not "trans-conceptual," "trans-congnitive" and "trans-phenomenal" as the three variants of TR believe it to be, as pointed out at the outset. These variants leave us with a purely metaphysical image of a thing with *some* constitution of its own *whatever* that be. It is doubtful whether such a stuff with a constitution which is "we know not what" can allow the word, initially fixed to it, to refer to it continuously, and also to things which presumably share the same constitution. The stuff which does contribute in reference fixation by helping the speakers to identify and reidentify it, and also by aiding the hearer's uptake, is *phenomenal*, not something which is absolutely independent of the way we take it to be.

This does not mean that the way we take it cannot be mistaken. Nor does it mean that such "taking" determines its being what it is. Rather, its being what it is explains why we take it in the way we do take it. The fact remains that such being, if it is to be meaningfully talked about and referred to, must not be something which is totally outside the sphere of things given to us in experience, unless of course by "meaningful" we merely mean "logically coherent." Saying that a thing's being what it is explains why we take it in the way we do, amounts to the claim: things really *are* the way they *appear* to us. This need not usher in constructivist irrealism. For to say that a thing *really has* certain properties, albeit *relationally* to whom they appear, is not to say that those experiencing subjects *impose* or *construct* these properties which the thing does not have. It is only when a thing is believed to be transcendent, having intrinsic non-relational properties which alone are to count as real, that one feels tempted to treat relational properties as unreal appearances.

How is reference fixed by such a phenomenal stuff? Not just by causal interaction with the stuff which directly produces and stores a concept or mental representation in the interacting individual mind. What is wrong with the picture Putnam challenges is that "it suggests that everything that is necessary for the use of language is stored in each individual mind. . . ."[28] Reference according to him, is *socially* fixed and not determined by conditions or objects in individual brains/minds. For example, an individual speaker may certainly interact with a metal she picks out and calls gold, but this by itself is unreliable for reference fixation, and the speaker knows that it is unreliable. That is why she goes to a jeweller or to a physicist or chemist to make sure that the word "gold" does really latch on to a metal which is gold. Reference, thus depending on "linguistic division of labour" is a social phenomenon.[29]

The immediate retort from those who subscribe to some variant of TR will be that IR is now sliding towards sociological constructivism. It is something in the experts' heads or minds this time that *imposes* or *projects* properties on things which do not have them. Moreover, even if we grant that a thing really is the way it appears, how can we say that all the different ways it appears, say to the scientist, or to the jewellers using one kind of test, and to the jewellers using another, are true of gold? Can one stress relativity to conceptual schemes of the scientist, the jewellers, the non-experts, and still avert the drift towards constructivist anti-realism?

Conceptual Relativity Need Not Imply Constructivist Anti-Realism

The answer to the question raised above would be "no" if one subscribed to any of the following contentions:

(i) Images in the heads of experts or non-experts by themselves fix reference.

(ii) There is no knowing whether all that appears, to experts or non-experts, is really the case. All that they believe or take as real may be false constructions.

The slogan "Meanings just ain't in the head" is an outright rejection of (i). Moreover, in the new account of reference as a social phenomenon, Putnam emphasizes that what fixes reference is not something stored in an individual mind. Even if he acknowledges the role of "experiential inputs" in reference fixation, the way in which the experienced data play this role, according to him, is very different from what the traditional theorists of meaning believe about it. The traditional theorists focus on the images or the data themselves, thinking that these have a magical power to get hooked to things outside. Putnam, by contrast, focuses not just on the images or data, but on the *ability* of the speakers who have them to relate and use them in a right manner in right circumstances. The BIV may have images of things even when the things cease to exist. For the images of things like trees in their case are never produced by real trees. So it does not matter whether real trees exist or not for them to have these images. If images could intrinsically refer, this would not have been the case. The reason why Real-worlders, unlike the Vat-worlders, can refer, is not just by having images, but by having the ability to use these in situationally appropriate and coherent ways. What restores the world-language link is the ability of the speakers to use, connect and coherently relate the data, and also the consequent ability to act appropriately in actual empirical transactions with things outside.

Yet, there may be misgivings about the possibility of restoring the referential link in this way. Perhaps this could be more solidly established if the conceptual link the mind or language has to the world is said to be "necessary," in the sense given to it by Kant's "transcendental idealism." But in that case IR will have to pay the price Kant paid. For with *which* world can we have a necessary conceptual link? It would only be the unreal world, since in Kant's dualistic metaphysics the "empirically real" world has the ontic status of mere appearance. If anything is real it is the world behind, the noumenal world.

Putnam rejects trans-cognitive and trans-phenomenal realism, and therefore will not endorse the noumenal/phenomenal divide. But even if we stay within the bounds of the phenomenal world, will it be possible to establish the link between mind/language and reality more solidy by taking the Kantian route of "transcendental idealism," in exactly the same way in which Kant had taken it? Putnam's later philosophy has been rightly described as an endeavor to "participate in a single project: to inherit, reassess, and appropriate Kant's philosophical legacies." However, though IR is a flowering of the overall Kantian perspective, it does not seek simply to rehabilitate the specific solutions Kant himself proposed.[30] And so, Putnam does not try to strengthen the link between mind/language and world, by tracing necessary truths which our beliefs and judgements about the world (supposedly) enshrine, to transcendental conditions in the mind. He does not hold like Kant that our beliefs and judgements, say, about persistence of substances, and causal relation between events, are necessarily true of phenomenal things and events because, all of us who experience these have certain innate concepts and principles in our minds. He does not think that beliefs and judgements of this sort are necessarily true inasmuch as it is impossible for us to experience substances as things which are not permanent, and events as happenings which are not caused. Nor does he say that it is impossible for us to do so because our minds work in the way they do, being equipped innately with certain concepts and principles.

Yet whatever Putnam holds or does not hold in this respect, must we make this assumption about the working of the mind at all, to secure stronger foundation for the mind-world link? Why must we assume that our minds must have innate concepts like "substance" and "cause," and innate principles like, all changes are merely changes in the states of permanent substances and "every event has a cause"? Is Kant's answer that these constitute the sole explanation of the possibility of our experience of enduring and causally inter-acting objects, plausible? There could be other alternative explanations of such experience? Moreover, it is doubtful whether Kant's argument proves that all human beings must believe these principles to be true. Kant, no doubt has gone beyond Hume when he contended that no experience like ours would be possible unless we did act in this way, while Hume admitted only that in practice we cannot help acting as if we believed the law of causation to be true. Still this seems to be "a supplement to Hume and not an answer to him," as long as it remains doubtful whether Kant's argument has proved beyond doubt what all human beings believe to be true.[31]

But then, if neither the coherently related data of experience, nor the transcendental necessity about phenomenal things and events can solidly establish the mind-world or language-reality link, must we say that all our beliefs, conceptual constructions and judgements are false? Certainly not. In fact this cannot even be articulated coherently, as Putnam shows by exposing the self-refuting nature of the skeptical claim. If the skeptic's statement "I know nothing" is true, then what she says is false, because to make this statement true, she must in fact know nothing, including her own statement.

However, for reinstating the realists' claim that we do have knowledge of the way things are, more is required than showing that skepticism is self-refuting. This is provided by a transcendental argument which both Putnam and Davidson give in defence of realism.[32] It is the argument that something must be assumed to be true if some of our beliefs, thoughts and discourses, and also the right use of the same, are to be rendered possible and intelligible. What has to be assumed is that most of our beliefs in a coherent total set of beliefs are true. But what is it that allows us to say that these beliefs are true? Mere coherence cannot; nor transcendental concepts and principles possessed by human minds. What does, is the argument that unless these cohering beliefs are assumed to be true, the coherence of the person's own beliefs and that of her beliefs with others' will not be possible or intelligible. The coherence is due to the fact that objects and events about which we have these beliefs are really what we believe or take them to be. What the transcendental argument must assume to be true in this case is something about *objects*, maybe phenomenal objects, but objects nonetheless. It is not something about human *minds*, and the way they presumably work, as in the case of Kant's "transcendental idealism."

Different believers may take the same object differently and hold different beliefs from different points of view, like jewellers using different tests for making sure that something is gold. This does not turn their accounts into false conceptual constructions. Take a bowl of soup, to take another example. Using a spoon of one size we may say that it contains twenty spoonfuls; using a bigger spoon we may say it contains half the quantity. Both accounts are true and what makes them true is how much the bowl contains objectively.[33] Unless it is assumed that it really contains a certain quantity, it would not have been possible to give these two, or many other measurements. Even when we say it has such and such quantity we are using one kind of description, different from some other, say, the physicists', in terms of its atomic constitution. But this does not render the kind of description used false any more than the alternative measurements depending upon it are false. The presumption of the transcendental argument is that the bowl really has a certain quantity of soup we believe it to have, though relationally to one way of taking it. Minus the presumption we cannot answer why we continue to hold on to this belief which tallies with many others.

To claim truth for this belief, and also for other beliefs which belong likewise to a coherent set, we do not need objects that are trans-conceptual, trans-cognitive and trans-phenomenal. Even if objects appear to our conception, cognition and experience in a certain way, that way does not forfeit its right to be considered objective simply because it *appears* to be such and such. Objects, about which a rich and adequate empirically meaningful discourse is possible, seem to be stubbornly phenomenal, but not unreal for being phenomenal. Conceptual relativity need not drift towards constructivist anti-realism. After years at the vanguard of realism Putnam has not abandoned the cause, just because he does not embrace Kant's "transcendent realism" or any other version of TR.

As long as one pledges support to Kant's "transcendent realism" and contends that if anything is real, it is the noumenal world behind, the threat of the drift towards constructivist anti-realism will loom large. The appearance will continue to be looked upon as an unreal projection or construction, perpetuating what has been described as the scheme and content dualism. But Putnam finds an answer that takes one beyond the polarized worlds of noumena and phenomena, beyond the content-scheme dualism, in Kant's own philosophy. He writes:

> Locke held that the great metaphysical problem of realism, the problem of the relation of our concepts to their objects, would be solved just by natural scientific investigation, indefinitely continued. Kant held that Locke was wrong and that this philosophical question was never going to be solved by empirical science. I am suggesting that on this subject Kant was right and Locke was wrong. . . . Since the birth of science thousands of years ago we have bifurcated the world into "reality"— what physical science describes— and appearance. . . . This is an error, and a subtle version of Locke's error. The "primary/ secondary" or "reality/ appearance" dichotomy is founded on and presupposes what Kant called "the transcendental illusion"—that empirical science describes (and exhaustively describes) a concept-independent, perspective-independent reality.[34]

Notes

1. This need not imply that a realist does not admit mind and mental states as pointed out in the text already. Mind-independence here pertains to a noetic relation. A thing, whatever it is, physical or mental, is mind-independent in the sense that it may or may not be known by the mind. The question: whether or not a mental entity *exists* is a seperate question from whether or not anyone *believes* it exists. This is held especially by those thinkers who reject both the "incorrigibility thesis" and the "self-intimation thesis" about the mental. Devitt however takes care to distinguish realism about the mental from idealism of different types. See Michael Devitt, *Realism and Truth* (Princeton, N.J.: Princeton University Press, 1984), 13.

2. I take this requirement as a distinctive feature of one variant of old-style "transcendent" realism which is described in the third section of this chapter as "trans-phenomenal realism." The notion of an "absolute conception of the world" from which the requirement stems, is explained by Bernard Williams in his book: *Descartes: The Project of Pure Enquiry* (Harmondsworth, Middlesex: The Harvester Press, 1978), 64-66, 236-46.

3. C. F. Delaney, "Presidential Address: Beyond Realism and Anti-realism," *Proceedings of the American Catholic Philosophical Association* (1985), privately circulated.

4. Paul Horwich, "Three Forms of Realism," *Synthese*, 51 no. 2 (1982), 181.

5. Ian Hacking, *Representing and Intervening* (Cambridge: Cambridge University Press, 1983), 95.

6. Richard Rorty characterizes this view as "Intuitive Realism." Exponents of this view contend that philosophers who contradict this thesis believe in the ubiquity of language.

They do not realize that problems that typically bother the realists arise where language and our concept-forming abilities prove inadequate to facts. See Richard Rorty, *Consequences of Pragmatism* (Brighton, U. K.: Harvester Press, 1982), xxiii.

7. These names were suggested by Pranab Kumar Sen.

8. Hacking, *Representing*, 27.

9. Hacking, *Representing*, 27-28. Hacking refers to Nancy Cartwright who holds such a view. Hacking's own realism about entities is similar to Cartwright's, for both controvert the contention that belief in entities depends on belief in a theory in which they are embedded.

10. Keith Donnellan, "Reference and Definite Descriptions," in *Naming, Necessity and Natural Kinds*, ed. Stephen Schwartz (Ithaca, N.Y.: Cornell University Press, 1977).

11. I owe the point I am trying to establish making use of Donnellan's distinction to Pranab Kumar Sen. Sen discusses the point in his book *Reference and Truth* (New Delhi: Indian Council of Philosophical Research in association with Allied Publishers, 1991), 37-42.

12. Sen, *Reference*, 42. This is not to say that there is any possibility of the object deviating from the description. But the point is that there is no independent evidence testifying to the nature of the transcendent entity. It is only from more general considerations regarding the phenomena we are trying to explain that it is inferred that there is or must be "such and such" a cause.

13. The point is discussed persuasively by Eric C. Sandberg in "Thinking Things-in-themselves," *Current Continental Research 603, Proceedings of the Sixth Interntional Kant Congress*, Vol. 11/2 (1989), ed. Gerhard Funke and Thomas M. Seebohm (Lanham, Md.: Center for Advanced Research in Phenomenology and University Press of America,1989), 24-26.

14. Gerd Buchdahl, "Kant: from Metaphysics to Transcendental Logic" in his book *Metaphysics and the Philosophy of Science*, (Oxford: Basil Blackwell, 1969), 534. Emphasis mine.

15. Jonathan Bennet, *Kant's Analytic* (Cambridge: Cambridge University Press, 1966), 24. The term "unamplifiable" highlights the fact that noumenon cannot be thought through any determinate predicate save those which follow analytically from the pure concept itself.

16. Saul Kripke, "Naming and Necessity," in *Semantics of Natural Language*, ed. D. Davidson and G. Harman (Dordrecht: Reidel, 1972), 313-14, 318-19.

17. "When a man says gold is *malleable*, he means . . . something more than this, . . . viz., . . . *what has the real essence of gold*. . . . But . . . by this tacit reference to the real essence the word *gold* . . . comes to have no signification at all, being put for somewhat whereof we have no *idea* at all, and so can signify nothing at all." This excerpt from Locke's *Essay*, III, ix and x, is borrowed from J. L. Mackie, *Problems from Locke* (Oxford: Clarendon Press, 1976), 95.

18. Devitt, *Realism*, 182.

19. Hilary Putnam, *Representation and Reality*, (Cambridge, Mass.: MIT Press, 1988), 19-20.

20. Hilary Putnam, *Reason, Truth and History*, (Cambridge: Cambridge University Press, 1981), 3-8.

21. Putnam, *Reason, Truth*, 1, 4.

22. Hilary Putnam, "The Meaning of 'Meaning'" in his *Mind, Language and Reality, Philosophical Papers*, vol. 2 (Cambridge: Cambridge University Press, 1975). See also chapter 1 of Putnam, *Reason, Truth*.

23. See Michael Devitt, "Meanings just ain't in the head," in *Meaning and Method, Essays in Honour of Hilary Putnam*, ed. George Boolos (New York: Cambridge University Press, 1990), 81-83, 85.

24. Putnam, *Reason, Truth*, chapters 2 and 3.

25. Putnam, *Reason, Truth*, 53.

26. Putnam, *Representation*, 30-31.

27. Putnam, *Reason, Truth*, 54.

28. Putnam, *Representation*, 25.

29. Putnam, *Representation*, 22-23. A comparable account of the social dimension of "reference" in actual communication situations involving much more than what a sign in the signifier's head is said to possess intrinsically, is given by D. P. Chattopadhyaya in his book *Anthropology and Historiography of Science* (Athens, Ohio: Ohio University Press, 1990), 103-7.

30. See introduction by James Conant in Hilary Putnam, *Realism with a Human Face*, ed. James Conant (Cambridge, Mass: Harvard University Press, 1990), xviii, xxiii.

31. C. D. Broad, *Kant: An Introduction*, ed. C. Lewy (Cambridge: Cambridge University Press, 1978), 15.

32. Donald Davidson, "A Coherence Theory of Truth and Knowledge," in *Kant oder Hegel*, ed. Henrich Dieter (Stuttgart: Klett-Cotta, 1983), 428-30.

33. This is Pranab Kumar Sen's example. He uses it to explain the point which Putnam is seeking to establish with the example of "mereological sums" in his book: *The Many Faces of Realism*, The Carus Lectures, 1985, Lecture I (La Salle: Open Court, 1987).

34. Putnam, *Realism, Human Face*, 162.

Chapter 2

The Way the Real Appears Is the Way It Is

Kant's insight into the incoherence of the idea of a concept-independent, perspective-independent reality became the corner-stone of Putnam's later philosophy. It culminated in the claim central to internal realism (IR), namely, the way the real appears is the way it *is*. This of course is not tuned to Kant's "transcendent realism," which in fact opposes the claim by perpetuating the reality/appearance divide. The insight to which the claim owes its inspiration is the one which underpins the "Copernican" or "transcendental" turn in Kant's philosophy, the turn which did away with the appearance/reality divide. The reality, needless to say, in this context is *phenomenal*, not *noumenal*. Putnam fell heir to this transcendental turn. The real which *is* the way it appears, according to him, is the "empirically real."

Conceptual Relativity and Constructivism in Transcendent Realism

It seems to me, as I have said, that as long as one adheres to Kant's "transcendent realism" and preserves the label "real" for the "noumenal," one will preserve the temptation too of treating "appearance" as an unreal projection. One will be tempted to treat it as something which we *impose* or *project* upon something else, namely, the noumenal, which does not have what we impose upon it. For to embrace dualism of noumena and phenomena is to stick to the assumption that there is a clear line of distinction to be drawn between properties which things-in-themselves have by themselves, and the properties which we *project* upon them. And if projection means what Putnam says it means, namely, "thinking of something as having properties it does not have," it seems obvious that noumena cannot have the properties we project upon them.[1] In fact even if we did not stop to consider what *projection* itself is supposed to be, we cannot say, within the ambience of Kantian philosophy, what noumena have, or have not got. They are unknowable.

We cannot even say that they have the properties we *think* they have, except those of course that follow analytically from the concept of "noumena." We cannot say on this reading of Kant, and within the bounds of "transcendent realism" that the real *is* the way it appears.

To repeat, on this reading, given the *noumenal* sense of the "real," the so-called "empirically real" appearance will be construed as a projection, as an "unreal" *conceptual construction*. Indeed, the insistence on the real character of "noumenal reality" and on the unreal character of "appearance" is not peculiar to the Kantian version of "transcendent realism," i.e., "trans-cognitive realism" alone. It figures prominently in other versions too, in what is characterized (in chapter 1) as "trans-phenomenal realism" for example. The insistence, in fact, is the expression of an intuitive idea that is passionately held by realists by and large. It is the idea that reality and truth about reality are *entirely independent* of our conceptions and beliefs. Since realists insist that these are entirely independent, they can even go to the extreme of holding that *all* our conceptions and beliefs may go wrong. For it is quite possible that "our beliefs might be just as they are and yet reality—and so the truth about reality—be very different."[2] According to this intuition about the total independence of reality and truth then, both reality and truth turn out to be "radically non-epistemic" (as Putnam says while characterizing "transcendental realism"). Or, in Dummett's phrase, they are "evidence-transcendent."[3]

But to view reality and truth in this way as "radically non-epistemic" is to maintain, as just stated, that they would be just as they are by themselves, totally unrelated to whatever belief we may have about them. And this means all our beliefs may conceivably be false. Paradoxically, in that case, the intuition so dear to realists of the "transcendent" stripe would make for skepticism, not realism. Putnam opposes "transcendent realism" of this kind, which maintains that realism is compatible with the *possibility* of *all* our beliefs going wrong. So, he cannot be accused of subscribing to a thesis which tends to treat our beliefs as erroneous, and what we believe as *false conceptual constructions*, on the pretext that "our beliefs might be just as they are and yet reality—and so the truth about reality—be very different." He does not hold like the transcendent realist that reality as conceived, believed and known is *not* the same as reality as it is independently of our conception and knowledge. In other words, he does not believe that the world as it appears is constructed by our minds, while the world as it is in itself alone is real. He holds on the contrary, that reality as known is *the same* as the independent objective world which is not our own making. The way we conceive and know it is not something we project or impose upon the way things are, independently and intrinsically.

Conceptual Relativity and Constructivism in the Immanentist Context

It seems that the kind of constructivist anti-realism which "transcendent realism" (TR) portends, dismissing "appearance" as unreal, has its genesis in a metaphysical conviction. The conviction is that only that can qualify as "real" which exists in itself, having features entirely independently and intrinsically. The way a thing *appears* to us, it follows, is likely to be construed as something *different*, different from the entirely independent real. Putnam defends conceptual relativity. He finds no sense in the talk about entirely independent transcendent realities. We can meaningfully discourse only about what appears to us, about what we view from within our conceptual schemes. "*What objects does the world consist of?* is a question," he writes, "that . . . only makes sense to ask within a theory of description."[4] Still, the kind of constructivism which TR portends, is not to be attributed to him. For he does not share the metaphysical conviction which seems to be the breeding ground of this sort of constructivism.

But constructivism may have a lineage which is not to be traced simply to a metaphysical conviction of this sort. It may have its genesis elsewhere, in Kant's theory of knowledge, for instance, and also in other works that have inherited the constructivist perspective of that theory. This is the kind of constructivism one reckons even in that context where we speak of *phenomenal* or *empirical* reality. Can Putnam be said to have accepted constructivism of the Kantian type which we confront in that *immanentist* context? In what follows I have tried to trace the lineage of constructivism in the immanentist context to Kantian epistemology, and I think even this brand of constructivism cannot be attributed to Putnam.

In the immanentist context, i.e., in the context where we speak of *phenomenal* or *empirical*, not noumenal reality, constructivism does not seem to be premised on the kind of reasoning that is emphasized by different varieties of TR as enumerated in chapter 1: "trans-conceptual," "trans-cognitive" and "trans-phenomenal." The reasoning of these varieties of TR, generally speaking, is that since things do appear to us in experience, we are bound by logic to admit something which appears. This something of which appearances are appearances, cannot itself appear to us in just the way it is *in itself*, for if it does, it will be an "appearance," not *that* of which the appearances are appearances. It follows then, that the thing of which an appearance is an appearance must be construed as something *different*. And the difference may be expressed by the advocates of different types of TR as follows:

(a) Reality which is beyond the reach of human conception could be very different from whatever we conceive or think of, for our thought, conceptual ability and language may be inadequate for giving a faithful description of it as it is *in itself.* (This is how trans-conceptual realism would express the difference between reality and appearance, between the *in itself* and *for us*.)

(b) The noumenal realities of which appearances are appearances, must be different from appearances. If appearance in the sense of phenomenal object is an object of experience, then noumenon which is different from phenomenon cannot obviously be the possible object of experience. It cannot be the object of knowledge also, to be which according to this version of TR, it has to be a possible object of experience. (This is how the difference in question is expressed in trans-cognitive realism.)

(c) Trans-phenomenal realism too shares the conviction concerning the dichotomy between the *in itself* and *for us* with other variants of TR. But it does not maintain that the in itself is *unknowable*. In this respect it controverts trans-cognitive realism. Nevertheless it retains the basic distinction, emphasized by all forms of TR, between what is real and what appears, between the real *as it is* and the real *as known*.

Prima facie this sounds paradoxical, because how can one say that the real *as known* is different from the real *as it is* when "to know" means to be aware of what really is the case? However, this will not seem paradoxical if we view the matter from the fallibilist perspective. From the fallibilist perspective one may say that one can *have* knowledge *in fact* of what really is the case and yet at the same time not *know that one knows.* A fallibilist is ready to accept something as knowledge even though it may not be *recognized* as such. She will not withhold the term "knowledge" from what a human inquirer regards as a *purported* true description of what really is the case. So, she may claim to know, in spite of being a fallibilist and in spite of the fact that "to know" means to be aware of what really is the case. This is the weaker sense of the term "knowledge" according to which even tentatively accepted knowledge, say "knowledge 1" may rank as true knowledge, i.e., knowledge revealing final truth, although it cannot be *recognized* as such. It is in this weaker sense that a fallibilist can claim to have knowledge of the real as it is, controverting trans-cognitive realism. However, the stronger sense of the term "knowledge" demands not only *having* knowledge of the real as it is, but also *recognizing or knowing that* one has such knowledge. Since the foolproof justification requisite for recognizing it as such is not available to the fallible inquirer, "knowledge" in the stronger sense of the term is not achievable. In the absence of a foolproof justification, "true knowledge" revealing final truth, characterized as "knowledge 2," remains an unattainable limit of inquiry. And in that case tentatively accepted "knowledge 1" can at most be said to *approximate*, and not count as true knowledge or "knowledge 2."[5] Such being the case, trans-phenomenal realism of the fallibilist brand has to admit a distinction which it does admit, the distinction between "knowledge 1" approximating "knowledge 2" on the one hand, and "knowledge 2" itself on the other. So the cut between *the real as it is in itself* and the *real as known* (in the weaker sense of the term "known") remains, the former being the object of true "knowledge 2," the latter the object of putative "knowledge" or "knowledge

1." The point has been eloquently expressed by Popper:

> The gods did not reveal, from the beginning,
> All things to us; but in the course of time,
> Through seeking we may learn, and know things better.

> But as for certain truth, no man has known it,
> And even if by chance he were to utter
> The final truth, he would himself not know it;
> For all is but a woven web of guesses.[6]

Constructivism in the immanentist context however, is not based on considerations and reasoning of this sort. Rather, it can be taken as a corollary of a particular theory of knowledge, as noted before, that is tagged typically to Kant's immanent metaphysics of experience. So construed, constructivism is to be understood against the backdrop of such a metaphysics—"a truly empiricist philosophy, freed, on the one hand, from the delusions of transcendent metaphysics, on the other, from the classical empiricist obsession with the private contents of consciousness."[7] In this "truly empiricist philosophy" and in the theory of knowledge that goes hand in hand with it, reason is not allowed to delude itself by supposing that it is possible for it to know things-in-themselves that are inaccessible to experience. However, how do we know the objects which are accessible to experience? In a philosophy freed from the classical empiricist obsession with private contents of consciousness, we cannot suppose that one starts with discrete and fleeting sense-impressions, and then reaches out to the objective world of durable objects, working outwards, as it were, from the private data of sense. But then, how can it be possible at all to have knowledge of durable, independently existing objects which are accessible to experience—of objects belonging to the ordinary world which we do know? Kant's answer is well-known. If experience offers nothing except fleeting and private sense impressions, then the classical empiricist endeavor of moving from this changing private basis to durable public objects is futile. The gap between the changing and the constant, the private and the public, the subjective and the objective, according to him, cannot be filled by imagination as Hume had suggested. Rejecting the classical empiricist answer, Kant answers the question by turning to a priori concepts and principles the use and application of which make knowledge of durable external objects possible. The a priori here has a special sense. It is not just that which is not derived from and independent of experience, and certainly not what yields an infallible intuitive grasp of objects inaccessible to sense experience. It is a priori in the *transcendental* sense, i.e., in the sense of being something which is the necessary condition of the very possibility of knowledge of the empirical objective world. And also, it is a priori, in the sense that it originates from the mind, for the concepts and principles, which are a priori in this sense, are integral parts of the structure and workings of minds of beings like ourselves. The a priori concepts and principles which make knowledge of objects possible are what our minds are natively equipped with. Kant's answer regarding the possibility of human knowledge of enduring interacting objects of the external world thus, is seen to depend on a thesis about the structure and working of the human mind. Investigation of the a priori ideas and principles presupposed in all our empirical knowledge is to be seen primarily as an investigation into the structure and workings of the cognitive capacities of human minds.[8] The answer to the question how we can have knowledge of durable external objects then, is that we experience and think about the world as having such objects because this is how *we are made* to think about the world.

I have pointed out already (in chapter 1) that even if we believe that the world has persistent substances and casually interacting objects and events, the truth of our beliefs need not be traced to transcendental conditions in the mind. Putnam does not hold like Kant, I said, that our beliefs and judgements about persistence of substances, and causal relation between events are necessarily true of phenomenal things and events, because all of us who have these beliefs have certain innate concepts and principles in our minds, or, because we are made in a certain way, to put it differently. In fact, he might not endorse the idea that it is impossible for us to experience substances as things which are not permanent, for this impossibility, implied by transcendental necessity, is something which an absolutist, not a pluralist like him, will rigidly maintain. Putnam embraces Kant's immanentism; he welcomes Kant's contention concerning the relativity of the (empirical or phenomenal) real to human thought, to a conceptual framework, but does not believe in the absoluteness of a single conceptual framework. He echoes Kant's claim that the object of belief or knowledge is not transcendent, and that such an object must be thought of as something which is indissolubly linked with our way of conceiving it. But he does not think that (a) there is only *one* way of conceiving it, and that (b) the object is in fact what we take it or conceive it as, *because* we are *made* to think of it as such. It is one thing to say that the real *is* just the way it appears to us, or even that it *is* what we conceive it as; it is quite another to say that it appears as such and such because we are made this way or that. It is in the latter case it seems that the way the real is (phenomenally), turns out to be a consequence of how we are made, and therefore something which we or our minds manufacture and project. Putnam's immanentism exalts conceptual relativity, but minus absolutism and constructivism.

It may be alleged that this is not a right reading of Putnam. For to deny the constructivist strain of his thesis of conceptual relativity is to go against the letter of his text. " 'Objects' do not exist independently of conceptual schemes" he writes. "We cut up the world into objects when we introduce one or another scheme of description.... 'Objects' themselves are as much *made* as discovered, as much *products* of our conceptual invention as of the 'objective' factor in experience."[9] Citations of this sort are invariably encountered in Putnam scholarship where critics chorus that he has turned renegade by paving the path for constructivist anti-realism. And so these would be hurled as textual counter-evidences at anyone who attempts to give an anti-constructivist reading of the kind I am trying to defend here. Still, I do not think that it is right to label Putnam's thesis of conceptual relativity as "constructivist" in any of the two senses of the term suggested above, i.e., in the sense given to it, in the context of transcendent realism (in the previous section), and in the sense given to it in the immanentist context (in this section).

Constructivism and Scheme Content Dualism

It is true that the thesis of conceptual relativity is widely believed to have a companion creed, "constructivism," by its side. But this is because the philosophers who hold this belief have been "held captive by a certain picture—the picture which Davidson calls 'the dualism of scheme and content' and which Dewey thought of as 'the dualism of Subject and Object.' "[10] The picture, generally speaking is of two disparate ontological domains, one containing pieces of thought or beliefs, and the other what these beliefs are about.

Thinkers "held captive" by this picture have to explain the relation between the two. The relation between the disparate items, beliefs and thoughts on the one hand, and what these beliefs/thoughts are about on the other, is construed as *correspondence*. To establish that such correspondence occurs, the beliefs and thoughts which are on the "scheme" or "Subject" side have to be confronted with the things which are on the "content" or "Object" side. But how can these items which are so disparate be related in a way that would make one the copy of the other? How can beliefs be confronted and eventually matched with non-beliefs? If the correspondence relation is to obtain at all between these items, then, the philosophers committed to the "scheme-content" or "Subject-Object" dualism must somehow show that the disparate items are homogeneous. No wonder homogeneity or similitude had been a key idea in the oldest form of the correspondence theory which many scholars attribute to Aristotle. The belief in an external object will be made true, according to this theory, if the mind's image of the external thing, namely, "phantasm" represents, or is *similar* to the external object in the sense of sharing its form. "The mind, in having available the phantasm, also has directly available the very *form* of the external object."[11] But then, the difficulties which plague the advocacy of scheme-content dualism, and also the effort to overcome the dualism in this way are obvious. Firstly can I have a three feet long *mental image* of a table which is three feet long? "Physical length and subjective length must be different."[12] Secondly, it is impossible for us to get beyond our thoughts, images, beliefs, to a vantage point from where we can compare these items on the "Subject" side with those that are on the "Object" side, to see whether the former correspond to the latter. Faced with such difficulties, and committed to "scheme-content" or "Subject-Object" dualism, the philosophers, per force, have to take constuctivist routes it seems. If they have to show that the disparate items do not fall apart, and that heterogeneous elements can be transformed into homogeneous ones, then, the courses available to them seem to be the following. Putnam however, does not avail of any such course.

Each course involves a constructivist maneuver:

(a) The only way to avoid the gap created by dualism, and save correspondence, some thinkers may feel, is to follow Berkeley's lead. So idealists generalizing Berkeley's point will say: "nothing can correspond to a representation except a representation."[13] That is, if no representation, mental image or idea can refer to anything save another representation, then all that these images correspond to will be representations. All that can be talked about, referred to, and thought to exist will be such representations. Now this may secure homogeneity, and so save correspondence, but only by having recourse to reductionism. The balance will tilt totally to the "scheme" side, ending in a re-description of reality as consisting of representations or ideas only. Physical objects, on the contrary, will turn out to be *projections* being treated as *constructions* out of what is really there, namely, ideas. Physical objects, that is to say, will be no part of reality. Berkeleyans consider physical object talk as a derived talk, which must be reduced to a talk about ideas. So far, these philosophers are reductionists with respect to one kind of things, namely, physical objects, and so far, reductionism entails constructivist anti-realism about physical objects. Berkeleyan reductionists however are not anti-realists all the way down. They reduce the list of what there really is, by applying Occam's Razor, but they are convinced nevertheless about the reality of the things constituting the reducing class, namely, ideas or mental representations. Putnam is not a constructivist of the Berkeleyan brand. He is a realist all the way down, with respect to both physical objects and mental representations, and many other things.

(b) Some philosophers may take the constructivist route which Kant took in the *transcendent* context. The gulf that divides noumenal content and human beings equipped natively with a conceptual scheme is unbridgeable. Given this dualism, every effort to match the scheme with the content is bound to be abortive. If the two are to be matched at all, then, not the real *noumenal* content but only an *appearance* constructed (partly at least) by the mind, can be said to be homogeneous to whatever there is on the "scheme" or "Subject" side. This is how thinkers taking the Kantian constructivist route, try to secure scheme-content homogeneity on the *phenomenal* level. There is no need to dwell on this point once again for it has been discussed in the first section. Putnam does not believe in "scheme-content" dualism in the sense of noumena-phenomena dualism. And so, he does not have to regard *noumenon* as "content," and then to render the content homogeneous to our "scheme" replace it by a *phenomenal* content, a *construction*.

(c) There is no need to dwell any more on the kind of constructivism discussed in the second section also, namely, the kind which philosophers may embrace in the *immanentist* context to resolve the problem stemming from scheme-content dualism. I will only reiterate that Putnam as a realist cannot subscribe to Kant's constructivist immanentism without qualification. He should not try to resolve the problem which scheme-content dualism generates by resorting to a constructivism that flows from the fount of Kantian epistemology, an epistemology which preaches that the way a phenomenal object is as an object of knowledge, is a *consequence* of how we are made.

The scheme-content dualism has been formulated in many ways. In the transcendent context, as stated above, it is a dualism of *noumenal* content and the scheme. In the immanentist context, it is a dualism of an "organizing system and something waiting to be organized . . ." of the scheme and the *empirical* content which is "explained by reference to . . . experience, sensation, the totality of sensory stimuli or something similar."[14] The only way to make such an empirical content conform to the scheme according to Kant-type constructivist immanentism is to make the scheme bestow form and structure upon this empirical content. The homogeneity which has to be established here is not between noumenal content and scheme with which humans are equipped. In fact this kind of homogeneity cannot be established at all, as noted before, if by "content" is meant the thing-in-itself. The scheme is to be matched not to the thing-in-itself but always to the thing as represented. "And the representation is never a mere copy; it always is a joint product of our interaction with the external world and the active powers of the mind. The world as we know it bears the stamp of our own conceptual activity."[15] In the immanentist context as opposed to the transcendent context then, the dualism is not between noumenal content and scheme, but between *empirical* content and scheme. In this context the world of unknowable things-in-themselves seems lost, and talk about them seems otiose. And so, "most philosophy that has followed Kant in insisting on our own conceptual contribution to constituting what we call 'the world' has refused to follow Kant in postulating a world of Things in Themselves."[16] The question is: can this "post Kantian" as opposed to merely neo-Kantian tradition, to which Putnam himself belongs, subscribe even to this kind of constructivism, which is supposed to resolve the problem generated by dualism of *empirical* (not noumenal) content and scheme? It is in this immanentist context that I want to reiterate that as a realist Putnam cannot accept Kant's constructivist immanentism without qualification.

The constructivist immanentism, which I feel he cannot accept, rests on the typically counter-intuitive Kantian claim that "objects in the world owe their fundamental structure—and, if they couldn't exist without displaying that structure, their existence—to our creative activity."[17] It may be unfair to suggest that Kant attributed *existence* of the objects of the world to "our creative activity." But note that the whole content of our experience, even *outer* spatiotemporally situated objects, distinct from *inner* temporally successive states of consciousness, have been regarded by him as being as much conditioned by features due to our own cognitive constitution as the inner states. I think Putnam cannot concur with the claim that even the fundamental structure of such outer spatiotemporally situated objects is a *creation* of our minds, a projection. He must not defend, as stated before, the typical constructivist claim that objects of the world have the structure they do have, *because* we are made in such and such a way. If he did, it would be tantamount to making a confusion between a criterial and a causal claim. The point of Putnam's immanent realism is that we cannot intelligibly talk about objects of the world unless the fundamental structure they do have is such that we are able to think about it or comprehend it. To put it differently, the objects have, and will be found to have, when inquiry is carried on long enough, the fundamental structure which we think they have. The homogeneity between beliefs/ thoughts and what these are about is not a matter of construction or constitution. It is not being suggested that if there was no enquiry, no mind constructing anything, then there will exist no object in the world. The indissoluble connection between thought and reality, belief and being, is *not* a *causal* connection in the sense that beliefs construct or bring into being the objects and their fundamental structure. Notwithstanding the often misleading use of constructivist metaphors in Putnam's writings, his immanent realist approach is different from Kantian constructivism in the immanentist context. The latter is while Putnam's immanentism is *not* vulnerable to the kind of criticism quoted above, which makes Kant's position drift towards Berkeley's despite disclaimer from Kantian quarters. In his own words, Putnam's post-Kantian view is:

> a view in which the mind does not simply 'copy' a world which admits of description by One True Theory. But (the) view is not a view in which the mind *makes up* the world either (or makes it up subject to constraints imposed by 'methodological canons' and mind-independent 'sense-data'). If one must use metaphorical language, then let the metaphor be this: the mind and the world jointly make up the mind and the world. (Or to make the metaphor even more Hegelian, the Universe makes up the Universe—with minds—collectively—playing a special role in the make up.[18]

The special role they play, I will like to add, is not casual in the sense mentioned above.

Quine and Constructivism in the Immanentist Context

Quine's "post-Kantian" view is also a legacy of immanentism which holds that "the world as we know it bears the stamp of our own conceptual activity." Like the other "post-Kantian" philosophers to whom this legacy has been bequeathed, he too refuses to follow Kant in postulating the world of things-in-themselves. He too abandons the dichotomy of conceptual scheme and a world behind, that is undescribed, undepicted and unperceived. The point about which the "post-Kantians" including Quine whole-heartedly agree is that, as Putnam writes (in chapter 1 of his book *Realism with a Human Face*) and Rorty approvingly quotes:

element's of what we call 'language' or 'mind' *penetrate so deeply into what we call 'reality' that the very project of representing ourselves as being 'mappers' of something 'language independent' is fatally compromised from the very start.* ... Realism is an impossible attempt, to view the world from Nowhere.[19]

In a later chapter Putnam quotes a few lines from Quine, which articulate the same point: "The lore of our fathers is a fabric of sentences. ... It is a pale grey lore, black with fact and white with convention. But I have found no substantial reasons for concluding that there are any quite black threads in it, or any white ones."[20]

The ideas which these excerpts express, and which have profoundly influenced American philosophy, typically reminisce Kant's immanentism as opposed to his transcendent realism. Note that the scheme-content dualism which these ideas shun is of that kind which has been characterized above as dualism between scheme and *noumenal* content. This formulation of the dualism pertains to the transcendent context, which is to be seen in contrast to another formulation which we find in the immanentist context. The second formulation speaks of the dualism between the organizing scheme and something waiting to be organized, between scheme and *empirical* content, as pointed out before. Quine debunks the dichotomy as construed in the first formulation, that is, the dichotomy between conceptual scheme and a world behind, undescribed, undepicted and unperceived. He may therefore avoid the kind of constructivism to which this first formulation of dualism leads. He does not shun however, the dualism in its second formulation. In point of fact he acknowledges this dualism.

This dualism is, as noted before, (in the third section) a dualism of an "organizing system and something waiting to be organized . . . ," of the scheme and the empirical content which is "explained by reference to . . . experience, sensation, the totality of sensory stimuli or something similar."[21] From this cluster of expressions "sensation" may be straightaway dropped, for Quine's naturalized epistemology switches "neural receptors and their stimulation" in place of "sense or sensibilia."[22] The empirical content is to be explained by reference to such neural stimulation. The empirical content of a testable sentence or a set of sentences is what Quine calls the set of all the "synthetic observation categoricals that it implies, plus all synonymous ones."[23] The observation categoricals are sentences of a generalized form: "whenever this, that." They are compounded out of observation sentences which are linked directly to stimuli of the stated sort. We have here then, the dualism of the (empirical) content, that is, synthetic observation categoricals and their component observation sentences tied to stimuli, on the one hand, and the scheme which connects stimuli, individuates, reifies, and thereby makes possible knowledge of external objects, on the other. For instance, we have sensory stimulation on the occasion of witnessing, say, a willow at the water's edge and also a willow leaning over water. The two "observation" or "occasion sentences": "there is a willow at the water's edge" and "there is a willow leaning over water" are directly associated with stimulation, inasmuch as on the occasion of stimulation these sentences command a forthright assent or dissent from us, the linguistically competent witnesses of the occasion. The stimuli, and the assent or dissent to sentences they occasion, are as yet unorganized, for the sentences do not say that the willow growing at the water's edge is the *same* willow which leans over water. This sameness emerges when we compound the sentences and form what Quine calls the "focal observation categorical," namely, "when a willow grows at the water's edge, *it* leans over the water."[24] Still there is no *objective reference*. There is need for further organization by some individuating device before we can apprehend a full blown, persistent self-same object or body, the *same* willow for instance, which grows at the water's edge and leans over the water. Observation sentences and categoricals, Quine says, can at most produce an expectation of continuity of a persistent feature, but reification and individuation of persistent bodies across time are beyond their reach. Of course, as he also says, the "early rumblings of reification" are signalled typically by the use of pronouns, of "it," for example, in the focal observation categorical: "When a willow grows at the water's edge, *it* leans over the water." The component observation sentences here, concentrate not just on the same scene but on the *same part* of the scene, on the same willow, a distinctively salient portion to which we may point. Moreover, there is a "coinciding of saliences" for *where* the willow is at the water's edge, *there* it leans over the water. When our language adds to pronouns further devices like predication, quantification, truth functions, that is, when it is regimented in the logical notation of the predicate calculus, and the role played by pronouns is played by bound variables, we may have the organization we had been seeking. The "early rumblings of reification" mature into individuation.[25]

The whole account shows how stimuli, and observation sentences associated with them, get ordered and organized by an organizing scheme, by a language with various individuative devices. The account reverberates Kant's contention of order being brought to sensa by pure contributions of the mind. To echo Quine's echo of Kant's thesis: "The assuming of objects is a mental act," or more precisely, a linguistic act, for words must accompany thought if it is to be tracked. This act or this talk is like a conceptual bridge of our own making for linking sensory stimulation to sensory stimulation. As Quine says in the opening sentence of *Theories and Things*: "Our talk of external things, our very notion of things is just a conceptual apparatus that helps us to foresee and control the triggering of our sensory receptors in the light of previous triggering of our sensory receptors."[26] The triggering is the only reliable source of information about external things. It is *given* to us, while the conceptual apparatus is our own making.

Yet, Quine claims that there is nothing we can be more confident of than external *things* like other people, sticks and stones although these are not given to us like the stimuli. All we have as evidence are triggering of sensory receptors. Still we may and do speak of *objects*, and while speaking of objects we are not being skeptical. What we speak of does apply to objects we are talking about. Critics refuse to accede to this claim pointing out that *what there is*, is a question of *fact* and not of language. But Quine does not think that the claim to objective reference is forfeited. In a similar vein perhaps, in Kant's idiom one might say, that even though the outer spatio-temporally situated objects are conditioned by features due to our own cognitive constitution, there are *empirically real* objects nevertheless, which are *outside* us. So despite their belief in conceptual relativity, it might be said, Kant did not succumb to "subjective idealism," and Quine to "linguistic idealism."

However, in Kant's case the "outness" of outer spatiotemporally situated objects is seen to depend on something *in* us, the forms of outer and inner sense. It is something from the "Subject" or "scheme" end so to say, that makes possible awareness of objects in space. In other words, if the subject has beliefs about bodies in space, and if the beliefs are to be matched to things about which she has these beliefs, so that they can count as justified true beliefs, then, the pure "forms" and "concepts" of the "scheme" which every subject possesses, have to play the role of match-maker. The mind through the intermediation of its "conceptual scheme" marries beliefs to non-beliefs (objects or bodies). Quine also has to marry them, and explain how, in fused phrases of Kant and Russell (as he says), our knowledge of the external world of physical objects is possible. How can our beliefs about such objects or "bodies" rank as justified true beliefs by being matched with what they are about? What is it that intermediates between them according to him? Quine finds the intermediary in observation sentences, which he calls "the primary register of evidence about the external world...."[27] It is the observation sentence to which the speakers of language assent in similar, recurrent, perceptual situations that constitutes the foundation of whatever objectivity there is. And on this hinges the soundness of the claim that his view about the external world can be given the Kantian title: "empirical realism" rather than "transcendental idealism." For the intermediaries in his view are *observation sentences*, not transcendental pure conditions of the mind. The plausibility of the "scheme" or the "organizing system" which assumes objects depends not on transcendental conditions, the pure "forms," "concepts" and principles of the mind, but on sentences directly linked with stimuli. The justification for the beliefs in bodies comes not from the "Subject" side but from stimuli coming from outside.

Let me recapitulate at this stage the main ideas that I have been trying to put across, while moving from point to point in this section and in the two preceding sections.

(1) Constructivism comes in the wake of commitment to the dualism of "scheme" and "content."

(2) The scheme-content dualism has been formulated in different ways: as (a) a dualism of conceptual scheme and *transcendent* or *noumenal* content, and (b) a dualism of an organizing system and something waiting to be organized. Vis-a-vis (b) in Kantian theory the unorganized content is comprised by *sensation*, and in Quine's ontology by *stimuli* and observation sentences linked with stimuli, and

also by "observation categoricals" compounded out of "observation sentences."

(3) (a)-type dualism is germane to the transcendent context, and (b)-type to the *immanentist* context. Type (b) itself has been classified into sub-types, which we come across in Kant's and Quine's immanent metaphysics respectively. (The third section is devoted to Kant's theory and the present section to Quine's.)

(4) Each type and sub-type of dualism plunge us into an abyss that divides two ontologically disparate domains of beliefs and non-beliefs, or beliefs and what these beliefs are about.

(5) Both Kant and Quine try to avoid falling into the abyss. Both erect bridges between the two disparate domains so that beliefs belonging to one domain can be matched to, and be proclaimed as true of objects belonging to the other. The bridge built by Kant is made up of pure elements of the conceptual scheme with which, he thinks, humans are endowed. The bridge serving as "intermediary" in Quine's theory, on the contrary, has as its planks the observation sentences/categoricals.

(6) The bridge gets its *epistemic* strength in Kant's case from pure/ transcendental conditions of the *mind*. In Quine's thesis the strength accrues from sensory stimuli given to us from *outside*. The strength comes from opposite ends, as I have said, in the two theories, from the "Subject" side in Kant's theory, and from the outer objective side in Quine's.

Both Kantian and Quinian Immanentism resort to constructivism to resolve the problem of matching ontologically disparate items. Quine's constructivism however, is seen to be free from the doctrinal fantasies of "transcendental idealism," especially in view of what has been said above about the source of epistemic strength of the bridge which is supposed to connect ontologically disparate items. But do observation sentences really have the epistemic strength required for establishing the truth of sentences expressing beliefs in physical objects? Do they provide the bulwark of evidence for the conceptual scheme we construct, positing such physical objects? In case they do not, how are we to counter the skeptical charge against Quine's physicalist claim?

Is Quine Able to Silence the Skeptic?

In order to silence the skeptic it is necessary to build a bridge across the gulf dividing beliefs and what the beliefs are about. More urgently, it is necessary to make the bridge strong enough to carry the beliefs from the "Subject" side to the world outside, so that these beliefs can latch on to what they are about, say, physical objects. Quine maintains that the support needed comes from observation sentences/categoricals which are tied to stimuli. Beliefs about bodies or physical objects, he is convinced, are to be *justified* by observation sentences which draw on the vigor of the triggering of sensory receptors. Sworn into truthfulness before "the tribunal of experience," these sentences are to be regarded as trustworthy witnesses testifying to the justifiability and truth of our beliefs about physical objects.

It is at this juncture that Quine's claim concerning the justifiability of one's belief in *bodies* is seen to be vulnerable to skeptical charges. To adjudicate the rival claims, Quine's own and that of the skeptic, we must ascertain under what conditions a sentence expressing one's belief in bodies is true. To find out whether the sentence is true, we have to find out whether the conditions making it true obtain. But how can we determine that these conditions have actually been fulfilled? The answer which Quine gives is that the truth of this sentence, or any other sentence for that matter, cannot be ascertained in isolation by confronting the sentences one by one with what justify their truth-claim. In other words Quine defends holism with respect to ascertainment of truth in this context. This holism is to be seen in contrast to the view that a single sentence in isolation can be confronted with what justifies it. Quine challenges this atomistic view, the classical foundationalist epistemology of the empiricist brand, which seeks justification for the belief expressed by a single sentence in something *beyond* the belief, namely, sense experience. But even when he questions atomism and sees himself as an antifoundationalist, he does not eschew foundationalism in point of fact. For he does not dispute the basic contention of foundationalism that justification for our beliefs is to be sought for in something *other* than beliefs. It is this contention which distinguishes foundationalism from coherentism, the latter subscribing to the exactly opposite thesis that justification for beliefs is to be found in other *beliefs* and not in something of a *different ilk*. Far from disputing the basic foundationalist contention, Quine defends it, and so, opposes coherentism. He refuses to call himself a foundationalist because he refuses to accept atomistic foundationalism of the classical kind. The fact remains that he holds steadfastly to its basic contention. But what has the vestige of foundationalism that still remains after shedding its atomistic dress got to do with making his thesis vulnerable to skeptical charges? Why cannot the observation sentences, which are justifiers of "another ilk," be sworn into truthfulness before the "tribunal of experience," so that our beliefs in bodies be proclaimed justified true beliefs?

The reason why observation sentences cannot be regarded as trustworthy witnesses testifying to the truth-claim of beliefs of this sort perhaps is that they belong to a realm of a different ilk. To qualify as reliable witness, the justifiers must belong to the domain of what they justify. If there is a gap between what is to be justified, that is, belief, and that which justifies, that is, "sensation" (in classical empiricist foundationalism) or "observation sentence" (in Quine's theory), then, the gap has to be reduced. Or else, we have to admit that the justifier and the justified are very different, the content of one exceeding that of the other. In that case the effort to ground beliefs on sensation will be suspect, for how can sensation with its meager content justify belief which has a much richer content? How can sensation which is subjective be evidence for belief in something that is objective? It is here that skeptical doubt is bound to cast its shadow on the possibility of having knowledge concerning physical objects.

It may still be said that the doubt does not cast shadow on Quine's physicalist claim, for he himself fully realized that the status of evidence cannot be given to atomistic sensation. The "notion of observation," he writes, "as the impartial and objective source of evidence for science is bankrupt."[28] Nevertheless, this would not silence the skeptic, for even when private sensation is replaced by "observation sentence," the sentence remains tied to sensory stimuli. Quinian foundationalism, even after expunging atomistic sensationalism, and being elevated as a chapter of "Naturalized Epistemology," still seeks to "anchor at least some words or sentences to non-verbal rocks."[29] So the question remains: how can observation sentences anchored to non-verbal rocks (sensory stimuli) justify belief in things belonging to the external world? To answer the skeptic therefore, the gap between sensation and belief which has a richer content must be reduced.

Two distinct moves may be made for reducing the gap. (1) David Hume, for instance, pointed out that the distinction between impression and idea, sense perception and thought or belief, is merely quantitative. So, for him there is hardly any difference between *perceiving* a color patch and *believing* that there is a color patch. Though he blamed Locke for an equivocation regarding the use of the term "idea," he himself did not move very far from Locke. Nor should he have done so. Otherwise neither Locke nor he would have been able to answer how a belief or proposition can be justified by sensation, since sensation is something very different, something of "another ilk." (2) The other move does not seek to elevate sensation to the status of belief following Locke and Hume. It makes belief collapse into sensation, by showing that a sensation is not simply a direct apprehension of say, a patch of color. Rather, a number of beliefs is nested in it like: (i) the belief that a patch of color is being given; (ii) the belief that the patch is green; (iii) the belief that it is of such and such a shade, etc. It is as though a number of nested beliefs is appearing in the guise of a direct apprehension or sensation.

The trouble is, neither of these two moves can make sensation justify beliefs and give them the support they require. For there seem to be two obstacles to this. (1) Even if sensations are elevated to the status of beliefs, these beliefs are never about the *objective* world outside, but are about *us* believers. Suppose that Hume was right in obliterating the distinction between perceiving a green color patch and perceiving *that* a patch is green. What does the latter statement "I perceive (or believe) that the patch is green" say? It says only that I have such and such a belief. That is, it says something about *me* the believer, not about something objective and external. From "I believe that the patch is green" one cannot infer "there *is* a green patch here and now which I am perceiving." (2) Secondly, beliefs cannot really collapse into sensations. For, as pointed out earlier, the epistemic content of belief exceeds that of sensation. What can be said about beliefs cannot be said about sensations. So, the very idea of belief in the guise of sensation is suspect.[30]

The lesson of all this seems to be that the gap between beliefs and what the beliefs are about, cannot be bridged by installing observation sentences as *epistemic intermediaries.* Notwithstanding Quine's ebullience in praise of observation sentences, the latter cannot play the role of *justifiers.* The sensations with which these sentences are directly related can at most *cause* beliefs, not *justify* them. In Davidson's words they are *causal,* not *epistemic* intermediaries. Moreover, if sensation is regarded as a source of justification, what does it justify? Even if sensations justify beliefs, they justify beliefs in *sensation.* For as noted above, from the statement "I perceive (or believe) that the patch is green" what can be justifiably inferred is something about myself, about my having some sensation or belief. We do not see how the sensations justify belief in external events and objects. On the contrary the sensations can be very misleading and deceptive. Davidson recalls Putnam's example of "the brain in the vat" (BIV) and urges: "a person's sensory stimulations could be just as they are and yet the world outside very different."[31] And since we cannot guard against such deception and therefore cannot swear sensory intermediaries into truthfulness, we should not allow intemediaries between our beliefs and their objects in the world.

If the skeptic is to be answered, the "intermediaries" or observation sentences must be established as true. But how can we determine whether these sentences are true? This is an epistemic question. To answer it we have to turn to theory of meaning for it is here that we specify what makes a sentence true. To determine that a sentence is true we have to understand what conditions make it true. Since these truth-conditions comprise its meaning, knowing its meaning involves knowing its truth-conditions. Mark that what is needed is merely knowledge of what these conditions *are.* Knowledge that such conditions have *actually obtained* is not required. Quine however, thinks that precisely this is what we need for understanding meaning. Knowing what a sentence means, according to him, involves not only knowing what its truth-conditions are, but also knowing how we can *recognize* these conditions when they actually obtain. This demands that for giving the meaning of a sentence we have to specify what would justify asserting it. The meaning of an observation sentence, we thus see, is the condition that justifies its assertion. This condition is sensory stimulation. What this "stimulus meaning" of the sentence allows it to say however, is that some sensory experience has occured. This is what makes the sentence true and this is what justifies its assertion. In fact what the speaker *recognizes* or *knows* in this case perfectly coincides with what the observation sentence she utters *says.* But by establishing the truthfulness of the observation sentence in this way one has to pay a price which Quine is not ready to pay. One has to say that all that the observation sentence can truthfully and justifiably assert here is that the speaker is having such and such sensory experience, and not that such and such a *physical object* exists. To swear the sensory intermediaries or observation sentences into truthfulness then, one has to capitulate to sensationalism or phenomenalism and forget physicalism. It seems that Quine cannot escape the horns of the dilemma. If he opts for physicalism which he does, then he has to anchor sentences expressing beliefs in bodies to something *beyond* non-verbal rocks, namely, sensory stimuli. But this will be tantamount to giving up the foundationalist claim: "our *only* source of information about the external world is through the impact of light rays and molecules upon our sensory surfaces."[32]

I will reconsider the question of whether Quine has been able to substantiate his physicalist claim in the next chapter. I want to do so because whatever tension there may be in his writings due to pull from opposite directions—empiricist foundationalism of some sort, and physicalism—I see him nevertheless as an ally of the kind of immanent realism I am trying to defend. Maybe he went only half-way, and won half the battle of realism versus Realism, defeating the latter with a big "R," that is, "transcendent or metaphysical" realism. Maybe, that is to say, he strengthened the hands of post-Kantians in carrying out their negative program of ousting transcendent realism. I still feel that his positive views too are realist in *intent*. I have therefore tried to *reconstruct* his ideas along pragmatist realist lines which Putnam develops. I have tried to do so generally, and also in a limited context, with reference to a specific subjectmatter, "universals," so that realists defending immanentism may venture to answer, from their standpoint, the question: what is it to be a realist about "universals"? A similar effort was made in chapter 1 to answer from their standpoint the question: what is to be a realist about entities, especially, theoretical entities?

Meanwhile, I wish to point out that Putnam does not install epistemic intermediaries to match the conceptual *scheme* which believes in "bodies," to the physical objects which exist outside.

Conceptual Relativity in Internal Realism

The need for installing intermediaries arises if the world is bifurcated ontologically into disparate domains. Conceptual relativity is a pervasive theme in Putnam's writings. But whatever this theme conveys and seeks to establish is not to be seen as an effort to answer problems produced by that bifurcation. Since he is not held captive by the picture which troubled Dewey, Davidson and other thinkers, his problematic is different from that of philosophers who were held captive by it. Putnam's thesis of conceptual relativity is not designed to resolve the problem born out of ontological bifurcation, the problem of matching items of disparate domains. So "conceptual relativity" in his case is not intended to install something which is intermediate, a tertium quid, which is supposed to bridge the gulf between "scheme" and "content," "Subject" and "Object" or the organism and its environment. In fact the main concern of his thesis is to reject the dualism which has assumed so many different forms.

(i) One such form is the dualism of noumenal content and scheme constructing the "phenomenal." This, as has been repeatedly stressed, is an anathema for immanent metaphysicians in general, and for the internal realist particularly.

(ii) Again, the dualism is typically and widely construed as one which divides utterly disparate relata belonging to different ontological terrains, pieces of thought, language, beliefs belonging to one side, and pieces of the outer objective world to another. To answer the skeptical challenge that the former can never be said to *correspond* to, or be *true* of the latter, the *idealists* we have seen, retained the representations only, which belong to the side of the former. For there will be no difficulty in matching ontologically homogeneous items, namely, representations.The *physicalists* on the contrary, left the matter to the outside world which has a hand in establishing a direct causal connection between the disparate relata. The third response can be Kantian, or Quinian, which seeks to install "intermediaries."

Putnam does not, and *need* not make any of these responses. For he erases the very picture which the skeptic uses for holding so many philosophers as captives, philosophers, who in their desperation to relate disparate relata, take idealist, physicalist and constructivist routes of various kinds. The picture of the ontologically bifurcated world is wrong, he urges, deeply influenced by Kant, whose thought marks a decisive break with the Cartesian tradition. That tradition perpetuated the divide between mind and the world outside. Kant did not believe in two *substances*— mind and body, as Descartes did. He said something of permanent significance when he suggested instead that there are dualities in our experience. The "relation between mind and body should not be pictured as a binary opposition,a dualism of two incommensurable kinds of entity, but rather as a *duality*: two complementary poles of a single field of activity—the field of human experience."[33] The "constructivist" strain of transcendental idealism aside, which treats bodies as parts of the field of human experience, the objection that is voiced here against the picture of a binary opposition between heterogeneous entities had a salutary effect on recent developments in the philosophy of mind, especially "functionalism" fathered by Putnam himself. Although he now disowns his very influential brain child, he does not give up the idea that was central to this thesis. The idea is that our *matter* is not more important than our *function*. Our *what* is not more important than our *how*. Irrespective of what the *matter* is, of a machine, a human being, a creature with a silicon chemistry, and a disembodied spirit, all or any of these can function in the same way.[34] So it does not really matter as to whether there is any heterogeneity between disparate entities. Putnam repeats the Kantian move of striking at the root of the binary oposition between mind and body which provided staple for skeptical thought. Since disparate entities can function alike, ontic heterogeneity does not pose any special problem of the kind we have been considering: how can *we* and our thoughts, beliefs and language, which are of such a different kind of *matter*, reach out to non-thoughts or non-beliefs in the world outside? The point which is sought to be established here is that the opposition between substances of different sorts, is not a block to our ability to reach out to the world outside. Ontic heterogeneity need not be taken to create the abyss which compels philosophers to erect conceptual bridges and install "intermediaries."

(iii) Yet another form of the dualism was seen to be the one between the unconceptualized raw material of sensa or sensory stimuli, and the "scheme" which is supposed to organize and bring order into these. Kant believed that despite this schism, order can be brought to the plurality of sensory elements and we can have *objective* knowledge. This is possible because although the sensory impressions are unorganized and merely serve as the *occasion* for awakening our faculty of knowledge into action, "the activity of our understanding [can] compare these representations, and, by combining or separating them, work up the raw material of the sensible impressions into that knowledge of objects which is entitled experience."[35]

The contribution of pure elements to experience by the "activity of our understanding," and also by our faculty of sensibility at the most rudimentary level, are Kantian themes that sprouted ages later into the thesis of theory-laden observation. Observables, even sensations, are shaped to some extent by our concepts, according to this thesis. Putnam himself supports the thesis. He does not think that a sharp line of distinction is to be drawn between observational and theoretical vocabularies. "Even our description of our own sensations, so dear as a starting point for knowledge to generations of epistemologists, is heavily affected (as are the sensations themselves, for that matter) by a host of conceptual choices."[36] And he thinks that even if sensations or experiential inputs are conceputally dressed, that does not mean we cannot have knowledge of external objects. He credits Kant for showing us how, despite the fusion of pure elements of the mind with impressions received sensorily, we have *objective knowledge*. We know many statements about individual objects, that is, empirical objects which are "things for us." And any of these is a true statement in the sense that it "is a statement that a rational being would accept on sufficient experience of the kind that it is actually possible for beings with our nature to have."[37]

Any realist who takes an immanentist stance will agree that:

(i) on sufficient experience of the kind that it is actually possible for beings with our nature to have, we cannot know things-in-themselves but only things-for-us.

(ii) Things are not "unreal" (the noumenal sense apart) because they are things-for-us.

(iii) The fact that the things-for-us are indissolubly connected with the ways in which we conceive them, does not turn them into "bundles of ideas" *in* the mind or head. Things-for-us are empirically real and are known as things existing *outside* us.

But staying within the Kantian framework is it possible to show that there is an unmediated and indissoluble link between things-for-us and ourselves, which is the central and most urgent concern of immanentism for rising above schisms of different sorts? It has been claimed of course, that "in whatever manner and by whatever means a mode of knowledge may relate to objects, *intuition* is that through which it is in immediate relation to them, and to which all thought as a means is directed."[38] And intuition takes place only insofar as objects are *given* to us. But even if we ignore the ambiguity of the term "object" here, and concede that a mode of knowledge is in immediate relation to it, what exactly is this knowledge immediately related to? Sensible impressions no doubt, but these impressions serve merely as the *occasion* for awakening the faculty of knowledge into action. They do not make "things-for-us" available to us straightway. It is as though the impressions by themselves are mute, amorphous, gaining voice and character only through the *meditation* of the faculties of sensibility and understanding which *impose* forms from within themselves. Once the schism is acknowledged between unordered impressions and the scheme supplying pure forms and constructing the object of knowledge (be it the undetermined object of an empirical intuition, or the determined object about which we have true judgements) "intermediaries" are unavoidable. Therefore forms of sensibility, pure concepts of understanding, and also the empirical criteria (schema) for applying and adapting pure concepts to sense impressions are pressed into service. This is done for achieving the match between the unconceptualized raw materials of sensa, and the object which our conceptual scheme believes in. But if the sensa are muted, and the sanction that we do know true statements about objects come *only* from the mind, from the transcendental conditions that make knowledge possible, then the match secured will not be between our beliefs and something which *is not* our own making, but between our beliefs and something which *is* our own making. This might be welcome to transcendental idealism, but not to immanent *realism*, which insists that the object of knowledge in spite of being for us is not our own making in the sense of being a mere projection. It is not what it is *because* we are made in a certain way imposing forms on data that are unformed. As has been urged repeatedly, the way a thing appears is the way it *really* is, but this does not mean that the thing is made to appear in the way it does because we are made in a certain way. What the immanent/internal realist is trying to secure is certainly the unmediated link between things-for-us and ourselves. But just as this link is to be construed as something which does not involve *confrontation* between us and things-in-themselves, so also it must be construed as something which does not involve *intermediaries*. And intermediaries will not be required if the schism is denied from the start.

Quine also seemed to have risen above the schism between unorganized factual data and organizing scheme when he stressed that the "lore of our fathers . . . is a pale grey lore, black with fact and white with convention," and that there are no quite black threads in it and no quite white ones either.[39] But the schism between unconceptualized data and scheme bringing order seems to surface nevertheless when observation sentences are seen to have two faces. "Seen holophrastically, as conditioned to stimulatory situations. . . ." an observation sentence is *theory-free*; seen analytically, word for word, it is *theory-laden*, according to him.[40] In its "pristine holophrastic freedom from theory" however, is not the sentence woven of threads which are quite black? Moreover, can the the quite black observation sentence conditioned to stimulatory situation be evidence for true statements about physical objects in the external world?

Following Davidson's and Putnam's suit, we have seen that sensations and also observation sentences tied to sensations can merely serve as causal, not epistemic intermediaries.

What all this shows is that the unmediated link between mind/language and the world cannot be secured by (a) admitting schism, and (b) by looking for a bridge either in pure contributions of the mind *alone*, or in "the impact of light rays and molecules upon our sensory surfaces" which is supposed to be the "only source of information about the external world."[41] We do know true sentences about objects. But to justify this truth-claim, neither sense impressions, nor thought and the concepts it uses, should be given exclusive privilege. What can establish the linkage between words and objects and help in justifying the claim that we do know true sentences about these objects include many things. There are the sensory data, dressed conceptually, constituting nevertheless the experiential inputs. The inputs put together are what were earlier described as the "contribution of the environment."[42] There is furthermore the ability of the knower to use experiential inputs in coherent situationally appropriate ways, both individually and in agreement with fellow inquirers, in actual transactions with things outside.

Usually, among several contenders for the position of evidence proper, high value is given to one to the exclusion of others. What will be excluded or deemed weighty, depends on what kind of epistemology one subscribes to. The brand names of these epistemologies: empiricist (classical), rationalist, verificationist suggest which contender wins and counts as evidence proper. What is being urged here on the contrary is that no single contender, sense experience or clear and distinct rational insight or estimation of degree of confirmation or operational techniques for applying terms, etc. should be considered specially advantaged for qualifying as good evidence. How language hooks on to the world, how words manage to refer, and sentences report truthfully what is the case, is not a individualistic activity drawing on any of these evidences taken singly. It is a form of cooperative activity involving fellow inquirers, as I have said, and a linguistic division of labour among them. Moreover, this cooperative activity itself draws on the cooperation, so to say, or the complementary relation between different sorts of evidences. On the basis of the multiple inputs provided by these evidences, reason can make an overall estimation of what can be justifiably accepted as true. Even when I utter the simple sentence "Hawks fly" for example, and take it to report truthfully what is the case, I do not intend my hearer to deduce that a hawk with a broken wing will fly. What I expect depends on a network of beliefs. When a whole corpus of statements, a scientific theory instead of a single sentence has to be tested, to ascertain whether it can be said to report truthfully what is the case, the testing cannot be done just by looking up the operational definitions of all the terms and verifying the sentences comprising the theory one by one. Reason has to make an overall estimation depending on a whole network of beliefs besides stray verifications and operational tests. It has to depend on many other intangible things too, such as estimating simplicity, weighing simplicity against our desire for successful prediction, and so on. And in making the estimation reason has "a nose for the 'right' trade-off" between the values which these intangible considerations have.[43]

The complexity of this notion of "being justified" by so many multiple factors might produce apprehension about the very claim that we do have justified true beliefs. The rating of what is the right trade-off between values which the multiple factors have, might even suggest complicity with verificationists who replace truth-conditions by assertability conditions. For what is rated assertable in one situation may not be judged assertable or rationally acceptable in another. No wonder Putnam has been blamed for turning truth into an epistemic concept. If calling a belief, or a sentence expressing a belief true depends on taking an episte-mological stance suited to a specific context, then the notion of truth itself would seem to be context-relative. And relativism about truth perhaps is "always a symp-tom of infection by the epistemological virus; this seems to be true in any case for Quine, Nelson Goodman and Putnam."[44]

I do not think that this is true in any case for Putnam. Firstly, he does not confound truth with justification. On the contrary he clearly distinguishes the two, saying truth cannot be lost while justification can be lost.[45]

Secondly, Davidson who blames Putnam for defending an epistemic concept of truth himself notes the difference between those who equate truth with "justified assertability" and Putnam who equates it with "*idealized* justified assertability.*" He points out that since Dummett does not insist on something similar to Putnam's "ideal conditions," he is subject to the criticism which Putnam levelled against him. For "if truth depends simply on justified assertability, truth can be 'lost,' that is, a sentence can be true for a person at a time and later become false because the conditions of justification change. This is wrong."[46]

Thirdly, Davidson's suspicion that justification conditions which are so ideal cannot have the intended connection with human abilities, is unfounded.[47] The notion of "*idealized*" justification condition is a *limiting* notion. It does not imply that human inquirers can actually be in a position to justify every true statement were epistemic conditions ideal. In fact Putnam is now ready to drop the notion of "ideal" altogether for it suggests a fantastic utopian situation in which conditions are simultaneously ideal for answering *any* question whatsover. This is something which does not make sense to demand. For instance, the epistemic situation in my study is surely "ideal," or if this word is misleading, it is good enough with respect to the statement "there is a chair in my study." For lights are on or daylight is streaming through the window; there is nothing wrong with my eyesight and I have an unconfused mind and so on. But will this condition be simultaneously ideal for answering any question, say, "is not the chair in the study a congerie of particles?" The point is that the *good* epistemic situation must be described with respect to some statements, not to others. Not any condition is good for asserting any statement. To claim of any statement that it is true in its place or in its context is to claim that it could be justified were epistemic conditions good enough with respect to that statement in that context.[48] So even if conditions of justification change, one need not say that the sentence "there is a chair in my study" which was true for me at the time when some conditions obtained, has become false when these conditions changed, when normal eyesight under normal conditions, for instance, is replaced by use of electron microscope. Truth is not lost after all when conditions of justification have changed. This would have been the case if truth depended simply on justified assertability. By insisting on *ideal* assertability conditions, and by construing "ideal" as "good epistemic condition" in a specific situation, Putnam escapes two charges:

(a) He does not have to say absurdly that a sentence once held true under one condition has become false under another, for it is the former condition which is ideal or good which establishes it as a true in *that context* with respect to which it is ideal.

(b) This non-utopian, context-relative notion of ideal condition shows that Davidson's remark and reservation regarding its not having a connection with human abilities are misdirected.

This account of how and when we can justifiiably claim to have true beliefs may invite other queries:

(i) Can a sentence expressing a belief justified by good enough epistemic conditions in a particular context, be established as true in that context in the sense that its revision or even rejection is impossible? Not necessarily. The epistemic conditions are not ideal in the utopian sense, and fallible humans may be mistaken in claiming that these are good enough. But *were* they good, ideal in the sense that is intelligible in the human situation, the sentence will count as *true*, and true in the substantial sense of the term. Alternatively if the perception of the fallible inquirers regarding goodness of the conditions is revised, the sentence which was believed to be true when the conditions were wrongly perceived as good, may itself be modified or even rejected as false. In any case this does not imply skepticism about the substantial notion of truth which is different from justified assertability.

(ii) Supposing two or more incompatible sentences are asserted in the same perceptual situation but from different points of view, can they be said to be correct in spite of being incompatible and true of the *same* object or event?

A full answer to this question concerning the constancy of the things or events being referred to by words figuring in incompatible sentences will not be attempted here. I will return to this, and to the problem of incommensurability which arises in this connection in the concluding chapter. For the present the answer is simply that in the same perceptual situation, incompatible sentences can be uttered depending on what perspective one opts for. And this perspectival character of utterances, or their conceptual relativity, does not debar one from claiming that they express justified true beliefs. To "claim of any statement that it is true, that is, that it is true in its place, in its context, in its conceptual scheme, is, roughly, to claim that *it could be justified were epistemic conditions good enough.* "[49]

The reference to good enough epistemic conditions does not import epistemological considerations which jeopardize the objectivity of the substantial notion of truth as critics allege. The reference to such conditions is intended to eliminate what some of the most eminent critics themselves want to eliminate, namely radically non-epistemic truth which totally outruns the possibility of justification. When Putnam says that a statement is true in its place, in its context or conceptual scheme, he means that it is as a *matter of fact*, asserting what the case is. There is a fact of the matter as to what is rightly assertable under certain conditions from a specific point of view. The fact of the matter is that the object which the sentence talks about, itself has the properties it appears to have from a perspective under certain specific conditions. The properties are real, and not mere projections.

Consider Putnam's own example (mentioned in chapter 1) of the question: "how many objects are there in a world which has just three individuals X1, X2 and X3?" (as encountered very often in Carnap's logic). But suppose like some Polish logicians, that for every two particulars there is an object which is their sum. Given that conceptual scheme and context of counting, the answer will no longer be three, as in Carnap's logic. It would be seven, namely, X1, X2, X3, and X1 + X2, X1 + X3, X2 + X3, X1 + X2 + X3.[50] Does it make sense to deny truth to any of these two assertions? There is a fact of the matter in relation to one system of counting in one context, and there is also a fact of the matter in relation to another counting system in another context, although to ask which *one* to the *exclusion* of the other is *really* the fact of the matter does not make sense.

Putnam's imaginary opponent Professor Antipode is violently opposed to the alternative scheme of Polish mereology. He will only allow assertions in an ordinary commonsense conceptual scheme and claim there are five objects, say a book, a bee, a human being, a nose of a person and a notebook in one part of a room. To talk of the mereological sum of the book and the nose and consider it as an object is simply crazy.[51] But what will Professor Antipode say if we are to count the pages of the notebook? If the nose attached to the body counts as an object, how do the pages attached to the notebook disqualify for being counted as objects? The point is that the reference to alternative standpoints, alternative contexts of assertion is hard to eliminate. Even in the common everyday context alternativity cannot be ruled out. Nor is there any need for eliminating it on the pretext of maintaining objectivity of the claim that we do know true sentences, though these sentences are true in their place, in their context of assertion. The resistance to alternativity or conceptual relativity may stem from the wrong conviction that these are conventional matters and objectivity is something totally different. There is certainly "an aspect of conventionality and an aspect of fact in everything we say that is true, but we will fall into a serious error if we commit a 'fallacy of division' and conclude that there must be a part of the truth that is the 'conventional part' and a part that is the 'factual part.' "[52] Putnam's doctrine of conceptual relativity demands that these two parts should fuse inextricably, as in the "pale grey lore"—in the fabric of sentences in which the threads are neither quite black with fact, nor quite white with convention. What these sentences talk about are things which really are the way they appear to us from different perspectives.

The controversial issues attending this doctrine of conceptual relativity, especially those that relate to incompatible assertions and the threat of incommensurability will be addressed later. Meanwhile, I will turn once again to an allied post-Kantian position which holds that the way things appear is indeed the way they really are. I will review the general metaphysical stance of this position to answer the question: what is it to be a realist in the immanentist sense about things in general? I will also review the more specific view this position has concerning a particular subjectmatter, universals, to answer the question just raised in a local context. The question in the local context is: what is it to be a realist in the immanentist sense about universals?

Notes

1. Hilary Putnam, *The Many Faces of Realism* (La Salle, Ill.: Open Court, 1987), 11. In case of projecting, Putnam says, we are imagining things to have properties they do not have without being conscious that this is it what we are doing.

2. Donald Davidson, "The Structure and Content of Truth," *The Journal of Philosophy* LXXXVII, no. 6 (June 1990), 298. Davidson too is as much skeptical about the plausibility of this transcendent or "metaphysical" realist position as Putnam.

3. Davidson, "The Structure and Content of Truth," 298.

4. Hilary Putnam, *Reason, Truth and History* (Cambridge: Cambridge University Press, 1981), 49.

5. See Ilkka Niiniluoto, *Is Science Progressive* (Dordrecht: Reidel, 1984), 43.

6. Karl Popper, *Conjectures and Refutations* (London: Routledge, 1963), 26.

7. P. F. Strawson, *The Bounds of Sense* (London: Methuen, 1966),19.

8. Strawson, *The Bounds of Sense*, 19.

9. Putnam, *Reason, Truth*, 52, 54. Emphasis mine.

10. See Richard Rorty, "Pragmatism, Davidson and Truth," in *Truth and Interpretation: Perspectives on the Philosophy of Donald Davidson* ed. Ernest Le Pore (Oxford: Basil Blackwell, 1986), 336.

11. Putnam, *Reason, Truth*, 57. Putnam refers to Aristotle's *De Anima* book III, chapters 7 and 8.

12. Putnam, *Reason, Truth*,59.

13. Rorty "Pragmatism, Davidson and Truth," 337.

14. Donald Davidson, "On the Very Idea of a Conceptual Scheme," in Davidson, *Inquiries into Truth and Interpretation* (Oxford: Clarendon Press 1984), 189.

15. Hilary Putnam, "The Way the World Is," in Putnam, *Realism with a Human Face*, ed. James Conant (Cambridge, Mass: Harvard University Press, 1990), 261.

16. Putnam, *Realism, Human Face*, 261.

17. This is a line from Alvin Plantinga's paper "How To Be an Anti-Realist," in *Proceedings of the American Philosophical Association* 56 (1982). I borrow the quotation

from Rorty, "Pragmatism, Davidson and Truth," 338.

18. Putnam, *Realism, Human Face*, 262. See also Putnam, Reason, Truth, 11.

19. Putnam, *Realism, Human Face*, 28. See also Richard Rorty, "Putnam and the Relativist Menace," *The Journal of Philosophy* XC, no. 9 (September 1993), 443.

20. W. V. O. Quine, "Carnap and Logical Truth," in *The Philosophy of Rudolf Carnap*, ed. P. A. Schilpp (LaSalle, Ill.: Open Court, 1963), 386-406. See also Putnam, *Realism, Human Face*, 262.

21. Davidson, "On the very Idea of a Conceptual Scheme," 189.

22. W. V. O. Quine, *Pursuit of Truth* (Cambridge, Mass.: Harvard University Press, 1990), 19.

23. Quine, *Pursuit*, 10, 17.

24. Quine, *Pursuit*, 10-11.

25. Quine, *Pursuit*, 10-11, 24-26. See also W. V. O. Quine, *Theories and Things* (Cambridge, Mass.: Belknap Press, 1981), 5-7.

26. Quine, *Theories*, 1-2.

27. Quine, *Pursuit*, 39.

28. W. V. O. Quine, "Epistemology Naturalized," in Quine, *Ontological Relativity and Other Essays* (New York: Columbia University Press, 1969), 88.

29. Donald Davidson, "A Coherence Theory of Truth and Knowledge," in *Kant oder Hegel* (Stuttgart: Klett-Cotta, 1983), 429. Reprinted in *Truth and Interpretation: Perspectives on the Philosophy of Donald Davidson*, ed. E. Lepore (Oxford: Basil Blackwell, 1986).

30. Davidson, "A Coherence Theory of Truth and Knowledge," 427. In developing these points suggested by Davidson, I have profited from discussions with Pranab Kumar Sen and Madhucchanda Sen.

31. Davidson, "A Coherence Theory of Truth and Knowledge," 428-29.

32. W. V. O. Quine, "The Nature of Natural Knowledge" in *Mind and Language* ed. S. Guttenplan, (Oxford: Clarendon Press, 1975), 68. The line is quoted by Davidson in his paper "A Coherence Theory of Truth and Knowledge." Emphasis mine.

33. See James Conant's introduction in Putnam, *Realism, Human Face*, xxii.

34. Hilary Putnam, *Representation and Reality* (Cambridge, Mass.: MIT Press, 1988), xiii.

35. Immanuel Kant, *Critique of Pure Reason*, tr. Norman Kemp Smith (London: Macmillan, 1933), 41, B1.

36. Putnam, *Reason, Truth*, 54.

37. Putnam, *Reason, Truth*, 64.

38. Kant, *Critique*, 65, A20, B34.

39. Quine "Carnap and Logical Truth," 386-406, and Putnam, *Realism, Human Face*, 262.

40. Quine, *Pursuit*, 7.

41. Quine, "The Nature of Natural Language," 68.

42. Putnam, *Representation*, 30-31; and Putnam, *Reason, Truth*, 54.

43. Putnam, *Representation*, 9,11, 25. Putnam thinks that *reason* has "a nose"—a capacity to make an overall estimation of what we can justifiably accept as true, drawing on multiple inputs and considerations. In a comparable way, D. P. Chattopadhyaya points out that the *human organism* itself has the capacity of acting in the right way. It has the ability, he observes, of adaptation for readjusting itself to changing environmental conditions, even repairing or totally dispensing with it's own inherited adaptation. Biology of the body has a "nose," so to say, for the right way of dealing with the world. This enhances the

cognitive worth of beliefs by strengthening the organism-environment linkage. See D. P. Chattopadhyaya, *Induction, Probability and Skepticism* (Albany, N.Y.: State University of New York Press, 1991), 76.

44. Davidson, "The Structure and Content of Truth," 298.

45. Putnam, *Reason, Truth*, 55. See also Hilary Putnam, *Realism and Reason, Philosophical Papers,* vol. 3, (Cambridge: Cambridge University Press, 1983), xviii.

46. Davidson, "The Structure and Content of Truth," 307-8.

47. Davidson, "The Structure and Content of Truth," 307.

48. Putnam, *Realism, Human Face*, vii-viii.

49. Putnam, *Realism, Human Face*, vii.

50. Putnam, *Many Faces of Realism*, 18.

51. Hilary Putnam, "Truth and Convention" in *Realism, Human Face*, 98. See also Putnam, *Representation*, 110-11.

52. Putnam, *Realism, Human Face*, x.

Chapter 3

Realism versus Nominalism: From Quine's Immanent Metaphysical Point of View

In the early history of philosophy, especially in medieval thought, the term "realism" was used in opposition to "nominalism." This opposition was about a *specific subject matter* "universals," and so, realists here may be seen as waging a war with their nominalist foes over a regional issue. The issue being regional both realism and nominalism can be viewed as positions which were labelled "local" in chapter 1.

Stated simply, and in their classical construal nominalism maintains that the only things that exist are *"particulars,"* whereas realism acknowledges the real objective existence of *"universals"* as well. The debate therefore revolves round the metaphysical question: what there is? Of course, the answers given also intend to explain our ability to see one "particular" resembling others. Moreover they seek to give an adequate account of our use of linguistic expressions that are general. But the thrust of the debate is not on what *we see* or *experience* or *know*, nor on what *we say*, but on the issue concerning the world, concerning *what there is*.

The question: "what there is?" as traditionally conceived, seems to be: is there in fact only *one* type of entities made and marked by the world *itself* as concrete "particulars" having definite space-time location? Or, is there in fact a pre-given division in nature between *different types* of entities, some of which are put into the natural slot of "universal abstract entities," and some others into the slot of "concrete particulars"? Traditional nominalism gives a forth-right answer: there are in fact no universal abstract entities. Realists by contrast maintain that there are in fact both types of entities, concrete "particulars" and abstract "universals." And whatever the adversaries admit as entities to be included in the inventory of "what there is," these are, according to them, *found*, not *made* by us. Nature makes what there is, people recognize.

The question "what there is?" however, was soon posed and phrased in a different way. It tended to get assimilated to questions like: "what do we *see, think* and *believe* there to be?" or "what can we *take* there to be?" or again "what do we, or our theories *say* there is?" These are questions typically framed in the immanentist idiom.

Preoccupation with these questions and the varying emphases they receive have permeated the whole course of the debate, traditional and modern. But the new way in which the old question was reconstrued from an *immanent* perspective, owes especially to the works of Quine, and also Nelson Goodman, with whom he took a joint step towards nominalism of a special kind.[1] For both Quine and Goodman, "what there is," namely, the world and things in it, are not *unconceptualized transcendent* realities. Whatever we are ontologically committed to, depends on what we, or our theories *say* there is.

My concern in this chapter is to discuss Quine's immanent approach to the problem of "universals" specifically, and the kind of metaphysics it has as its backdrop generally. Vis-a-vis both aspects of the issue: general and specific, occasional reference will be made to Goodman's views to highlight where the two authors agree, and where they disagree. I wish to discuss the issue in two stages. The first confines itself to making few remarks on some aspects of the traditional debate. The second focuses on Quine, who reiterates some of the old questions though in a new way.

Realism versus Nominalism: From the Traditional Standpoint

Realists by and large insist that "what we say" and the different types of linguistic expressions we use for saying, must be mapped directly on to the irreducibly different features of the real world. Take, for instance, the general word "red." There must be some reality independent of our language to which the word corresponds. Or else we cannot explain why one word can be used legitimately in many cases and be applied to many things. That it does apply to *many* things shows that a *generality* is built into its meaning. This is its irreducibly distinct feature which sets it apart from the semantically opposite expressions like singular terms. To what in the world can this feature of generality be mapped? In other words, what in reality gives the term its generality and justifies its use in many cases? In order that the word "red" is true of such things as the setting sun, roses, cherries, etc., must there be, in addition to these particular things, an *entity* which can be said to be the real counterpart, of the generality inherent in its meaning? This real counterpart, or the "universal" as it is called, had been construed differently. Plato conceived it as the *archetypal form* to which things of the same kind approximate. Aristotle took it as a *common property* which these things possessed. The universal in one case is conceived as an *entity* existing objectively in a realm apart from the particulars that "participate" in it, or "approximate" it. It is construed in another case as a *common property* that is identically present in the particulars, not in separation from them. In both cases the question sought to be answered is: what basis in reality is there for the generality inherent in experience, thought and language? What we think and say there is, must have a basis in what there is.

The nominalists reverse the order of emphasis. They refuse to seek the basis for generality *in language*, in a reality *beyond language*. To answer the question how words are general, one need not postulate an extra-linguistic entity, mental or extramental. In its extreme form, nominalism maintains that there is nothing common to a class of particulars called by the same name except that they are called by the same name.

Extreme nominalism does not explain why or how words are general. Its application of a word to more then one thing seems arbitrary. However, to have an explanatory worth which its extreme version lacked, nominalism in its moderate form resorted to *resemblance,* on which the use of general words was to be founded. But if nominalism is to survive as an independent position, opposed to realism, tha resemblance cannot be given the status which "universals" enjoy according to realists. Nominalism of both shades, extreme and moderate, must deny the universality of *thing* and *property* and insist instead on the universality of the *word*. If resemblance is reified and taken as a thing or even as a property present identically in things called by the same name, then, nominalism even in its moderate form, is likely to collapse into some kind of realism.

But can nominalism really eschew references to an independent reality if it has to explain generality in thought and language? Realists found the locus of generality of thought and language in the world, in *what there is*. In nominalism the emphasis shifts to *what can be experienced, thought or known,* and to *what can be said* beyond which it need not seek the basis of generality.

Indeed, the regional war about the specific issue of "universal" seems to have a global implication. As it has been very appropriately observed, "the real issue is: what is *first philosophy*—metaphysics, epistemology or philosophy of language?" Are we going to find a justification of generality inherent in experience and language, in the world? Or, should we take an account of knowledge or of language as primary, and then derivatively get our picture of the world? There is no good ground however, why any one area should be considered "first." As the same author expresses: "there are no second-class citizens in the kingdom of philosophy. Metaphysics, epistemology and philosophy of language should live together cooperatively in a manner that will be mutually beneficial and fulfilling."[2] But philosophers generally have not taken this equalist stance, which they would have, had they defended the immanentist standpoint insisting that there is an indissoluble link between what we *say* and *know* on the one hand, and what there *is* on the other.

Thus, in resisting multiplication of needless entities besides particulars, nominalism, especially in its older form, has been guided by an empiricist epistemology.

Sense-experience, considered as an unmistakable source of knowledge, provides immediate access to, and is always associated with particulars, which therefore must be included in the inventory of "what there is." Apparently, there is no similar compulsion for admiting "universals." So, epistemic questions like "what are we justified in believing about the world" are believed to hold the key to the question "what there is."

Thus, if all we have in our minds are particular images when we think of something, then in reality there are only "particulars," according to nominalists wedded to Berkeleyan epistemology. Even if "triangle" for example, is a general (common) noun, in thinking of it one does not think of anything besides the image of a *particular* triangle. When the word is used to talk about triangles in general, the image we have of a particular triangle is taken to represent all other figures of the *same sort*. To Berkeley, ideas which general words may signify are actually *not general,* but *particular* images that become general by being made to represent all other particular images of the same sort. Almost a verbatim quotation is found in Locke's *Essay*: (book iii, ch.3, sec.13): "Ideas are general when they are set up as representatives of many particulars things . . . (They) are all of them particular in their existence . . . their general nature being nothing but the capacity they are put into, by the understanding of signifying or representing many particulars."[3] It may be pointed out however, that particulars have this representative capacity by virtue of common properties they share with other particulars of the *same* kind. And these common properties are "universals" masquerading as "resemblances."

The nominalists, in their turn will point out that "resemblances" are as much *particular* as the "particulars" which resemble. Particular things and relations are all we can and do perceive. Moreover, although all things resemble in many different ways only some can be selectively picked out by the mind for grouping certain things. In this sense the selected "resemblances" are "creatures of understanding" functioning as *man-made* principles for classifying things. There is no need to reify resemblance as a mind-independent "universal," not even for the fear of an infinite regress. We tend to get involved in such a regress when two particular resemblances, say, between a and b, and between c and d, resemble each other. But that third resemblance too may be a *particular* relation. Of course an *ultimate resemblance* may still have to be admitted as a *relational universal* of which particular resemblance relations are instances, in order to stop regress, as Russell demanded.[4] But this ultimate *relational universal* can hardly be said to have the *explanatory value* of universals of *quality* which can serve as the basis of classifying things. However insofar as the classification or sorting of things under names on the basis of selected universals of *quality* is due to the workmanship of understanding, as pointed out above, the nominalists are apparently under no compulsion to admit mind-independent "universals".

It may still be urged however, that nominalists have not been able to eschew references to mind-independent realities after all. Resemblances or similitudes serving as the basis of classification are in respect of *qualities* or *properties*. These may be selectively picked out no doubt, and the picking out is certainly the workmanship of understanding. Nevertheless properties themselves are not the handwork of the mind. On the contrary the mind must have some given data to work on. In fact, nominalism in its moderate form, resorting to similitudes in respect of properties has a close associate in Locke's conceptualism. And what is said about conceptualism in this context would also be applicable to nominalism. Thus although it is "the work of the mind that some resemblances . . . are recorded in language . . . the mind has something *real* and *natural* to work from. . . ."[5] This reference to "real" shows that at some point there must be an interface between the so-called rival approaches, each trying in vain to secure the status of the first "philosophy" for its preferred area.

But the philosophers concerned apparently are not interested in the interface, in cooperative exchanges between approaches that focus primarily on "what there is," and those which unduly emphasize "what we experience and say there is." They would rather remain within their own chosen preferred field, which, to them seems "first." For instance, both Locke and Berkeley recognized that ideas have the capacity to represent particulars of the same sort. But while Locke regarded ideas with this representative capacity as "general" and took them to be the mental counterparts abstracted from properties of things out there in the world, Berkeley rejected the view that we need "abstract ideas," the so-called real mental counterparts of real properties, to explain why words are general. We do not need to admit general or abstract ideas in the ontic inventory of "what there is" because what we know or sensibly experience are only particular images. The question "what there is?" in Berkeley's philosophy then, is in this context subsidiary to the question: "what do we know?" or rather "what do we sensibly experience?"

On What There Is: Quine's Immanent Metaphysical Approach

Centuries later the question reappeared in Quine's philosophy, asking in the same way how we are able to fathom the *generality* of words, and *resemblances* between objects. "There are those who feel," he writes, "that our ability to understand general terms, and to see one concrete object as resembling another, would be inexplicable unless there were universals as objects of apprehension. And there are those who fail to detect, in such appeal to a realm of entities over and above the concrete objects in space and time, any explanatory value."[6]

Quine's strictures about the admission of "universals" or abstract objects, "the twilight half-entities," are well-known, and leave little doubt as to which group he has chosen to take as an ally. Still it is hard to give a straightforward answer to the question: is Quine a nominalist who holds that there really are no universals at all?

Quine raised the question: "are there universals?" in a new way. The question is broken up into the following: are there such entities as attributes, relations, classes, numbers, etc.? He took these entities as instances of universals. And in raising the question he believed himself to have asked specifically, what is asked by the general question "what objects exist?" or "what there is?" He returned to the question repeatedly in various essays phased over decades. Does this indicate a shift once again, reversing the order of emphasis which we had reckoned in Berkeley's philosophy? In other words, is there a reversal in respect of emphasis from the question "what we *know* or *experience*?" to "what there *is*?" and consequently, from epistemology as a preferred field to metaphysics or physics?

I will discuss Quine's treatment of the general question "what there is?" first, and then, keeping this as a backdrop in view turn to the specific issue of "universals" in the section that follows.

The question "what there is," needless to say, is the concern of "ontology" and also of "metaphysics," which, in spite of being a term fraught with ambiguity, is often used synonymously with "ontology." And if the concern of "metaphysics" is with being, with reality, with "what there is," then, insofar as Quine himself has taken it to be a major problematic, it seems that he too is assigning a special status to this enterprise (metaphysics/ontology). Of course there is the disclaimer that there is no "first philosophy." But the "first philosophy" which is sought to be eliminated is speculative metaphysics as distinct from science. And the metaphysics which still seems to be given a special status is one that is not distinct from, or is at least continuous with science, as Quine says in a vein reminiscent of Kant. It seems then, that one cannot give a straightforward "yes" or "no" answer to the question: "is Quine a metaphysician" also, just as one cannot give a similar answer to the question: "is Quine a nominalist?" To the former question the answer seems to be both "yes" and "no." This depends on what sense is given to the term "metaphysics." It is "no" if metaphysics is *transcendent*, concerned with being *qua being* or ultimate reality. It is "yes" if metaphysics is *immanent*, as it came to be conceived especially since Kant took the "transcendental" turn, which showed how futile it is to try to discover what being *qua being* or being *in itself* is.

My persistent effort to regard Quine as a Kantian may anger Quineans themselves. How, for instance, can a thinker vehemently opposed to "mentalism" be placed in the tradition that makes the (phenomenal) "world" a *construct* of the mind? If Quine did take a turn then it was linguistic, semantical, not transcendental. Moreover, this linguistic turn itself may suggest on first blush that there is a slant in a different direction, towards philosophy of language, even to that extent that makes ontology seem subservient. It may seem so in spite of the fact that Quine himself has repeatedly characterized his philosophical concerns as being concerns with ontology.

However, the moot point of comparison is whether, in one case we can *know* something that is transcendent, which is not the object of possible experience, and whether in another case we can *say* there is something transcendent, which does not depend on our use of language. The answer in both cases is "no." We cannot ever *know* "what there is," without certain conditions under which alone such knowledge is possible, that is, without the contributions of the "forms of sensibility" and "concepts of understanding." And we cannot *say* what there is without referring to a discourse within which a theory *says* what there is. And a theory can *say* what there is, if and only if, some of the entities it assumes are counted among the values of the variables it uses, in order that the statements it affirms are true. Both Quine and Goodman, who held a similar view, urged that it is in the values of the variables that the ontology of a theory is to be sought.

To explain how we *know* "what there is," why do we have to refer to certain *conditions*, as Kant maintained, under which alone such knowledge is possible? The reason as noted in the previous chapter is this: things which we do *know* experientially are fullblown objects, extended in space, persisting in time, interacting with other objects in a regular manner. But these are not what we *find* given in experience, just as such. What is *given* in experience, in Kant's terminology is "matter," the manifold of sense, shades of red and blue for instance, not even *extended* patches of red and blue surfaces *in time*, characterizing different sides of objects. However, if spatiotemporal order, unity, regularity etc., requisite for the empirical cognition of inter-acting objects are not *given* or *found* in experience, where are we to get them from? We get them from within us, from forms of sensibility and pure concepts of understanding like unity, substance, causality etc. . . . These are the conditions, the ineradicable transcendental elements of human cognitive faculties which *bring* unity to experience and thereby make possible our grasp of fullblown objects. Since unity is *brought* to the manifold of experience by these transcendental concepts or categories, and the object is just that in the concept of which the manifold is united, the so-called physical objects may be simply called "functions of the Table of Categories."[7] They are conceptually imported as posits in order that some unity in the manifold may be effected. The object which we know "there is" then, is *not* an unconceptualized reality, given by a transcendent nature to be *found* and recognized by us. What is given, to repeat, is the flux, the manifold of experience. Yet if "objects" are included in the inventory of "what there is" as far as we *know*, then, we have to admit that these are not what we *find given* but *construe* or *take* our experienced items to be.

Kant's "transcendental idealism" finds resonance in Quine's doctrine of "ontological relativity" and also in the allied thesis sponsored by Goodman. In fact the constructivist stance which Goodman takes seems more radical than that of Kant and Quine. He is an "activist" about activism, as has been aptly observed, in maintaining that there is no such thing as unstructured absolutely immediate sensory data free from conceptualization.[8] The mind is active in perception at *all* levels. Of course Kant himself, from whom these thinkers derive inspiration in their (avowedly) anti-foundationalist epistemologies, considered only the spatialized and temporalized sense-manifold, the dressed data, as "appearance." But he left the "matter" minus the "form" of "appearance" free of all contribution from the mind.

The inclusion of an element that is altogether a posteriori (though not a posteriori in the received sense of the term), cannot be endorsed by Goodman's rejection of the "given." There is nothing to be received passively from any *transcendent* end in his brand of anti-foundationalism. I wonder whether anything like "stimulus" even can be admitted that comes from the world, though not from the *noumenal* world, if we are to keep close to the letter of his text.

Goodman rejects the conception of knowing "as a processing of raw material into a finished product. . . ." He says that the issue is not *what* is given but *how* it is given."[9] In Kant's case however, the "what" of the "given" may be identified with the *matter* of sensible intuition and the "how" with its form. Again, what is given according to Quine, is the *stimulus*, which is fired or triggered from without, from the world-end. The response which this elicits is a *function* of *what is given,* and *whatever is added* from our side. There may be multiple responses which fit equally with the stimulus given. But not only is there a given sensory stimulation; it even plays the key role, as we have seen, in the preference we exercise in choosing one out of the many responses. "Physical objects" for instance, are to be posited rather than abstract ones on the ground of comparative directness of association with sensory stimulation.[10] Goodman, on the contrary, holds that "we can get no light on the way the world is by asking about the way it is given." He does not think that "any sense can be made of the phrase 'given as'. . . . The nearest we could come to finding any meaning to the question that the world is *given as*, would be to say that this turns on whether the material in question is apprehended with a kind of feeling of wholeness or a feeling of broken-up-ness."[11] Strictly speaking then, one should not even ask whether we can come near to finding any meaning for the expression "given as." For the meaning of the so-called expression "given as" depends not on *anything given as anything* but on *how we apprehend*, on our "feeling of wholeness . . . or broken-up-ness." In other words the "given as" is a product of "given how" and not a function of "*what* is given" and "*how* it is given."

It may be said that this ultra-constructivist interpretation is wrong. For it seems to suggest misleadingly that in Goodman's thesis the notion of reference to anything whatsoever evaporates into thin air, and we are only left with our ways of apprehending and feeling. But in fact Goodman does not eschew the notion of reference. He points out that reference makes sense only within the bounds of one or other "version" which we construct in accordance with the ways the world appears to us. However, the notion of *the* world outside the "version" as a transcendent reality is a misnomer. If we do refer, we refer to a world relative to a "version" and its way of apprehending it. We do not refer to the world which is (allegedly) version-neutral. So, though none of the versions tells us "*the* way the world is, . . . each of them tells us *a* way the world is."[12] It follows that if Goodman was an "irrealist" then this irrealism has to be understood *contra* Kant's *transcendent realism*, or any other cognate view that believes in a fixed inherently structured world that is independent of our ways of apprehending it. But insofar as he does refer to version-relative worlds, and also to things within them, his view can be said to be *pro* Kant's empirical realism.[13] And in that case the line that I wish to draw between the two allied doctrines of ontological relativity, Quine's and Goodman's is hard to draw. Both can be treated as immanent realistic ontologies.

Still whatever might have been Goodman's intention, the letter of his text suggests a contrary reading, "I by no means insist that there are many worlds—or indeed any.... Of course, we want to distinguish between versions that do and those that do not refer, and to talk about the things and worlds, if any, referred to; but these things and worlds ... are themselves fashioned by and along with the versions ... World-making begins with one version and ends with another."[14] There are various ways of organizing in various versions. "But what is *it* that is so organised? When we strip off as layers of convention all differences among ways of describing *it* what is left? The onion is peeled down to its empty core."[15] No wonder, Quine reads Goodman's pluralism and constructivism as follows: "...Two versions of the world? But what world is that? To describe it we must retreat into one or the other version; they share no neutral description. Recognize the two versions, Goodman says, and leave it at that."[16]

Quine, I think, does not leave it at that. Both his and Goodman's allied doctrines can be viewed in Goodman's words: "as belonging in that mainstream of modern philosophy that began when Kant exchanged the structure of the world for the structure of the mind...."[17] But apart from the difference that Quine favors a physicalistic "version" and Goodman does not, there is the further distinction, the distinction in respect of the greater emphasis laid by Goodman's thoroughgoing constructivism on Kant's "transcendental idealism."

Quine too speaks of the flux of experience which does not make full-blown physical objects directly available to us. It is we who hit upon the device of positing physical objects "for working a manageable structure into the flux of experience."[18] This indeed is an echo of the sound of the wave of "transcendental idealism" that has surged since "the mainstream of modern philosophy began with Kant." Still there is another echo that seems more vibrant, that of the sound of the wave of "empirical realism" of the same mainstream.

Kant's unformed manifold of sense lacked unity and order. He felt obliged to explain how our experience of unity and order is still possible. Hence the obligation to *import* or *posit* objects by applying the relevant categories deduced from the "Table of Judgements" to the sense-manifold. Unless we assume ourselves to have these categories and posit object with their help, the fact that we do have experience of unified, enduring and interacting physical objects would remain unexplained. The method used for justifying the assumption about the constitution of the human mind and its ineradicable categorial framework is, needless to add, *transcendental.*

Quine surely does not believe in the ineradicability of Kant's *single* categorial framework. And the justification of the choice of *some* out of various conceptual frameworks in his case is explicitly stated to be *pragmatic* not *transcendental.* Yet the way in which he tries to render intelligible our experience and discourse about the world has nevertheless the main thrust of the *transcendental* method of justification. Our understanding and account of the things of the world have to be justified. If they cannot be explained by the flux of experience only, we have to fall back upon conceptual scheme. To put it differently, if they cannot be justified or made evident by something given from outside—"surface irritations," "the firing of nerve endings," then we have to turn to ourselves, our ways of conceiving and speaking and to our conceptual schemes. Unless we assume that our chosen conceptual scheme and the "myth of physical objects" it posits, constitute the best device "for working a manageable structure into the flux of experience," we cannot discourse meaningfully about our world. It does not matter if "Speaking of Objects" is a "myth" chosen on purely *pragmatic* grounds. The method of justifying the choice still seems to be *transcendental* in a pragmatic guise. For what is a transcendental method of justification after all? To make some facts of experience intelligible we must assume something to be the case, without which the facts concerned remain inexplicable. In Kant's case the "Table of Categories" derived from the "Table of Judgements" positing "objects" was the *sine qua non* for the possibility and intelligibility of our experience of unity in the manifold of sense. In Quine's case the "myth of physical objects" which pragmatically evolves as the best conceptual scheme perhaps, is the sine qua non for meaningful discourse about our experience of "what there is."

What ontic status however, does this transcendental method give to "physical objects"? Are they things in a real world out there, which our conceptual scheme is supposed to reflect? This amounts to asking a question which Quine says, is spurious: How much of our "scheme" is " ... merely contributed by language and how much is a genuine reflection of reality?" To answer it "we must talk about the world as well as about language, and to talk about the world we must already impose upon the world some conceptual scheme peculiar to our own language."[19] Even if we change or improve the "scheme," we would be in the same predicament of not being able to detach ourselves from the improved or different "scheme." And so we would continue to impose upon the world such changed or fresh "schemes." The "scheme" cannot be compared with objects *in themselves* in an unconceptualized transcendent reality. What the scheme *says* there is then, object in this case, is an *imposition*, a myth comparable to Homer's Gods. But if this is the status assigned to "objects" then, the wave of "transcendental idealism" would seem to swell into a tide, just in the way it did in Goodman's constructivist thesis. And "what there is" in that event will be reduced to what the "scheme" says there is.

Should Quine give up "the very idea of a conceptual scheme" then, and also the effort of fitting that "scheme" or "organising system" to something "waiting to be organised," namely, the "content" in Davidson's language?[20] I do not think so, for the following reasons.

(1) As Quine conceded to Davidson, one may drop the notion of "conceptual

scheme" and speak instead simply in terms of language and the world?[21] But why should Quine, or anyone for that matter, give up the effort to fit "language" to the world. Even if the two cannot be *compared*, the non-linguistic transcendent "original" on the one hand, and its alleged linguistic "copy" on the other, one may try nevertheless to ascertain the relationship in other ways between language and the world we experience. One may try to do so on empirical, pragmatic and transcendental grounds, as suggested before. The intention is to secure a hook-up between words and objects, between "what we say there is" and "what there is," and the objects to which words are to be hooked are things-for-us, not "transcendent" originals which language is supposed to copy.

(2) What exactly is meant by "content" with which language is to be linked? As just stated, "content" is not a *transcendent* noumenal reality to which the "scheme" has to be fitted in order to be regarded as something more than a "transcendentally ideal" construction. Neither Quine nor Davidson holds that we can get outside our beliefs and our language. Yet we are able to talk about an objective world which is *not our own making*. Davidson says so explicitly and rightly. Quine however, thinks that speaking of objects is a myth, though the *best* myth worthy of belief. In any case the fact that the hook-up is not with a *noumenal* world cannot be a pretext for renouncing efforts of fitting the "scheme" to "content."

(3) Alternatively, the "content" may signify "the totality of experience," "surface irritations," "the facts" and "the world." Davidson puts them all on a par. Quine does not accept this conflation though he does agree with Davidson that none of these make sentences, theories or schemes *true*. But then, should this compel us to give up the effort of fitting the "scheme" on to the "content"? No. For we seek in such "content," in "the totality of experience" "a basis not for *truth* but for *warranted belief*".[22]

The "scheme" or "the man-made fabric" is not sustained merely by internal coherence. It has to face the tribunal of experience, "the firing of the receptors," so that a link is forged between it and the world outside. Even if nothing makes it *true*, it is not a free-floating myth either, something that cannot be hooked on to the world. Had it been such a free-floating myth according to Quine, he would not have stressed the need of facing "the firing of the receptors." And mere internal coherence, and the convention of choosing the "myth" in question, would have sufficed to justify its adoption. But Quine retains and insists on retaining the appeal to the "tribunal of experience "in addition. Empiricism as a theory of *truth* may be dismissed, but it remains intact as a theory of *evidence*.[23] Experience may not be a "maker-true" of "what we say there is." But it certainly can *warrant* our belief that "what we *say* there is," is in all likelihood the way it *really* is. The emphasis on experience as something which issues this warrant springs from the conviction that sensations are what connect the world and our beliefs. In such epistemological matters Quine's position is unequivocal. Notwithstanding Davidson's and Putnam's assault against foundationalism, as we have noted (in chapter 2), Quine does not renounce the basic idea of this thesis, namely, justification for a belief is to be found not in other beliefs but in something of a "different ilk," in sense experience. No wonder he wishes to retain empiricism as a theory of *evidence*, albeit not as a theory of truth.

But why should Quine say that it may be dismissed as a theory of truth, especially when he favors a view of language in which knowing what a sentence means involves not only knowing what its truth-conditions are, but also *recognizing* these conditions when they actually obtain? If the conditions recognized to obtain are the conditions which make the sentence true, then what justifies asserting the sentence will presumably establish its truth as well. Still if Quine hesitates to characterize empiricism as a theory of truth, that hesitation is probably due to a problem which he has raised and which has exercised many philosophers. The problem is indeterminacy of translation. The problem and the example used to bring up the same are so well-know that I will be very brief in stating it here. The problem is: even if in the same perceptual situation a native speaking a jungle language says *gavagai* prompted by the sight of a rabbit, and denies *gavagai* prompted by the sight of a non-rabbit, one cannot conclude that "*gavagai* " means "rabbit." For the native may view the world from within a conceptual scheme, which Quine and other anothropologists and linguists (Whorf and Sapir) think, is very different from the scheme which we use, positing concrete full-blown objects. Consistent with the native's speech behavior, these thinkers urge, *gavagai* may be taken to mean "rabbithood exemplified," or "undetached rabbit parts" etc. So we cannot be sure that *gavagai* means "rabbit" and refers to the same thing to which the word "rabbit" refers. And if not, is there any sense in asking what *really* does the native mean or refer to when he utters *gavagai*? Confronting indeterminacy, Quine contends that there is no fact of the matter as to what a word refers to. Hence the hesitation in taking sense experience as a "maker-true" perhaps, of what the native and we as well say in the same perceptual situation. If this situation justifies the native's belief in a concrete living object, it justifies his belief in an abstract exemplification too.

But is there no way in which one can avert this problem and try to secure the word-object link? Quine himself showed the way. It is only when we analyze utterances finely and demand a determinate parsing into objects, relations, etc., that the problem seems so formidable. But if the utterances are taken holophrastically, as unanalyzed wholes, they can be viewed as tokening the same situation. They can be viewed thus because English speakers would assent to an utterance in just the same situation in which natives assent to others. Observation sentences, which have determinate holophrastic meaning according to Quine, issue the warrant for our beliefs in things which words talk about.

Still, one may not find Quine's answer satisfactory on more than one ground. (a) The appeal to sense experience, or even to observation sentence reporting the experience, as the ultimate source of warrant for our beliefs is untenable; it may be pointed out. For it is not at peace with Quine's avowed anti-foundationalism. (b) In case it is argued that such an experiential base is not intended to transmit certitude to an *isolated* sentence, and therefore, the appeal to it does not hark back to foundationalism, the immediate retort will be that even holism has not given up the basic foundationalist claim. As stated earlier, as opposed to coherentism, foundationalism of the Quinian holistic variety also seeks justification for a belief in sense experience, not in other beliefs. So the appeal to the "tribunal of experience" does hark back to foundationalism in one sense after all. (c) Finally, as discussed in chapter 2 taking cues from Davidson and Putnam, sense experience or even observation sentences cannot be said to *justify* beliefs, although they happen to *cause* these beliefs. Especially they cannot justify beliefs in physical objects.

(4) It does not seem to me however, that in the absence of foundational experience providing direct empirical evidence for our belief in objects, we have to be driven into saying that the "scheme" positing objects is an unwarranted myth. The empirical evidence at hand may not provide support that is direct and immediate. Quine himself maintained that the strength of a given sensory stimulation does not settle whether we are to posit objects of one sort or another.[24] Still, "experiential inputs" or the "contribution of the environment" to borrow Putnam's expressions, may and do help in exercising the right choice taken conjointly with other considerations, though not singularly, by themselves. Quine was wrong to insist that "our *only* source of information about the external world is through the impact of light rays and molecules upon our sensory surfaces."[25] He was therefore vulnerable to skeptical charges. Nevertheless, one can reconstruct Quine's arguments along pragmatist lines to explain how the language world linkage can be established notwithstanding skeptical questions. In fact he himself moved along such lines to explain why the (so-called) myth of "physical object" is to be preferred to other myths.

"Physical objects" are to be preferred to abstract objects because they are directly associated with sensory stimulation. The link between the stimulus and the verbal response, i.e., the sentence containing terms for physical objects, is forged through ostention, conditioning and habit formation. Of course, an association of this sort with sensory stimulation may allegedly shift preference to *sense data* instead of *physical objects*. This in fact is a reason for saying that sensory stimulation by itself cannot settle whether to posit objects of one sort or another. But as Quine pointed out, sense data cannot be regarded as better candidates for ontic admissibility on a different ground. Stimulus may warrant belief in both, but *objects* are to be preferred because in their case the warrant issued by stimulus is strenghtened and supplemented by other considerations. (i) There are utility considerations. We do not need "sense data" for explaining illusions, uncertainties, etc. For words expressing propositional attitudes like "seems that" appended to physical object sentences may do the same job. (ii) More importantly, "objects" have a stronger claim to *ontic admissibility* being readily *identifiable, reidentifiable* and *intersubjectively observable*. (iii) Consequently they "are at the focus of the most successful . . . communication."[26] In lieu of a warrant issued by the stimulus *singly* for an isolated sentence then, we have here not a conflict of two or more standards of which one is foundationalist. Rather, the weight of the warrant issued by direct association with sensory stimulation accrues through repeated conditioning, and also through the additional strength it gains through its compatibility with other supporting considerations mentioned in (i), (ii) and (iii) above. All these put together may help in weaving our web of belief in "physical objects" as the most eligible candidate for inclusion in the inventory of "what there is."

It is to be noted that it is not because we respond, identify, reidentify objects, and communicate about them, and enter into actual successful transactions with them, that these objects are brought into existence. It is rather the other way round. It is because these objects *have identity, or fulfil identity conditions* that the fact that we respond, identify, reidentify, communicate, and successfully interact with them becomes intelligible. What we "*say* there is" would obviously depend on our abilities of the mentioned sort. But "what there is" does not depend upon these abilities and upon what we say on their basis. What we *say*, or our language, or conceptual scheme decide what we can *ontologically commit* ourselves to. But what our language *commits* itself to, ultimately depends upon what we can *admit* in our ontology. The principle of *ontological admissibility* pertains to "what there is," while the principle of *ontological commitment* to "what we *say* there is." What is *admitted* must be assumed to have a nature that makes it possible for us to identify it. It cannot be something that is unknown and unknowable, i.e., "noumenal" and "transcendent" in Kant's sense. But what makes identifying possible is not itself brought into existence, by the act of identifying. It exists as an "empirically real" entity.

This immanent realist strain of Quine's treatment of the question "what there is?" does not seem to be captured by Goodman's metaphors of "world making," "fabricated fact," etc.. Going by the letter of the texts which I have cited, and others similar to them, the accent in Goodman's thesis seems to be on what we apprehend, feel, take or construe to be there. The difference in accent which I have tried to highlight with respect to the general question: what there is? surfaces in the treatment of the specific issue of "universals" as well.

Are There Universals?—Quine's Immanent Metaphysical Approach

I have tried to show why Quine can be reckoned as an immanent metaphysician of the Kantian stripe. Despite difference, the "linguistic turn" he took, is comparable to the "transcendental turn" in Kant's philosophy. The spirit of the turn in each case seems to represent the quintessence of the immanent metaphysical approach. This is the emphasis laid on the inseparable nature of the bond between mind and the world-order in one case, and language and the world-order in another. So far, Goodman's works too, typically represent the same spirit.

The moot point of comparison, I suggested, is that we can not *know* what there is, without referring to some conditions under which such knowledge is possible, and we cannot *say* what there is without referring to a discourse within which a theory says what there is. Prima facie this sounds trivial. But just as in the former case there is no suggestion that *being* or *existence* of things depends only on *us,* similarly, in the latter case there is no suggestion that being or existence depends upon *language.* As Quine says: "What is under consideration is not the ontological state of affairs, but the ontological commitment of a discourse. *What there is,* does not in general depend on one's use of language but what one *says there is* does."[27] In both cases the notion of "existence" or "being" referred to, has *empirical meaning.* Since such meaning can emerge solely in the context of possible experience, we cannot even think of "noumena" as "existing" or "not existing" if "existence" is said to have meaning only in the empirical sense of the term. Of course, once this is made clear, Kant held that we are free to "think" of noumenal existence, in another sense of the term "existence," in another context. "This suggests that Kant is operating with a double sense of 'meaning.' "[28] Quine is not. He sticks to *empirical meaningfulness of the* concept of *being,* of "what there is." But even such "existence" or "being " is not legislated by us. It is not simply a matter of manufacturing or making. Goodman's constructivism on the contrary, is couched in the idiom of *making, constructing, fabricating,* etc. This difference, as I said, surfaces in their respective treatments of the specific issue of "universals."

Initially,both Quine and Goodman took a joint step towards constructing a nominalism that renounces abstract entities, as stated at the outset. They reiterated the old resolve of traditional nominalism of not including universal abstract entities in the inventory of "what there is." But Goodman reconstrued nominalism as a thesis that "does not involve excluding abstract entities . . . [It] requires only that whatever is admitted as an entity at all be *construed* as an individual."[29]

What, however, can be *construed* as an "individual"? Not anything to be *found* in a transcendent world, which by itself, has allegedly marked entities as "individuals." The question is not what *in fact is* an "individual" but rather what we or our theories ("versions") *take* as, or *say* is an "individual." For "ultimate constituent" in terms of which the concept of "individual" is explained, is itself *system-relative.* An "ultimate constituent" is a minimal atomic element in the system which contains no other element that is simpler than it. "Depending on the system, an electron or a molecule or a planet might be *taken* as an atom."[30] Suppose we choose the concrete physical object planet as "constituent." Then, things which are identical being made of the same "constituents," namely planets, would count as "individuals." For "individuals," according to Goodman, are those things which are *identical* whenever they are constituted of the same "ultimate constituents." If such is the case, then, even abstract entities, say, "the class of 9 planets" and also "the class of class of 9 planets" can be construed as "individuals," for the two classes are identical being constituted of the same "ultimate constituents," namely, 9 planets. Of course "class" here is not understood in its standard sense as something *over and above* its members. It is not supposed to belong to a kind of entities *different* from that of its members in the type hierarchy. Thus whether the entity, "class" in this case, can be admitted in the nominalist's world of individuals depends on whether it can be *construed* as an "individual" in Goodman's sense. And whether it can be so construed depends on *how it is taken*; yes, if it is *not taken* as an entity different in kind from that of its members; no, if it is *taken* as such. To put it differently, an abstract entity like "class" can be admitted if it is construed as an "individual" in the sense mentioned. It cannot be admitted if it is construed as a "non-individual." All depends on how we construe a class or an abstract entity. The nominalist's slogan is no more: No abstract entities per se, but rather: No non-individuals. And what is or is not a non-individual, to repeat, is a matter of *taking* or *construing* not *finding*. The question "what there is?" is to be answered by answering what we or our theories or systems *say* there is.

This way of drawing the line between "individuals" and "non-individuals" however, may be contested even by those who support Goodman's rejection of the schism between the so-called *world-in-itself* and the *world as it appears*. Grant that the world-in-itself does not put some entities into a natural given slot, the slot of "particulars," as believed by traditional nominalists. Can we, instead of a transcendent world, draw the dividing line in the way suggested by Goodman? Apparently not. Not at least if things are to be treated as "individuals" for a system *only in case* they are taken as values of variables of the lowest type in that system. For as Quine pointed out, not only a "particular," a particular horse for example, but also the *class* of horses, which is non-particular, can be taken as an appropriate value of an individual variable within a system. Of course a "particular" does not mean what an "individual" means for Goodman. Nor is "non-particular" a surrogate for "non-individual." But the point debated is that being the value of the variable of the lowest type is not the exclusive differentiating mark of "individuals" *only* (even in Goodman's sense of the term "individual").

What however are to count as appropriate values of variables? This is explained in Quine's account with the help of the concept of a "name." A name in the semantic sense of an expression designating something is that with respect to which existential generalization is possible. Only a name in this sense can be a substituend of a bindable variable according to him. The named entity is the value of such a variable. Initially no expression like "class of horses" was permitted to function as a name in this sense, and consequently, as a substituend of a bindable variable. This is just what nominalists generally prefer. But later, Quine had to change his mind. Since he would not renounce mathematics, and mathematics was irredeemably committed to quantification over abstract objects,"[31] abstract entities like "classes" too were posited as values of variables. And since such abstract entities can be named, the expression "the class of horses" was allowed to function as a name, and therefore as a substituend of a bindable variable. What it names, namely, the abstract entity—"class of horses" was taken as an appropriate value of the bindable variable in question. But this shows that being the value of a variable of the lowest type in a system by *itself* cannot be the exclusive differentiating mark of what is an "individual" as I have said. In a realistic language of the sort Quine seems to favor, both "particulars" and "non-particulars" also are treated as values of individual variables. In other words, entities of different kinds, not made out of same "constituents," (in Goodman's sense of the term "constituent") can count as values of variables.

This is just where the step towards nominalism taken jointly by Goodman and Quine seems to lead to different directions. Goodman allows only such entities to rank as values of variables of the lowest type within the *same* system, which are made out of the same "ultimate constituents." "The class of 9 planets" and "the class of class of 9 planets" accordingly, can qualify as values of variables of the lowest type inasmuch as they are made of the *same* constituents. As such, they qualify as "individuals" too, for as Goodman says: "to treat entities as individuals for a system is to take them as values of the variables of lowest type in the system."[32] As long as "the class of 9 planets" and "the class of class of 9 planets" are construed as *identical* "wholes" or "sum individuals" being made of exactly the same parts or constituents, namely 9 planets, they can be accommodated in the system in question. So construed "class" is an "individual." But if "the class of class of 9 planets" is construed as an *additional* entity, it cannot be admitted in the same system. Goodman does not permit composition or generation of a *different* entity out of the *same* constituents. For that would amount to admitting not only "class of class of 9 planets" but also "class of class of class of 9 planets" and so on ad infinitum. His refusal to admit such an endless chain of additional entities is imperative, he thinks, in view of "the traditional injunction against undue multiplication of entities."[33] Hence the kind of nominalism he advocates, countenances nothing but "individuals" as entities. However, though the nominalist countenances only individuals, he may take *anything* as an individual. As pointed out already, "whether a system is nominalistic depends *not* upon whether the entities admitted are *in fact* individuals ... but upon whether they are *construed* in the system as individual ... Nominalism is defined not by independent standards of what constitutes an individual but by independent standards of what constitutes *taking* entities as individuals."[34] The question: "what there is?" or more specifically: "are there classes?" then depends on what we or our system *take* there to be or *say* there is.

However, when Quine asks "what kinds of entities we have to *admit* into our universe?" and also "are universals like attributes, classes, numbers, etc., to be counted among such entities?" the questions raised are typically about "what there is." They are not about what a theory "says there is." The answer he gives in the form of one of his key precepts is: "no entity without identity." If there is a "disagreement on whether there are wombats, unicorns, angels, nutrinos, classes, points, miles, propositions,"[35] he writes, what settles the issue is this key precept, which serves as the standard of *ontological admissibility*. Only those entities should be recognized for which adequate criteria of *identity* can be given. Undue multiplication of entities thus, in Quine's case is sought to be arrested by a criterion different from Goodman's principle of individuality.

Can we allow ourselves then, to introduce or admit into our ontology universals like attributes, classes, etc.? We can, the answer would obviously be, if the entities in question satisfy the criteria of *identity*. A river, "Cayster" for example, is a single concrete object extended in space and time, said Quine, way back in the fifties, in which you can bathe twice, notwithstanding Heraclitus's problems, namely: "you cannot bathe in the same river twice."[36] The river does have an identity and therefore does fulfil the criterion of *ontological admissibility*. We can point at it at various times and places and say "this is Cayster." By doing so we can also improve our listener's understanding as to what portions of space-time we intend our word "Cayster" to cover. But does this mean that the river has identity and is therefore ontologically admissible only because we are able to do this? No. On the contrary it is only when we affirm identity of the object from ostension to ostension that we cause our ostensions to refer to the same large object. Without identity pointing, ostending and referring would be ambiguous. For pointing itself does not tell us, as Quine says, *which* object/objects or momentary stages thereof, are intended. Rather, it is the *prior* concept of a time-consuming spatially extended process, or *one* distinctive form of summation of momentary stages, as in the case of the "river" including such stages, that makes reference and ostension intelligible. "The imputation of identity is essential . . . to fixing the reference of the ostension,"[37] and not the other way round. What has an identity and consequently *is* does not therefore seem to be *derived* from what we *say*.

Physical things, including spatio-temporally spread objects like "river" are *concrete objects* par excellence, and are the strongest bona fide claimants perhaps to ontic admissibility. But can whatever is signified by a general word, say, "red" be admitted in the same way? Is not what it signifies a "twilight half-entity" that can hardly be said to have any identity? Quine does not think so. We may say "This is red" just in the way we say "This is Cayster" (river) and the general term "red" may receive the same semantic treatment. By pointing and saying "this is red" at various times and places, we progressively improve our listener's understanding as to what portions of space-time we intend our word "red" to cover as in the case of the "river" mentioned above.

Quine has argued that "red" as an example of the category of "universals" can be treated on a par with "river" as an "ordinary spatiotemporally extended particular . . . the scattered total thing whose parts are all red things."[38] But the theory of universals as concrete particulars which happens to work for "red" breaks down in general. This becomes patent when we consider other *attributes*, different geometrical shapes like "square," etc., for example. Quine illustrates this with the help of a simple figure of visibly outlined convex regions:

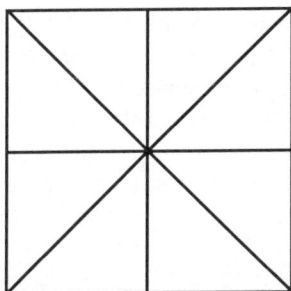

There are 33 such regions. These convex regions however can be interchanged with other geometrical regions, namely: isosceles right triangle, the square, the two-to-one rectangle, and two forms of trapezoid. The two regions, convex and geometrical regions other than convex, constitute different subject matters. But as per the maxim of identification of indiscernibles, we are entitled to speak of the *identity* of the two subject matters, "convex regions" and "geometrical shapes" represented by x and y respectively. Saying x = y apparently does not lead to trouble. But trouble ensues if "square" or "triangle" are semantically treated on a par with "red," that is, if the universals signified by these terms too are equated with single concrete objects like "red" and "river." For just as "red" is construed as the total spatio-temporal thing made up of all red things, so also the shape "square" here should be construed as the total region made up by pooling all the five square regions. The same holds in case of the other shapes with the result that all the five shapes reduce to one, the total region. "Treating the five shapes as universals, and treating these universals as single concrete things absurdly implies that all the triangular regions give simply the total square region . . . ; and similarly for the other . . . regions. We should end up, intolerably, by concluding identity among the five shapes."[39]

There is no need, warns Quine, to proceed on a faulty analogy and suppose that general terms like "square," "triangle," etc., purport to name a single entity that remains identical between different pointings or ostensions when we say "this is square" or "this is triangle," as in the case of "red" or "river." All that is required is that we and our listeners learn when to apply the word to an object and when not. In other words, (i) the general word "square" need not be a name of a separate single temporally spread object, supposedly remaining identical from pointing to pointing. (ii) Nor need we suppose that there is a separate entity *squareness* which is pointed to as the reference of this general word "square." Quine stresses the need of maintaining the traditional distinction between general terms like "square" and abstract singular terms like "squareness." In introducing and using the general term "square" it need not be supposed that it names either a *concrete entity* or an *abstract entity as attribute*. The attribute squareness he holds, comes to much the same thing as "the class of squares."[40]

The preference for *class* rather than *attribute* is patent. Quine's imaginary philosopher McX however, is ontologically committed to the existence of attributes, and in his conceptual scheme there would be variables to take attributes as values. Vis-a-vis this scheme by which he interprets his experiences, it is as obvious to say there are attributes like redness, squareness, etc., as it is to say: "there is red square," "there are big and small squares" and "there are red houses, roses and sunsets."[41] Quine, on the contrary, would admit *classes* rather than *attributes* into ontology, for classes satisfy the criterion of *ontological admissibility*. We can apply the maxim of identification of indiscernibles in case of classes because classes are identical when they have the same members. "Attributes by contrast may be distinct even though present in all and only the same things."[42]

Why however should one accept the conceptual scheme favoured by Quine, it may be asked, and dispense with *attributes* in the sense he dispenses with them? Are we to accept his scheme and not McX's just because it recommends a *clearer manner* of *speaking*? For instance, when we say "some dogs are white" and what we say is true, what is meant is simply that "some things that are dogs are white." In order that the statement be true, the things over which the bound variable "something" ranges must include white dogs, but not doghood or whiteness. In addition to white dogs—the sundry individuals, there is no need to posit any entity, individual or otherwise, which the variable can take as its value. The statement "some roses are red" will similarly commit us to saying there are red roses, but not redness as anything *additional*, which the roses have in common. If anyone presses for an answer to the question: "What do they have in common?" one may just say "if they are all red, that is what they have in common. If they are all red, then they are all red." This obviously is a platitude. And the platitude may be said to provide or recommend a clear manner of speaking, or at most, an alternative philosophical account of the generality of words, different from that of McX's. But how can the platitude provide an answer to the controversial question: what is that which makes it correct to call many things by one and the same name? Moreover, can the platitude settle the existential question? Quine has in fact been held guilty of having confused the platitudinous with the metaphysical.[43]

This charge is too harsh and unfair. Quine does not suggest a dependence of *being* upon *language* as mentioned earlier. Of course a clear analysis of language resulting in paraphrases is necessary, or else we may be ensnared into fallacious ontologies. Indeed, the fundamental ideal of classical analysis was to bring out the true meaning of propositions that lay hidden beneath the form they have in ordinary parlance. Quine therefore was right in undertaking the task of analyzing, translating and reformulating them into better wording which would be logically and conceptually satisfying. Hence the need for treating the letters "F," "G," etc., which stand for *predicates* or general terms in quantification theory as *schematic letters*, and not as *variables* taking *attributes* as values. Treating "F" and "G" and similar predicate letters as bindable variables produces not only a conceptual muddle; it also leads to a false account of the ontological commitments of our discourse. Still this does not mean that what a clearly formulated language is ontically committed to, determines the *being* of whatever there is.

Such a language forbids treating "F" and "G" as bindable variables for this leads to conceptual muddle, as just stated. It produces a conceptual muddle because a variable is like a pronoun and its function is like that of a noun. It cannot accordingly be replaced by a verb or a verb phrase. Predicates are either verbs or verb phrases. A verb or a verb phrase obviously cannot be substituends for individual variables which function like nouns. Predicate letters "F" and "G," etc., must not therefore be treated as variables of quantification. If they are "thought of as names of certain entities and 'F' is treated as a bindable variable, then the values of 'F' are such entities as predicates are names of. But if we treat 'F' as a schematic letter, an unbindable dummy predicate, then we drop the thought of namehood of predicates, and of values for F."[44] Taking predicates as names would be precipitating "a torrent of universals." It would be tantamount to admitting into our ontology *attributes* like doghood, whiteness, etc., over and above concrete individual things like white dogs, and similarly, redness, squareness, etc., over and above concrete individuals like red and square objects. It may still be urged that if Quine could and did admit entities like *classes*, and thought that there is good reason for admitting not only names of classes but also bindable variables which take classes as values, then *attributes* like squareness, etc., should also be admitted.

Against this, Quine's reservations, already noted, are as follows:

(i) *Attributes* like squareness, etc., do not satisfy the identity conditions requisite for ontic admissibility.[45] Classes do and may therefore be admitted.

(ii) If predicate letters like "F" and "G" are allowed to quantify over abstract entities like *attributes* then the conceptual, logical and grammatical disadvantage that results, ought to be avoided.

(iii) If letters like "F" and "G" on the contrary are given a *schematic* status, then they can be taken as variables with *classes* as values. This would not embroil one in the logical, grammatical and conceptual muddle as in the case of treating the letters as *predicates*, and predicates as names of attributes. But is this the reason why Quine *admits classes* and not *attributes*?

I do not think so. For what a right use of words forbids at most is the *ontological commitment* of a sort that may lead one to a bloated Platonic universe or a Meinongian jungle. The right use of words helps one in choosing that which one is ready to be *ontologically committed* to, without being led to such a "bloated universe" or a "jungle." But the *choice* and the consequent ontic *commitment* does not determine *being* and *non-being* of objects chosen and posited.

Goodman, referring to Quine's criterion of *ontic commitment*, had said: "If we use variables that we construe as having entities of any given kind as values, we *acknowledge* that there are such entities."[46] But saying that we *acknowledge*, *recognize* and *commit* ourselves to such and such entities does not answer the question: what entities are we willing to recognize at all? What we are willing to recognize as entities require criteria *other than* that demanded by nominalism for construing "individuals" and "primitives" of a system. As Goodman says: "Whatever we are willing to recognize as an entity at all may be construed as an individual." But this does not help in settling what we are willing to recognize and acknowledge as entities. "Important as the question is, nominalism does not decide it."[47]

In Quine's case, what we are willing to and do acknowledge as entities depends ultimately on whether the entities acknowledged *have identity*. Thus it is not the choice of a language and whatever the language chooses to acknowledge as an entity that determine the *being* of the entity chosen. On the contrary, it is because the entity *has identity* and thereby enables us to identify it that we acknowledge it in our ontology. Even if a clear "platitudinous" manner of speaking of a particular language is recommended, the "platitudinous" has not been mixed up with the "metaphysical."

Could Quine's principle of "ontological admissibility," namely "no entity without indentity," be included among the "other criteria" Goodman referred to, which are needed for acknowledging the entities we do acknowledge? Perhaps yes. Quine did not speak of the indentity of a *transcendent* reality that is *unrelated* to discourse. The identity conditions of "what there is" vary from case to case. Being a spatiotemporally extended concerete object may be the requisite condition in some cases. "Having the same members" constitutes such a condition in other cases where we speak of identity of "classes" for example. So we cannot meaningfully speak of entities, of "what there is," without reference to some specific universe of discourse. But what does this *relativity* to discourse, "version," "conceptual scheme," etc., mean and amount to?

Does it mean that admitting any entity in our ontology depends on our selection, organization, way of taking, in a sense that tends to lapse into Berkeleyanism, or to some other variety of constructivism? I do not think so. One may stress the necessity of describing the world or entities in it from within a framework or "version." But this could still be an objective enterprise in a realistic sense. Ontological relativity could simply mean that a thing has the specific kind of identity which *we think* it to have. This is not tantamount to saying that the thing has such an identity *intrinsically, non-relationally* and *absolutely*, which both Quine and Goodman dismiss straightaway. But this is not tantamount to saying either that whatever identity a thing is *thought* or *taken* to have, must therefore be a *construction* or *imposition* of thought itself. The identity a thing *has relationally* is still something which the *thing* has. It does not have it *by itself*; but nor have we, or our thought, or way of taking, *made* it so. Rather, it is because the thing *really* has the identity albeit *relationally* that it becomes possible for us to *take* it in a certain way. This relational nature of "what there is" is stressed by those who believe in the "empirical meaningfulness" of the notion of "existence."

If Goodman endorsed the same view, he too could be regarded as an "empirical realist." But this sounds discordant in the face of the renunciation of the idea of anything that is *given* to us as anything. In his self-styled "irrealism" the accent is on *taking* something as something. As pointed out earlier, "what there is" seems to be a function of *how we take or feel*. The overworked metaphor of "world-making" which begins *with* one version and ends with another, seems to suggest that relativity to versions is *constitutive* of "what there is."

At times the hesitation to refer to a world and things in it surfaces conspicuously. Yet on many occasions, in stark contrast to some earlier pragmatists, Goodman refuses to reduce the talk of *truth* to a talk of *acceptability*. Suppose we do grant that as in the case of cognate theories of ontological relativity, Goodman too reiterates the Kantian point concerning conceptualization. By means of some kind of selection and organization we can achieve reference as well as *predication* within the bounds of a language. For instance, in a "version" that takes "qualia" as primitive, one can say: "That chair is brown," the chair being constituted of the "constituent" "quale" brown in this case. What would be the truth-condition *internal* to the version in question? Since Goodman does not favor "classes" he cannot apply Tarski's concept given for the language of the calculus of classes. But one can adapt it to his system perhaps, and say "the quale brown is in or is a part of some quales denoted by the phrase chair" if the quale brown is in or is a part of some quales denoted by the phrase chair. So far, one may claim to have achieved reference and truth in spite of *relativization* of referential and truth-claiming assertions *within* language. But why should relativization stop here? May we not ask: How we can refer *simpliciter* to the "versions" themselves? What are the "systems" or "versions" to be relativized to, when these "versions" are taken as values of variables? In which system can these "systems" be taken as values of variables?[48]

Relativization should not stop in Goodman's pluralisitic and radically relativistic thesis. But unless the inter-systemic relationship is clearly explained, there would be a proliferation of "different worlds" in Thomas Kuhn's sense, and the attendant threat of crypto-absolutist system-centricity. Even if coherence between the versions is somehow shown, unless there is a further support given by the kind of transcendental argument attributed to Quine in the previous section, can his coherently interlocked "versions" be regarded as something more than idealistic constructions? In that case would it be proper to regard Goodman as an "empirical realist"?

Quine's ontology by contrast, has a realist strain despite its austerity. He does caution us against one manner of speaking, which treats predicates as names of attributes. He cautions us against taking predicate letters "F," "G,"etc., of quantification theory as bindable variables. He recommends instead another manner of speaking where a distinction is drawn between variables for individuals and variables for classes. The letters "F" and "G" should be given a schematic status, as noted before. Indeed he is even prepared to accommodate abstract singular terms like "squareness" subject to the standard behavior of singular terms such as the law of putting equals for equals. This may *commit* us to an abstract entity named by the singular term. But can we really *admit* into our ontology what we can apparently *commit* ourselves to? Preference for, or adoption of one conceptual scheme and its language in lieu of another, does not seem to be able to provide an answer to this question. Nor is it intended to do so in Quine's philosophy. There is the *separate* precept, "no entity without identity" to decide *admissibility*, and the precept may apply independently or autonomously in the sense that it does not require commitment to any particular conceptual scheme or discourse.

Class is accessible to identity conditions and therefore is. For as pointed out already, classes may be said to be identical if they have the same members. But class is an abstract entity. A class of stones cannot be identified for instance with a concrete heap, a heap of stones. For if it could be so identified, then another class, the class of molecules of stones in the heap could be identified with the same heap. But obviously the two classes are not identical. In admitting classes as abstract entities Quine advocates a mixed ontology, and for this, extreme nominalists may wish to withhold the brand name of their philosophy in characterizing his position. Yet, insofar as his reduced ontology does not find a place for such abstract entities which are supposedly designated by predicates, entities like whiteness, redness, etc., over and above sundry individuals, his position cannot be labelled as realism about universals either.

Even with respect to the kinds of entities he does admit in his ontology, notwithstanding my realist reading, it is hard to say straightforwardly how that ontology should be characterized. Being, as has been repeatedly asserted, following Quine, does not depend on the use of language although saying what is and is not, does. And it is identity which things must have, to have being, which makes intelligible reference, identification and ostension, not the other way round. It appears then, that being is transcendent in some sense. However it is *not* transcendent in the sense of something that is entirely beyond conception. On the contrary, things which have being, though not at the mercy of language and language-users for having that being, must nevertheless be such, or have such an identity that makes identification or reference possible and intelligible. Otherwise their admissibility into ontology would be suspect. It is this harmony of the world-order on the one hand, and language, experience and conceptual scheme on the other, that typically characterize the whole genera of immanent metaphysicians. Quine seems to belong to this genera of thinkers.

Throughout this chapter I have tried to highlight the "empirical realist" strain of Quine's immanent metaphysical standpoint, with respect to the general question, "what there is?" (in one section), and the specific question, "are there universals like classes, attributes, etc.?" (in the section that followed it). In both cases I seek support for my realist reading of his position in the distinction he draws between two precepts: "no entity without identity" and "to be is to be the value of a variable." It is with respect to the latter particularly, and our "*ontological commitment*" which it expresses, that the dependence on language and conceptual schemes is most pronounced. Insofar as it *relativizes* what we *say* there is to language and conceptual scheme, it seems to suggest that Quine is making existence parochial. And this in turn may give the impression that the thesis of ontological relativity is closer to "constructivism" of some kind or to "transcendental idealism," not to "empirical realism."

To defend what I take as Quine's immanent or empirical realist metaphysics, I can only recapitulate the points discussed already.

(a) Even if we grant that "to be is to be the value of a variable," we must admit nevertheless that what the variables of true statements of a theory range over are real things. If they are to count as values of variables of true statements, they have to be real things because the kind of quantification Quine deploys is *objectual*.

(b) Quine does not believe in *absolute* denotation based on an *interpretation-independent* reference relation between sentence parts and items of the world. The "real things" referred to by the theory must be understood in relation to language, and the conceptual scheme we use when we *say* what there is. So far things can be said to have *relative* denotations. But this only shows that Quine adheres to the "empirical meaningfulness" of the notion of existence. However even what is *said* to *exist* is not brought into being by language or conceptual scheme.

(c) Even "appearance" which is "formed matter" (to borrow a phrase from Kant) has the necessary condition of its being in something that is *given*. In Kant's dualistic metaphysics the "given" comes from a world of things-in-themselves. In view of the gap between "noumena" and "phenomena" in that dualistic metaphysics, the "pure contributions of the mind" seem to be more in the nature of an *imposition* or *ascription* on something independent. In Quine's ontology which is fully immanent, the "given" in the form of "firing of the receptors" comes from the world of experience. That world which is *ontologically admitted* is *not transcendent*. It is conceptually and experientially relatable to our understanding and language in the sense that it *has a nature* or *identity* which makes possible *reference* and *identification* from within a conceptual scheme. In view of this relation between the identity a real thing *has*, and what we *say* or *take* it to have, that which we say from within our "scheme" does not seem to be much in the nature of an *imposition* or *ascription* on something totally transcendent.

(d) Insofar as *ontological admissibility* is determined by *indentity*, and not by *our ability* to *identify*, "what there is" is not our ideal construction. Such identity is testified to by successful *reference*. However, can we feel assured about such "indentity," and the consequent stability of what we *ontologically admit*, even if reference becomes *unstable* and infirm? The whole edifice of what is claimed to be *real*, at least *empirically* if not *transcendently*, would seem to be erected on quicksand if reference becomes infirm. I cannot discuss Quine's thesis of ontogenesis of reference here, within the bounds of this chapter. Still, it seems that the uneasiness about the realist reading stems from the search for something which Quine thinks, one should not look for.

(e) One must not look for a referential link between sentence parts of a language peculiar to a conceptual scheme and items of a world beyond *all* conceptual schemes, that is the transcendent or noumenal world. But as per the "empirical meaningfulness" of the notion of "existence" one can speak of a word-object hook-up, albeit within a "scheme." Since there are many schemes, can we say that what we refer to, namely tables, rivers, galaxies, classes, etc., from within our "scheme" could also be referred to by our interpreters from within their scheme? There may be translational hazards no doubt. And there may be conflicting ontological claims about what is to be *admitted*. But just because McX *commits* himself to attributes, are we to *admit* attributes together with "classes"? A clearer manner of speaking free of conceptual muddles may convert McX and change his ontological commitment. Whether he can be made to refer to, or indentify, and therefore *admit* what we *admit*, say classes, would depend ultimately not on McX or on us. It would depend on the fact that what is admitted *has an identity*. As for our feeling assured about the success of translation and reference despite conceptual differences, we have to appeal to empirical evidence (association with sensory stimulus), in the first place, and to the transcendental argument that renders intelligible our ability to identify, and also to other pragmatic considerations. All put together may form a web of belief regarding what we, not McX, admit there to be.

Notes

1. Nelson Goodman with W. V. O. Quine, "Steps toward a Constructive Nominalism," in Goodman, *Problems and Projects* (Indianapolis, Ind.: Bobbs Merrill, 1972).

2. C. F. Delaney, Presidential Address: "Beyond Realism and Anti-Realism," *Proceedings of American Catholic Philosophical Association* (1985).

3. The lines are quoted by A. D. Woozley in his article "Universals," in *Encyclopedia of Philosophy*, ed. Paul Edwards, vol. 8 (New York: Macmillan & Free Press, 1967), 201.

4. Bertrand Russell, *The Problems of Philosophy* (Oxford: Oxford University Press, 1912), 55.

5. J. L. Mackie, *Problems from Locke* (Oxford: Clarendon Press, 1976), 112, 136.

6. W. V. O. Quine, "Logic and the Reification of Universals," in Quine, *From a Logical Point of View* (Cambridge, Mass.: Harvard University Press, 1953), 102.

7. Henry B. Veatch, "Is Quine a Metaphysician?" *the review of metaphysics* (March 1978), 418-19.

8. See the Introduction by Geoffrey Hellman in Nelson Goodman, *The Structure of Appearance*, 3d.ed. (Dordrecht: Reidel, 1977), xxiii. Quine on the contrary, one should remember, had contended that seen holophrastically, as conditioned to stimulatory situations, an observation sentence is theory free.

9. Nelson Goodman, "The Way the World Is," in Goodman, *Problems and Projects*, 26.

10. See W. V. O. Quine, "Ontic Decision," in Quine, *Word & Object* (Cambridge Mass.: MIT Press, 1960), 235. Though playing a key role, the stimulus by itself does not attain a bigger score however, for belief in physical objects, as we shall see presently.

11. Goodman, "The Way the World Is," 26.

12. Goodman, "The Way the World Is," 31.

13. See Hilary Putnam, "Reflections on Goodman's Ways of Worldmaking," in Putnam, *Realism and Reason, Philosophical Papers*, vol. 3 (Cambridge: Cambridge University Press, 1983), 163.

14. Nelson Goodman, *Ways of Worldmaking* (Indianapolis, Ind.: Hackett, 1978), 96-97.

15. Goodman, *Ways of Worldmaking*, 118.

16. W. V. O. Quine "Goodman's Ways of Worldmaking," in Quine, *Theories and Things* (Cambridge Mass.: Belknap Press of Harvard University Press, 1981), 97. Emphasis added.

17. Goodman, *Ways of Worldmaking*, x.

18. W. V. O. Quine, "Two Dogmas of Empiricism," in Quine, *From a Logical Point of View*, 44.

19. W. V. O. Quine, "Identity, Ostension and Hypostasis," in Quine, *From a Logical Point of View*, 78-79.

20. See Donald Davidson, "On the Very Idea of a Conceptual Scheme," in Davidson, *Inquiries into Truth and Interpretation* (Oxford : Clarendon Press, 1984), 189.

21. W. V. O. Quine, "On the Very Idea of a Third Dogma," in Quine, *Theories and Things*, 41. Quine agreed to drop the notion of "conceptual scheme." I have tried to show (in chapter 2) following Putnam that conceptual relativity does not frustrate efforts to establish linkage between mind/language and the world. So one need not make the concession.

22. Quine, "On the Very Idea of a Third Dogma," 39. Emphasis added.

23. Quine, "On the Very Idea of a Third Dogma," 39.

24. Quine, "Ontic Decision," 236.

25. W. V. O. Quine, "The Nature of Natural Knowledge," in *Mind and Language*, ed. S. Guttenplan (Oxford: Clarendon Press, 1975), 68.

26. Quine, "Ontic Decision," 234.

27. Quine, "Logic and the Reification of Universals," 103. Emphasis added.

28. See Gerd Buchdahl, *Metaphysics and the Philosophy of Science* (Oxford: Basil Blackwell, 1969), 534.

29. Nelson Goodman, "A World of Individuals," in Goodman, *Problems and Projects*, 157. Emphasis added.

30. Goodman, "A World of Individuals," 158.

31. Quine, "Ontic Decision," 269.

32. Goodman, "A World of Individuals," 157.

33. Goodman, "A World of Individuals," 163.

34. Goodman, *The Structure of Appearance*, 28. Emphasis added.

35. Quine, "Ontic Decision," 233.

36. Quine, "Identity, Ostension and Hypostasis," 65, 67.

37. Quine, "Identity, Ostension and Hypostasis," 66-69.

38. Quine, "Identity, Ostension and Hypostasis," 72. We can give an identity condition for the entity corresponding to the general term "red" only if we consider it to be a concrete particular. No identity condition can be given if we treat it as the property of being red. If such a condition could be given for a universal property then that would have enabled us to determine when two distinct predicates could both refer to the same property. But predicates refer to the same property only when they are synonymous. However, as Quine pointed out in "Two Dogmas of Empiricism," giving a coherent account of synonymy is impossible. Hence general terms should not be taken to stand for abstract universal properties.

39. Quine, "Identity, Ostension and Hypostasis," 72-73.

40. Quine, "Identity, Ostension and Hypostasis," 75-76.

41. W. V. O. Quine, "On What There Is," in Quine, *From a Logical Point of View*, 10.

42. Quine, "Logic and the Reification of Universals," 107.

43. Ilham Dilman, *Quine on ontology, necessity, and experience: A Philosophical Critique* (Albany, N. Y. : State University of New York Press, 1984), 68, 69.

44. Quine, "Logic and the Reification of Universals," 110.
45. Quine, "Identity, Ostension and Hypostasis," 72, 75, 76.
46. Goodman, *The Structure of Appearance*, 24, 28. Emphasis added.
47. Goodman, "A World of Individuals," 157.
48. Goodman, *The Structure of Appearance*, Introduction by Geoffrey Hellman, xlii.

Chapter 4

Skepticism against Realisms

In chapter 3 I highlighted the salient features of Quine's ontology with special reference to one particular subject-matter, universals. It seems to me that these features provide a scaffolding for the immanent realistic metaphysics I am trying to build. The search for a scaffolding in what seems to be the realistic component of Quine's philosophy however, might meet resistance, and reasons for this resistance may be found in some of his own convictions.

Skeptical Doubts Concerning a Realistic Interpretation of Quine's Metaphysics

I tried to build my case for a realistic interpretation of Quine's (immanent) metaphysics by drawing mainly on his precept concerning *ontological admissibility* in contradistinction to what he calls *ontological commitment.* Insofar as ontological admissibility is determined by identity, and not by our ability to identify, I said, "what there is" is not our ideal construction. Indeed all would have been well if we could also feel assured about such identity, by virtue of having which things (including universals like classes) are ontologically admitted as real, as what there is. And we could feel assured about such identity if this could be testified to by successful *reference.* But if reference is inscrutable, as Quine says, can we have the assurance we are seeking about the stability of things to be admitted ontologically? Even if variables are not uniquely referential expressions, they must be vehicles of reference nevertheless. The notion of reference has immense importance for Quine's views concerning objectual quantification and ontological admissibility. When his thesis of ontogenesis of reference makes that notion of reference a suspect, the account he gives of ontic stability of things admitted as real becomes enervated. What is required to strengthen that account and thereby dispel misgivings about a realistic interpretation of Quine's metaphysics is a firm word-to-thing relation. But it is doubtful whether we can legitimately claim within the framework of Quine's theory that there is such a relation for the following reasons:

(a) An ambivalence marks Quine's view about ontological admissibility and the importance of the notion of reference for it on the one hand, and his holistic view of language rendering that very notion of reference problematic on the other.

(b) Given this holistic view of language, one has to follow Quine and say that we do not understand sentences as isolated units, parts of which refer to interpretation-independent items in the world. To understand the alien sentence "gavagai," to take the famous example previously alluded to, is to understand how the alien assents to it in response to certain stimuli, in this case coming from a rabbit being seen. The trouble is, as I have mentioned before, there are many ways of translating this sentence, each of which is compatible with the alien's disposition to assent to it when the rabbit is around. For there are many ways of assigning reference conditions to the sentence parts which are compatible with the totality of the alien's speech disposition. Since there is no neutral interpretation-independent fact of the matter to decide which translation is true, there is no knowing whether the alien and the interpreter are referring to the same thing. How, in that case, can we have the firm word-to-thing relation we are seeking to establish?

(c) There is no relation of reference, it seems then, between sentence parts of a language within a conceptual scheme, and items in the world beyond the bounds of such a scheme, to which sentence parts of other languages too may refer. In fact, reference here is not a word-to-thing relation at all where the thing is supposed to be transcendent, interpretation-independent. But when Quine gives up the notion of such a transcendent reality and still claims, saying that he is a robust realist, there are tables and chairs, galaxies and black holes, what are we to understand by existence of such things? As per the thesis of ontological relativity we have seen, such existence is parochial, immanent, or internal to a language or scheme. So the alien's notion of whatever reality she refers to is parochial within her own scheme, but inscrutable and non-existent for the interpreter unless an appropriate translation manual is found.

(d) However, even if reference is sought to be construed in this way as *relative,* it seems doubtful whether there can be a word-to-thing relation of the kind we are looking for. The hook-up with the things, particularly a physical thing, cannot be established, through the intermediation of sensory stimuli as Quine suggested. Recall Davidson's and Putnam's stricture against taking sensation as *justifier* of belief in physical objects. Quine of course did not retreat in the face of such an attack, and continued to rely on observation sentences, which taken holophrastically will establish the language-reality link, he believed ardently. The arguments marshalled by Davidson and Putnam against such a claim (discussed in chapter 2) need not be stated here all over again. Observation sentences, taken singly, that is, without additional strength derived from *other* considerations, cannot justify belief in objects in the external world. How then can we justifiably assert that the sentences "there are black-holes," "there are rabbits," etc., are true?

(e) Quine himself has not been consistent in answering the question. On some occasions he urges that within a scheme, asserting that the sentence "there are black-holes" is true, is just assenting to, or reaffirming the sentence. Truth is immanent. But can just assenting to the sentence or mere reaffirmation of the same make the sentence true? Should we not look for the maker-true of the sentence in something beyond the scheme within which it is affirmed or reaffirmed?[1] How else can the sentence be hooked on to things outside about which it speaks? Things outside need not comprise a neutral interpretation-independent hard fact of the matter. But if the sentence has any rightness, it must transcend the speaker's own subjectivity or his own scheme. Quine's retaliation here will obviously be what has been stressed repeatedly. He does seek the source of objectivity and truth in something outside. The truth of some sentences at least, i.e., observation sentences is tied directly to patterns of excited nerve endings. Other sentences derive their empirical content and strength from their connection with those observation sentences and their logical inter-relations. But I do not know how far this retaliatory move can succeed in securing the firm word-to-thing relation which we require to establish sentences as true.

Firstly, as noted previously, Quine himself concedes that sense experience is not the maker-true of sentences expressing beliefs, especially belief in bodies. Empiricism, he admits remains intact as a theory of *evidence* though not as a theory of *truth*.[2]

Secondly, suppose we ignore for a while Davidson's and Putnam's criticism that observation sentences cannot serve as evidence for justified true beliefs. Suppose also that Quine is able to stave it off by arguing how observation sentences taken as unanalyzed wholes can circumvent translational hazards and secure word-to-thing linkages. But resolving the problem due to *indeterminacy* is not resolving the problem due to what is called the *under-determination* of theory. A theory can be justifiably called true, according to Quine, if it explains or predicts true observation sentences. But the hypotheses which the theory contains "are related to observation only by a kind of one-way implication; namely, the events we observe are what a belief in the hypothesis would have led us to expect. These observable consequences of the hypothesis do not, conversely imply the hypothesis. Surely there are alternative hypothetical substructures that would surface in the same observable ways."[3] This leads to the peculiar situation of scientific theories being under-determined empirically. For two alternative theories can be *equally capable* of accounting for all true observation sentences, and therefore be *empirically equivalent* although they are *logically incompatible* and *irreducible* in the sense that each theory contains at least one predicate that cannot be defined by using the resources of the other theory. "Under-determination says that for any one theory formulation there is another that is empirically equivalent to it but logically incompatible with it, and cannot be rendered logically equivalent to it by any reconstrual of predicates."[4] Facing this peculiar situation, will Quine say that both theories in spite of being logically incompatible are *true* because both can equally well explain and predict all true observation sentences on which their truth depends according to him? His answer shuttles between two opposed positions from time to time. On one view, a speaker at a given time operates with one theory which she accepts as true dismissing the other logically incompatible but empirically equivalent theory as false. In case she shifts to this second alternative theory, it is this theory which becomes true while the theory previously accepted as true becomes false. This view illustrates the position which holds: truth is *immanent*. But as Putnam observes, "Quine the logician is not willing to say of incompatible theories that *both* can be true."[5] The other position maintains that both theories being empirically equivalent are true or false together. Even if they are incompatible, they can be equally correct. This position, which is also advocated by Nelson Goodman, is in Quine's words "ecumenical."

These considerations, and the vacillation that marks the two conflicting moods, logical and ecumenical, lead to skeptical animadversions. The objective constraint which Quine thinks can remove skeptical doubts is the constraint of enabling us to predict successfully our sensory inputs. Since the strength this constraint supposedly has as evidence is itself challenged, and since even if it does serve as evidence that evidence is *indistinguishable* in relation to incompatible theories, it is questionable whether it can remove skeptical doubts after all. I still maintain that Quine's immanent metaphysical approach can provide a scaffolding for the kind of internal realistic thesis I am trying to build. But if that scaffolding is shrouded by an advancing fog of skeptical doubt, it would be hazardous to set one's foot on it to erect a realistic structure. Those who believe in a world which is not our own making and yet insist that the question "what there is?" cannot be meaningfully formulated without reference to what we know, believe and say about it, will readily embrace Quine's immanent metaphysics. Difficulty arises when the focus shifts from the metaphysical question "what there is?" to the epistemic question "what do we *know* there to be?" Quine's empiricist epistemology which is basically foundationalist, though disavowedly, has grown effete it seems, when exposed to Davidson's criticism. It does not provide sufficiently strong planks for the scaffolding, which one requires to set one's foot firmly, to build a realistic edifice. At this juncture and against the background of such an epistemology one should ask afresh: can one be realist, even of the immanentist or internalist type, in the face of the challenge mounted by the skeptic?

Skepticism against Realisms

Few questions in philosophy merit a simple yes or no answer. The question I want to ask afresh falls within that category. In fact one cannot begin to answer it without reconsidering the question what it means to call anyone a "skeptic" or a "realist," for each term has been applied to a variety of views. When varieties and sub-varieties are identified, the answer vis-a-vis some of them seems to be an emphatic "no," to others a grudging "yes," to still others a paradoxical mix of "yes" and "no." I will not try to classify types of skepticism here, but I can identify a skeptic who may not be hostile to internal realists. As for "realism" some varieties and sub-varieties were enumerated at the very outset (in chapter 1) under two main labels: transcendent and immanent.

Transcendent realism (TR for short) I suggested, could be classified into three sub-varieties: (a) trans-conceptual, (b) trans-congnitive, and (c) trans-phenomenal. Both TR and internal realism (IR for short) focus primarily on the *metaphysical* question: what there is? Both seek to answer this question by turning to a plethora of items to be included in the ontic inventory. If the inventory included *all* items, realism of both varieties should be termed "global." If the inventory turned out to be selective, retaining some items and excluding others, they would be termed "local" (as discussed earlier in chapter 1).[6] Realism however, can be given an alternative construal with the focus shifting from the purely metaphysical question "what there is?" to the *epistemological* question "what do we know there to be?" This construal is not antithetical, but complementary to the first. While the former talks mainly about the objective world, the latter concerns itself with the account of our ability to acquire the knowledge of that objective world. A third construal is *semantical.* In it realism is formulated not in terms of entities, but in terms of *statements,* a disputed class of statements about different subject-matters. Its main contention is that the statements falling within the disputed class, or for that matter any statement which is not vague, must have a determinate objective truth-value independently of our knowledge.[7] This too is not antithetical to the first formulation. In fact it is like one side of the coin which has transcendent metaphysical realism of some sort on the other side. If one wishes to find out what stance a skeptic will take towards realism, one should consider these types and sub-types which I have tried to indicate below in tabular form with the help of two figures. Figure 1 gives the three main construals, *metaphysical, epistemological* and *semantical,* and subdivisions under each rubric. Figure 2 gives a classification of sub-types of the epistemological formulation which one usually comes across in the literature on the subject, which of course is not exhaustive.

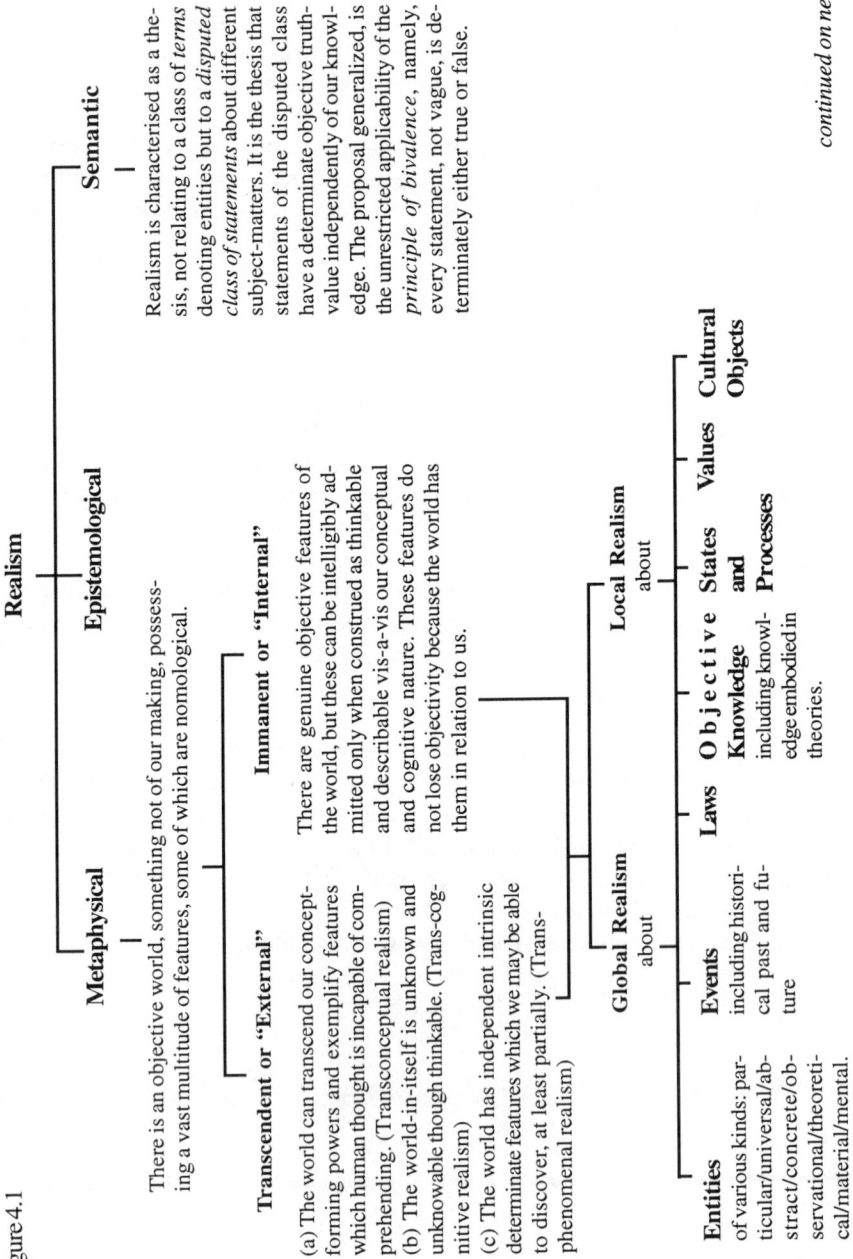

Figure 4.1

Realism

Metaphysical

There is an objective world, something not of our making, possessing a vast multitude of features, some of which are nomological.

Epistemological

Semantic

Realism is characterised as a thesis, not relating to a class of *terms* denoting entities but to a *disputed class of statements* about different subject-matters. It is the thesis that statements of the disputed class have a determinate objective truth-value independently of our knowledge. The proposal generalized, is the unrestricted applicability of the *principle of bivalence*, namely, every statement, not vague, is determinately either true or false.

Transcendent or "External"

(a) The world can transcend our concept-forming powers and exemplify features which human thought is incapable of comprehending. (Transconceptual realism)
(b) The world-in-itself is unknown and unknowable though thinkable. (Trans-cognitive realism)
(c) The world has independent intrinsic determinate features which we may be able to discover, at least partially. (Trans-phenomenal realism)

Immanent or "Internal"

There are genuine objective features of the world, but these can be intelligibly admitted only when construed as thinkable and describable vis-a-vis our conceptual and cognitive nature. These features do not lose objectivity because the world has them in relation to us.

Global Realism
about

Local Realism
about

Entities	**Events**	**Laws**	**Objective Knowledge**	**States and Processes**	**Values**	**Cultural Objects**
of various kinds: particular/universal/abstract/concrete/observational/theoretical/material/mental.	including historical past and future		including knowledge embodied in theories.			

continued on next page

Figure 4.1 *Continued*

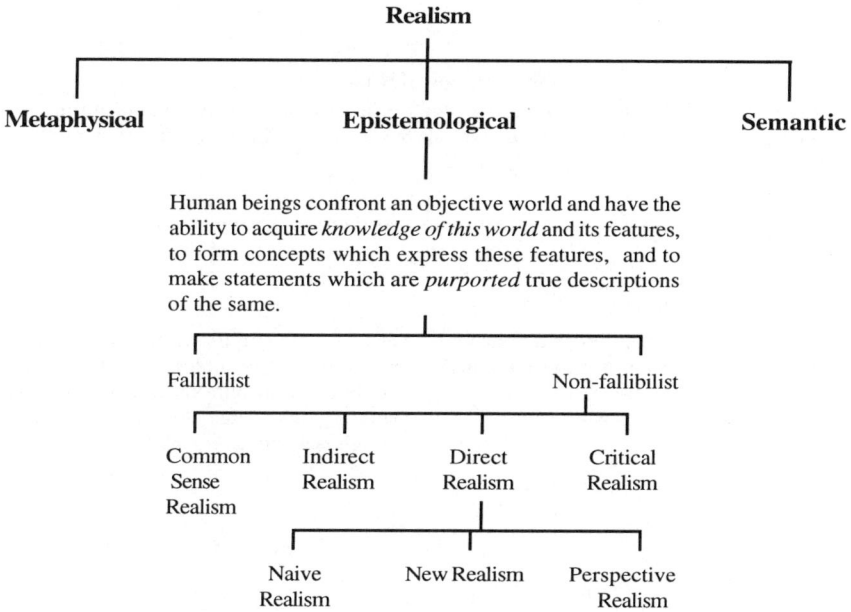

Realism

Metaphysical   **Epistemological**   **Semantic**

Human beings confront an objective world and have the ability to acquire *knowledge of this world* and its features, to form concepts which express these features, and to make statements which are *purported* true descriptions of the same.

Fallibilist   Non-fallibilist

Common Sense Realism   Indirect Realism   Direct Realism   Critical Realism

Naive Realism   New Realism   Perspective Realism

Figure 4.2

Epistemological Realism

We have the ability to acquire knowledge of the external objective world, form concepts which express its features, and make statements which are purported true descriptions of the same.

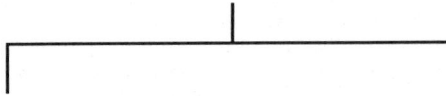

Fallibilist

We claim to have such knowledge despite fallibility. It does not matter if we fail to know that we know in the absence of a criterion which marks unmistakably what is true.

Non-Fallibilist

Varieties of this type within the empiricist framework are more optimist about our cognitive abilities to acquire knowledge of external material things either directly or indirectly through perception.

continued on next page

Figure 4.2 *Continued*

Non-Fallibilist

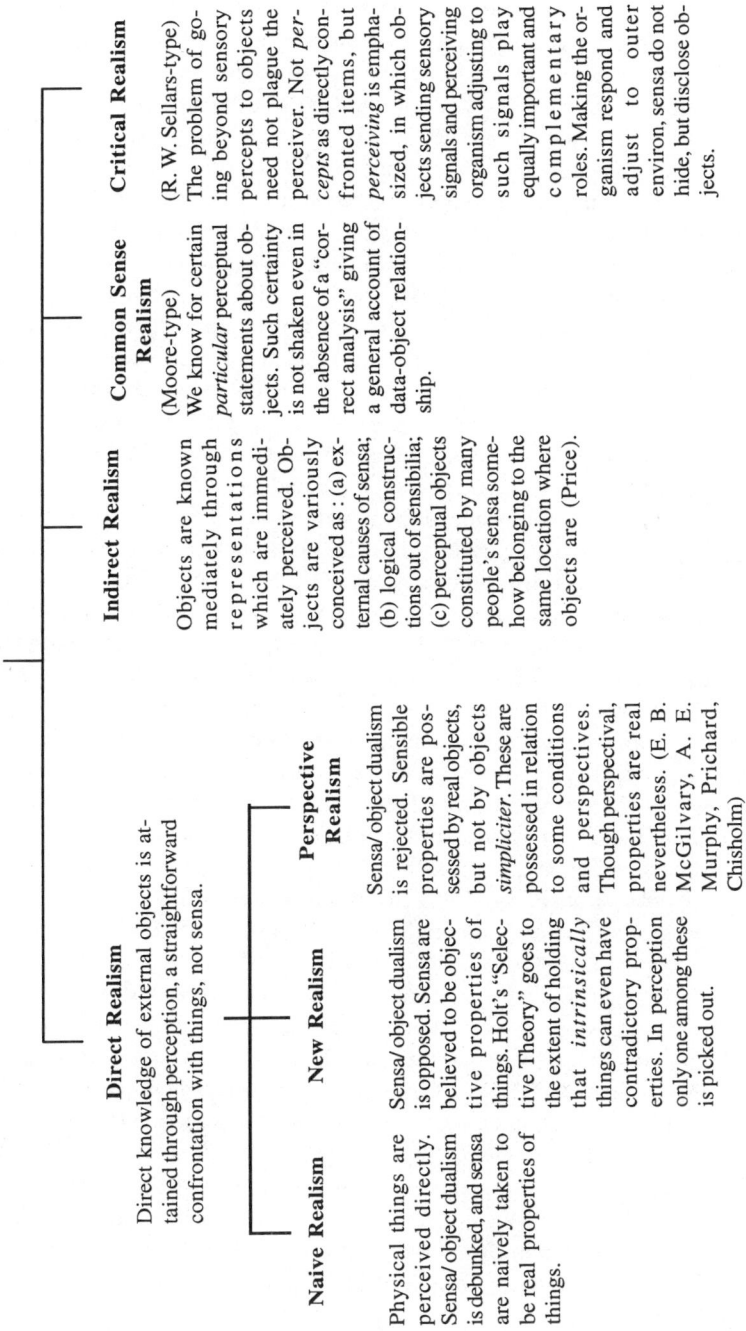

Direct Realism

Direct knowledge of external objects is attained through perception, a straightforward confrontation with things, not sensa.

Naive Realism

Physical things are perceived directly. Sensa/object dualism is debunked, and sensa are naively taken to be real properties of things.

New Realism

Sensa/object dualism is opposed. Sensa are believed to be objective properties of things. Holt's "Selective Theory" goes to the extent of holding that *intrinsically* things can even have contradictory properties. In perception only one among these is picked out.

Perspective Realism

Sensa/object dualism is rejected. Sensible properties are possessed by real objects, but not by objects *simpliciter*. These are possessed in relation to some conditions and perspectives. Though perspectival, properties are real nevertheless. (E. B. McGilvary, A. E. Murphy, Prichard, Chisholm)

Indirect Realism

Objects are known mediately through representations which are immediately perceived. Objects are variously conceived as : (a) external causes of sensa; (b) logical constructions out of sensibilia; (c) perceptual objects constituted by many people's sensa somehow belonging to the same location where objects are (Price).

Common Sense Realism

(Moore-type)
We know for certain *particular* perceptual statements about objects. Such certainty is not shaken even in the absence of a "correct analysis" giving a general account of data-object relationship.

Critical Realism

(R. W. Sellars-type)
The problem of going beyond sensory percepts to objects need not plague the perceiver. Not *percepts* as directly confronted items, but *perceiving* is emphasized, in which objects sending sensory signals and perceiving organism adjusting to such signals play equally important and complementary roles. Making the organism respond and adjust to outer environ, sensa do not hide, but disclose objects.

Among the types enumerated in the charts I concentrated on two, mainly, transcendent or "external realism" and immanent or "internal realism" (hereafter ER and IR respectively). Occasional reference to other types and sub-types may be there but the scope of the book is delimited to these two broad types. So I may now consider the reaction of a skeptic to transcendent realism or ER and its three sub-varieties: (a) trans-conceptual, (b) trans-cognitive and (a) trans-phenomenal, and also to IR. However, is there a single figure whom we can call *the* skeptic advancing a single thesis, whose reaction to these varieties of realism is to be appraised?

Even in antiquity we come across different versions of skepticism. The extreme or out-and-out skeptics believed that nothing can be known, not even the fact that nothing can be known. But if this extreme Pyrrhonian version is correct, then the skeptic is contradicting herself in claiming to *know* that nothing can be known. Equally inconsistent is the attempt to *prove* that nothing can be proved. The more moderate version called "academic skepticism" sought to reformulate the thesis as the view that nothing can be known except the fact that nothing can be known. However, while out-and-out skepticism is contradictory, academic skepticism seems to be false. For the obvious question about it is that "if one thing can somehow be known, then why cannot other things be known in a similar way? . . . [But] if anything else can be known, then academic skepticism is false [for it says that only academic skepticism can be known], and being false it cannot be known either [for we cannot know a falsehood.]"[8] Sextus did not meet the objection regarding the self-refuting character of out-and-out skepticism by embracing moderate or academic skepticism. He tried to answer it in a different way. The skeptic arrives at the thesis by means of argument proving the non-existence of proof, he urged, and having arrived, may throw away that very argument in a manner in which a man throws away a ladder after using it for reaching a high place.[9] I do not think that this makes things better for out-and-out skepticism. Whether the skeptic's argument is thrown away or retained, its usefulness is acknowledged. So far, the skeptic's own argument proving the non-existence of proof does escape demolition, and is therefore an exception to which skepticism should not extend. And this means one has to embrace academic skepticism instead of out-and-out skepticism. Yet Sextus did not uphold academic skepticism and tried to defend Pyrrho. But then, a total, out-and-out skeptic who opposes every view can hardly be said to take a stance towards any version of realism enumerated above. Even her own view, no matter what that says, cannot be taken seriously by her. She herself cannot live by it. No wonder the same Sextus, who declared the impossibility of establishing any position as true, including his own, did not universalize the scope of doubt *in practice*. In contrast to his theoretical position, his practical position simply stressed the possibility of doubting what is not *sufficiently evident*. Hundreds of years later, the arch-skeptic Hume persuaded in a similar vein that doubting, which is so devastating theoretically, is a mere philosophical argument not to be taken seriously in practice.[10]

The radical skeptic, who opposes all positions then, cannot be said to take any stance, I think, towards ER or IR. The so-called negative stance which she can take towards her own thesis must eventually end in silence. It is Sextus's doubt concerning something that does not seem *sufficiently evident* on the contrary, that has to be taken seriously. In consonance with the original Greek meaning of the term "skepsis" as seeing, watching, scrutinizing, skeptical doubt should be viewed as an integral part of an active noetic process, not as a matter of extravagant theorizing. It is what human inquiry caught up in the cross current of despair and hope encounters, finds frustrating and still takes up as a challenge to be overcome in its arduous task of seeking something that would be considered "sufficiently evident." More the doubter doubts, the greater would be the effort to secure adequate grounds for stable, sufficiently evident beliefs, the cherished desiderata of our cognitive enterprise. Such a doubting skeptic is a friend and not a foe of the knower.[11]

Skepticism then may be classified into two main types: (1) theoretical, and (2) methodological. Just as theoretical skepticism has sub-types, extreme and moderate, methodological skepticism has it own varieties, the Castesian variety and a strong fallibilist variety. It is with respect to these two methodological versions that I wished to ask the question raised at the beginning of this section: can one be a realist (in the "externalist" sense, and also in the "internalist" sense) in the face of the challenge mounted by the skeptic? What stance, in other words, will a methodological skeptic of both varieties take towards ER and IR? The answer, it seems to me, depends on what is considered *adequate* for making a belief "sufficiently evident" by the methodological skeptic.

If the skeptic adheres to the Cartesian formulation of the *adequacy condition* deemed essential for justifying knowledge claim, then her answer to the question above will be an emphatic "no" in relation to both ER and IR.

Cartesian Skepticism against External Realism

The best known skeptical argument of the Cartesian variety concerns the external world. It is the argument that on the basis of subjective experience of the external world we cannot prove its reality. The adequacy condition which Descartes demanded for our knowledge concerning the external world was that "one must know that one is not dreaming if one is to know something about the world." He found this condition unsatisfiable because "there are no certain indications by which we may clearly distinguish wakefulness from sleep."[12] That is to say, there is no foolproof method of differentiating between a dream-world or a world of hallucination and the real world. An updated version of this formulation states how, consistent with everything we experience, we can imagine that "all sentient beings are brains in a vat...." (BIV). The BIV think they are experiencing real things in a real world while merely hallucinating, being victims of a deception not of the Cartesian demon, but of an "evil scientist" who has switched them to a super-computer which causes these deceptive experiences.[13]

I will assume for a while (though mistakenly) that the adequacy condition of the Cartesian skeptic is the sine qua non for knowing anything about the world around. It seems in that event, that the skeptical foray against each of the variants of ER listed in the chart will drive them into silence.

The Cartesian skeptic will straight away dismiss version (a) of transcendent or external realism, that is, the version characterized as trans-conceptual realism. In the absence of adequate grounds for holding beliefs, she will point out, the trans-conceptual realist must refrain from asserting even existence *simpliciter* of totally transcendent reals. Secondly, exasperated raising of one hand followed by another, taking cue from G. E. Moore, to show that one is not dreaming, will not help. For Moore's experience or anyone else's experience could be just the way it is without eliminating the possibility of its being a dream experience.[14] Thirdly, the appeal to Moore's argument is pointless in this context, for trans-conceptual realism is not addressing a problem concerning the existence of *empirically given* things like right and left hands at all.

Can raising hands, make ineffective the skeptical challenge against version (b) of ER, namely, trans-cognitive realism? It cannot. Firstly, trans-cognitive realism under its easily recognizable Kantian banner believes in noumenal realities that are *thinkable*, and not *knowable* in so far as they lie beyond the bounds of sense. Moore's proof, as just noted, is intended to establish empirical realities like your hands or mine, and not transcendent realities that are unverifiable by experience. When Moore asks for instance, whether he knows a certain thing, a human hand, it is "just the question whether that thing is already included among the things one knows. . . ," things that are empirically verified.[15] The question here is "internal" in the sense that one can answer it from within one's knowledge about other things already known. But the question which version (b) asks about external noumenal things is "external," in as much as it requires a withdrawl from the whole body of knowledge we already have. When Moore advances his proof of the external world, he employs only an *empirical* concept of "reality." What (b) believes on the contrary, is a transcendent world of things-in-themselves which one cannot know by appealing to things empirically verified.

Secondly, it is true that the skeptic's dream argument is premised on the gros. mistake of taking sensory representations as *epistemically prior* to external objects which are known (if at all) only indirectly. This is what makes her argument look invincible for the data being knowable (allegedly) without the knowledge of objects, there is no knowing whether these data are veridical or illusory. But even if this kind of indirect realism which the skeptic may utilize to make her own argument seem invincible is wrong, can b-type trans-cognitive realism be shielded from skeptical blows? It cannot. For suppose that realists are right in renouncing indirect realism in favor of direct realism in so far as the former seems vulnerable to skeptical assault. Moore, for instance, rightly favored direct realism in his naive realistic moments when he held that we perceive *objects* directly. This is reminiscent of Kant's contention that our experience is of *objects,* not discrete sensory representations.[16] Still the Kant-Moore type belief which takes one in the right direction does not undercut skeptical reasoning in spite of the fact that this reasoning is premised on the wrong view concerning the supposed epistemic priority of sense data. For what direct knowledge sanctions is the belief in external objects in space, which are only empirical realities or objects of everyday experience. These are not unknown and unknowable *noumenal* realities which b-type trans-cognitive realism admits into its ontology.

Thirdly, b-type trans-cognitive realism seems to surrender to skepticism in voicing its belief in realities which are *thinkable*, not *knowable*. For the skeptic will be the first to hail the idea of inaccessibility of transcendent objects to knowledge. One may still ask: will not the skeptical argument be weakened by Kant's belief in noumena which though not *known* through sense are *thought* none the less as objects through pure understanding? It is difficult to answer the question although the claim that we can, and even must be able to *think* things-in-themselves have become a part of the accepted reading of Kant. It is difficult because not merely *thought* but *knowledge* of some kind will be necessary if thinking things-in-themselves is to weaken the skeptical argument. But no non-sensible knowledge is possible within the Kantian framework, which is requisite for establishing that there are such things with a nature which they have in themselves. So this line of argument which appeals to the thesis of pure thought of things-in-themselves will prove abortive in meeting the skeptical challenge. Against this argument I want to rehash the ideas I put across in chapter 1.

(i) What exactly are we able to think of with the help of pure, unschematized categories—just the logically possible *thought* of a noumenal object, or the *object* itself? Mere absence of contradiction enables us to think of *logically possible* thoughts but not of the possible object itself. The *real possibility* of an object can be thought with the help of categories only in case the object is *given in experience*. And this means that the schematized categories alone can ensure this possibility, for they alone can apply to things given in experience. Needless to add that the object given in experience, thought with the help of schematized categories, is not noumenon, the intelligible object of a pure unschematized category.[17]

(ii) But what does this intelligibility of the object of an unschematized category amount to? Being completely outside the sphere of things given to us, it cannot be thought through any determinate predicate. If it signifies anything it is only "the unamplifiable logical possibility that there should be atemporal data...."[18] But this, as I said before, is a far cry from objectively existing things with built-in features of their own.

(iii) Suppose we ignore the above interpretation exposing the emptiness of the idea of the object of the pure unschematized category. Grant instead that there must *be* something which appears, (the noumenon) and even that a kind of knowledge *might* be possible in which there is no sensibility through which this noumenal object can be known. But then one will immediately put forward the following objections:

(1) What lies beneath the reach of *sensible* intuition could be known by an intellectual, i.e., non-sensible intuition in case there is such an intuition. The possibility of such an intuition is dubious, and it is not a form of human cognition within the Kantian framework.

(2) Even if we do not have this kind of intuition it may be said, we can think of noumena. But this takes us back to the logical possibility that there could be an atemporal reality, and no vocabulary, no concept (except what analytically follows from its definition) to describe such a reality.

So if version (b) of ER has to describe meaningfully a transcendent reality which exists and has properties by itself, then it must be able to explain the possibility of a kind of knowledge which does not distinguish between appearance and reality. It has to say that the thing in question appears in knowledge in just the way it is *intrinsically*. But few, and least of all Kant who had taken the Copernican turn would have been ready to admit the possibility of ideas which correspond exactly and infallibly to things as they are by *themselves*.

Fourthly, version (b) cannot score a point against the skeptic even if, in the absence of an infallible intuition of the kind mentioned, one maintains that noumena are not utterly unknowable after all. This is the most liberal interpretation perhaps of the thought about noumena, under which they can be described as "things apart from relation." In this case "in itself" seems to contrast with "in relation to other things (or to us.)" This only means that they are unknowable in *themselves*. In other words "what is denied us is not any access whatever to those things, but just knowledge of their non-relational or qualitative aspects."[19] But this confirms the point I am laboring to establish. Version (b) cannot meaningfully say: there are noumenal things which have *intrinsic properties* by themselves. Even if it is conceded that we do not merely think of logically possible concepts but also of things-in-themselves as *real existents*, and state in addition that these things are not utterly unknowable, the most we can say is that these noumenal things exist *simpliciter*. We cannot specifically say *what* they are intrinsically or non-relationally.

It seems to me that version (b) can stake its claim to know things as they are only at the cost of its *transcendent* standpoint. That is to say its proponents have to erase the distinction between appearance and reality. But this they cannot do. First, if they erase the line and assert that things really are the way they appear, then the things can no more be labelled transcendent having properties *by themselves* in contradistinction to properties they *appear* to have. Second, they cannot assert either in complicity with direct realists that these things appear in knowledge in just the way they are *intrinsically,* for if they do they will be abandoning the Copernican cause which accompanies version (b) of the sort Kant defended. Since (b) cannot opt either for the move towards obliterating the distinction between appearance and reality, or for direct realism for its anti-Copernican implication, it has to retain the noumena-phenomena divide. Indeed, if it does not retain the divide, it will not retain its distinctive status as a type of transcendent realism or ER. It will tend to merge with IR

Curiously it is this belief in the appearance-reality divide which the enemies seem to share. Both transcendent realists defending ER and Cartesian skeptics believe that the world has *intrinsic* features apart from how it *appears* to us. It is against the backdrop of this strange alliance that their feud is to be understood.

ER holds that it is the deep cut between what the mind *projects* (as in version (b) of ER) and what the world intrinsically is in itself, that makes its *independence* intelligible. Even version (c) which does not have the constructivist component of (b) will insist on retaining the cut. The cut, it maintains, is between things as they intrinsically are and things as they appear, though what appears need not be a projection. How else, versions (b) and (c) may ask, can the realist say, which she has to say to be a realist, that the world is real, and not a "dream-world" or a "vat-world"? How else can she also say that our beliefs can truly describe this world if not by checking them against something that is independent of belief and thought? This of course is a question which may be asked only if she subscribes to version (c) which stakes the claim that we may be able to discover, partially at least, the independent built-in features of things of the external world: So even version (c) which confesses ignorance and fallibility of cognitive inquiry, refuses to give up the conviction that (i) the transcendent world has *intrinsic* features, and (ii) knowledge proper is a *purported* true description of such a world with *such* built-in features. Epistemological realism of the fallibilist type which seems to merge with (c) articulates the same conviction notwithstanding its fallibilism. Semantic realism too joins the chorus and holds that it does not matter whether we have a criterion which can enable us to *recognize* knowledge proper when we have it. "Truth" for this shared "externalist perspective" is recognition-transcendent.

The skeptic in her turn has to maintain the same deep cut between appearance and reality. How else can we make sense of her claim that we do not know the real world and can only experience what appears in the "dream world" or the "vat-world"? This is a claim which is aimed at proponents of version (c) of ER which makes this knowledge-claim. Against them the skeptic seems to be saying that she is not skeptical about the *existence per se* of the world, but only about the possibility of *knowledge* of the same as it is *by itself.* But then, the skeptic who is advancing a doxastic thesis, that is, a thesis concerning the knowledge-claim of c-type realism, comes very close to version (b) of ER. In other words the skeptic who flings an emphatic "no" at realists who claim to *know* the real world has to concede with a grudging "yes" perhaps, when asked whether she is ready to take sides with trans-cognitive realism, that is, type (b) of ER which maintains the sharp cut between noumenal reality and phenomenal appearance. She is an ally of (b) in so far as (b) preaches unknowability of noumena, and an enemy of (c) which claims knowledge of the same despite it's fallibilism.

But suppose that the skeptic goes beyond the bounds of the doxastic formulation of her thesis and denies not only *knowledge* of transcendent realities, but also the very *existence* of such realities. Can she still be ensnared into a position where she has to concede with a grudging "yes" to b-type realists when they ask:

is not there a world behind appearances? It seems she cannot afford to say "no" and question even existence *simpliciter* of the world in which she has to be stationed to raise her skeptical question. The retort that her skepticism here merely requires her *own* existence and not of the world hardly helps. Indeed she alone must exist at least, to doubt other existences. But in that case she could have only chanted the Cartesian first truth: I doubt (think) therefore I am, and then remained silent. She need not have referred obliquely to other things when she said nothing exists. Of course these other things are mere appearances and not realities. But this means she is once again driven into saying what b-type ER says, namely, there is a cut between reality and appearance. So the skeptic of the Cartesian type cannot give a blanket "yes" or "no" answer to realists of various shades. To ER itself generally speaking, her answer will be a paradoxical mix of "yes" and "no," an emphatic "no" to version (c), and a grudging "yes" to (b).

In short, the skeptic sustains the reality/appearance dichotomy to make sense of her own position and to silence the dogmatists voicing the claim that it is possible to *know* the real as it is in itself. The realists too sponsoring ER of various stripes sustain the dichotomy even when that dichotomy makes the skeptical threat loom large, because giving it up meant for them giving up realism itself.[20]

In the chapter that follows I wish to discuss why ER has to give up this *externalist* conviction in its own interest, that is, to show how its aim of knowing the real world can be fulfilled. For this, ER should be skeptical about the impossible aim it hitherto had, of giving a true description of the real as it is *intrinsically*. The skeptic in her turn should also change her stance. She has to part company with the Cartesian skeptic and advance the strong fallibilist thesis, which, recalling what Sextus and Hume contended from the practical standpoint I said, was of deep philosophical concern to human inquirers. Such a fallibilist skeptic seems to me to be a friend not a foe of the realist, who has turned skeptical about her own dogmatic claims. Charles Sanders Peirce, Karl Popper and Hilary Putnam are three major figures representing three stages of the route to that kind of realism which seeks to banish skepticism by embracing fallibilism. Popper and Putnam are today's Peirceans reviving Peirce's fallibilist realism which takes one beyond skepticism and dogmatism.

Notes

1. Many philosophers have regarded Tarski's work on truth as a technical improvement on what is basically a redundancy theory. Putnam counts Quine and Rorty among them. He thinks that Quine and Rorty themselves subscribe to this thesis which is called the "disquotational view." According to it, to call a sentence "true" is just another way of asserting the sentence. See Hilary Putnam, "A Comparison of Something with Something Else," *New Literary History* xvii (1985), 74, 76-79. Reprinted in Hilary Putnam, *Words and Life,* ed. James Conant (Cambridge, Mass: Harvard University Press, 1994).

2. W. V. O. Quine, "On the Very Idea of a Third Dogma," in Quine, *Theories and Things*, (Cambridge Mass.: Belknap Press of Harvard University Press, 1981), 39.

3. W. V. O. Quine, "On Empirically Equivalent Systems of the World," *Erkenntnis* 9 (1975), 313.

4. Quine, "On Empirically Equivalent Systems of the World," 322.

5. Hilary Putnam, "The Way the World Is," in Putnam, *Realism with a Human Face*, ed. James Conant (Cambridge Mass.: Harvard University Press, 1990), 264. See also Donald Davidson, "The Structure and Content of Truth," *The Journal of Philosophy* LXXXVII, no. 6 (June 1990), 306. Davidson does not accept this position. It is not easy to see, he writes, how the same sentence (with interpretation unchanged) can be true for a given person at one time and not at another. Quine, he says, imports epistemological considerations into the concept of truth.

6. Items with respect to which one may embrace global or local varieties of realism, both transcendent and immanent, are indicated in figure 4.1.

7. This is how Michael Dummett characterizes realism.

8. Alan Musgrave, *Common Sense, Science and Scepticism: A historical introduction to the theory of knowledge* (Cambridge: Cambridge University Press, 1993), 20.

9. Musgrave, *Common Sense, Science and Scepticism*, 21.

10. David Hume, *Enquiry Concerning Human Understanding*, ed. L.A. Selby Bigge (London: Oxford University Press, 1902), 160.

11. My understanding of skepticism here is largely influenced by the view advanced in this connection by D. P. Chattopadhyaya in his book *Induction, Probability and Skepticism* (Albany, N.Y.: State University of New York Press, 1991), 252-53.

12. Barry Stroud, *The Significance of Philosophical Scepticism* (Oxford: Clarendon Press, 1984), 12, 23-24.

13. I have already alluded to this science fiction example in connection with Putnam's theory of reference. The focus here is on its skeptical implications. See Hilary Putnam, *Reason, Truth and History* (Cambridge: Cambridge University Press, 1981), 6-7.

14. See P. F. Strawson, *Skepticism and Naturalism: Some Varieties* (New York: Columbia University Press, 1985), 6-7.

15. Stroud, *Philosophical Scepticism*, 117.

16. Stroud, *Philosophical Scepticism*, 130-31, 138.

17. This point, which I have discussed before (in chapter 1) is borrowed from Eric C. Sandberg, "Thinking Things In Themselves," *Current Continental Research 603, Proceedings of the Sixth International Kant Congress*, vol. 11/2, ed. Gerhard Funke and Thomas M. Seebohm (Lanham, Md.: Center for Advanced Research in Phenomenology and University Press of America, 1989), 24-26.

18. Jonathan Bennet, *Kant's Analytic* (Cambridge: Cambridge University Press, 1966), 24.

19. Jim Van Cleve, "Incongruent Counterparts and Things In Themselves," ed. Funke and Seebohm, *Current Continental Research 603*.

20. I am indebted to Amita Chatterjee for the critical observations she made while commenting on my paper "Skeptical Realists" (paper presented at the All India Seminar on "Is the Skeptic a Realist?" organized by Rabindra Bharati University and Indian Council of Philosophical Research, Calcutta, March 1992).

Chapter 5

Peirce's Halfway House between Two Realisms

I wish to discuss now how two opposed perspectives of two realisms, "external realism" and "internal realism" (ER and IR), represented by Popper and Putnam respectively, can be said to have contributed to the Peirce renaissance. The answer suggested is that the double nature of Peirce's concepts of "truth" and "reality" may breach the wall between the two perspectives.

Peirce and Popper upheld the "externalist" ideal of achieving a true description of the totality of real things. But while Popper conceived the "real" as having an intrinsic nature independently of how it appears to us, Peirce maintained that "reality" is not a thing existing independently of all relation to the mind's conception of it. He intends his notion of the "real" to improve upon, or even prove fatal to, Kant's negative concept of noumenon, the incognizable cause of appearances of sense. Moreover, the mind referred to should be understood as the mind of the ultimate community of inquirers, who will presumably reach final agreement in the long run.[1]

I will return to Peirce's notion of reality shortly. Let me point out at this juncture that the answer to the question: can a "skeptical realist" be a realist at all in spite of being a strong fallibilist, is "yes." She can be a realist, I think, if she renounces the old realist creed ER, and pledges allegiance to IR instead, towards which Peirce's concept of reality seems to move. Moreover, though this conception refers essentially to the mind of the ultimate community of inquirers, it does not require (i) a redefinition of "truth" in terms of *consensus*, nor (ii) a renunciation of the aim of knowing the real as it really is. It does not because:

(1) A guarantee, though not provided by private individual sensation, is not absent. For some beliefs that what *appears is real* must be assumed, since we cannot coherently say *all* beliefs are false. This sustains the hope of knowing the real as it really is. Note that the notion of "the real as it really is" need not be confounded with the notion of the "real as it is in itself."

(2) The assumption that we can know the real is the best explanation of coherent experiences of the inquirers, and of scientific success.

The Externalist Perspective in Peirce and Popper

Charles S. Peirce has been widely acknowledged as a predecessor of Karl Popper. Realism, fallibilism and evolutionary epistemology are well-known areas in which the trail blazed by Peirce was followed and enlarged by Popper. Popper's philosophy however, is not the only contemporary work in which Peirce's thoughts "reached full flower,"[2] as noted before. Putnam too has been regarded as "today's Peircean."[3] But how can two philosophical perspectives which are basically opposed, "external realist" and "internal realist," be said to have a common parentage? Is there anything in Peirce's works that can breach the wall between the two perspectives?

The "externalist perspective," as characterized by Putnam, involves three basic beliefs or doctrines to which he gives the names "metaphysical realism$_1$," "metaphysical realism$_2$," and "metaphysical realism$_3$." He says that "these doctrines have been held by philosophers of every historical period, and one can think of a rich filigree of ideas, doctrines, and detailed arguments which flesh out these abstract theses in different ways."[4] Stated flatly, apart from specific philosophical traditions and controversies which can give them a clear content, the doctrines are:

(1) The world consists of a fixed totality of mind-independent objects (metaphysical realism$_1$).

(2) There is exactly one true and complete description of such a totality (metaphysical realism$_2$).

(3) Truth involves correspondence between words or thought signs and external things (metaphysical realism$_3$).[5]

Putnam says that there may be several ways of giving sense to these stray sentences by situating them in appropriate philosophical contexts. For apart from a philosophical tradition it hardly makes sense to speak of objects, let alone a "fixed totality of all objects." So he explains how in one such way we can clarify the notion of a "fixed totality" of individuals/objects of which the world consists, and the notion of a "fixed totality" of properties and relations (of each type), by assuming an ideal theory of the world. This ideal theory, one can say, is the unique complete description of the world following "metaphysical realism$_2$." The clarification of the aforesaid notions may be achieved by identifying the totality of individuals with the range of the individual variables, and the totality of properties and relations (of each type) with the range of the predicate variables (of that type) in that ideal theory. In other words what Putnam is suggesting here is that "metaphysical realism$_1$" can be understood by assuming "metaphysical realism$_2$." He also says that the order can be reversed and the latter may be stated clearly by assuming the former, i.e., "metaphysical realism$_1$."[6]

I am not trying however, to weld the three sentences here to any "rich filigree" of ideas belonging to a particular philosophical doctrine. I am only making a flat remark about a minimal contention which external realists, or even internal realists are ready to share. Indeed all realists will stake the claim about independent exist-ence of things, objects, events, processes, generally speaking. Surely, human minds did not create stars and mountains. So the belief expressed in (1) (minus the as-sumption about a *fixed* totality) seems unexceptionable. The belief numbered (2) seems to many to be a corollary of this unexceptionable contention. What *exists* independently must be *described* too in terms that have nothing to do with hu-mans. For only such an independently existing thing can have a *uniquely true* and *complete* description which is described in its *own* terms, that is, in terms of prop-erties which it possesses *intrinsically,* not as experienced or interpreted by some mind. Since variations in description are due to the intervention of the mind experi-encing and interpreting the object in different ways, the "one true and complete description" must be of properties which the thing has by itself apart from and independently of such experience and interpretation. This is how many of the hard-core realists might think that the notion of mind-independent existence is linked with and leads to the idea of a uniquely true and complete description. Thus, "metaphysical realism$_2$," which asserts that there is such a unique description may be seen as leaning on "metaphysical realism$_1$" proclaiming the mind-independent existence of the totality of things of which there is this unique description. Many realists would also add that the truth of such a uniquely true description of the world should be construed as an interpretation-independent hard fact of the matter. It should be construed as *correspondence* between bits of language and bits of reality which obtains independently of interpreters, and also of whether they know when it obtains (metaphysical realism$_3$).

Popper is an externalist ardently supporting (2). Peirce too, in a sense, may be said to have accepted (2) and to that extent was an externalist. But while Popper asserts the possibility of a uniquely true and complete description of real things as they are *intrinsically*, Peirce conceives reality as something which does not exist independently of all relation to the mind's conception of it. So the uniquely true and complete description which the community of inquirers aspire to achieve ultimately is a description of such realities as Peirce conceives them. Besides, Popper ac-cepted (3) while Peirce did not, although (2) seems to lead to (3). Thus what Putnam describes as the "externalist perspective" is defended wholly by Popper and partly by Peirce.

The main problem of inquiry in science and philosophy according to Popper is the problem of cosmology: the problem of discovering inherent and structural features of the world as it is by itself. This is maintained throughout, for instance, in the earlier period of his philosophy when we are asked not to despair even if basic statements being testable are declared refutable, and therefore unable to disclose infallibly the inherent features of things in the world. It is also maintained in the later period, when cognitive Darwinism embarks on an unending quest for truth through blind groping by trial and error. We are not to despair because the failure to *attain* the "one true and complete description" does not imply that there cannot *be* any such description." On the contrary, we have to assume that there *is* an independently structured "trans-phenomenal" reality (as in version (c) of TR discussed earlier) of which there *is* such a description. Or else we cannot give sense to falsification, and to the whole idea of the trial and error enterprise. For the very fact that the falsifying data are themselves falsifiable shows that falsification (as opposed to verification) has a compulsiveness—a brute fact element that resists, controls and baffles our thought forcing us to give up one assumed description in place of another. The resistance to thought must obviously come from the independently structured world. A structureless reality would hardly resist and compel us to revise and relinquish one assumed description in place of another.

Peirce too entertained the externalist perspective in some sense. He believed that "there are Real things, whose characters are entirely independent of our opinion about them . . ." and " we can ascertain by reasoning how things really and truly are; and any man, if he has sufficient experience and he reason enough about it, will be led to one true conclusion."[7] Note that by "our opinions" here, of which characters of real things are entirely independent, Peirce means *our present opinions* in contradiction to what will appear to the *mind of the ultimate community* of inquirers. This optimistic image of science as advancing progressively towards the "one True conclusion," which will be disclosed to the ultimate community of inquirers, was unflinchingly held, even though doubts raised by fallibilism seemed to cast shadow upon it. Peirce did not abandon the route of self-corrective inquiry which he thought would ultimately reach the "externalist" terminus of the "one true description" even if doubts make the journey hazardous. He did not give up his optimism in the face of skeptical doubts, even of the fallibilist sort he himself raised, for the following reasons:

i) He thought that doubt is not natural and irremovable. This as Putnam observes, is one of the central contributions of pragmatism, particularly of Peirce's pragmatism. Peirce rightly pointed out that "Descartes only *thought* he doubted the existence of the external world . . . real doubt . . . requires a justification; it is not only beliefs that need to be justified, but also challenges to belief."[8] Doubt arises when what we expect and how we act get disrupted by events outside. But being endowed with the power to correct or readjust our habits of action and expectation, we may remove such doubts temporarily at least, and continue our self-corrective endeavours to achieve the ultimate desideratum—stable belief about the real world. That we do have these self-corrective and adjustive habits as a part of our biological endowment must be assumed to explain our survival, and also the historical reality of our ever more successful intellectual pursuits.

This has a modern ring: it sets the stage for the pioneers of a very new approach, a biologically based, scientifically oriented approach to human knowledge and epistemology. No wonder Peirce is counted among the precursors of the contemporary cybernetic conception of evolutionary/scientific knowledge dynamics.[9]

The new evolutionary conception challenges ideas that gripped generations of epistemologists, the ideas that knowledge must *reflect or represent* reality, and truth lies in the accuracy of *mirroring*. Such ideas involve a passive view of mind and of perception, the latter overstressing immediacy or directness, as understood by laymen uncritically, and also by many philosophers. Such a passive view typically regards whatever is immediately encountered as a finished, confronted item where perception ends. To what this idea of direct encounter leads, has been discussed at length. Carried away by this idea, foundationalists were seen to be at a loss when asked to discriminate between veridical and non-veridical perceptual data, which insofar as they are given, are indiscriminable. The passive view of perception drawing on the idea of confrontation then, is a very vulnerable victim of the skeptic. But the new evolutionary approach is starkly opposed to such a passive view.

In a manner reminiscent of critical realism (of the type R. W. Sellars sponsored) it focuses not on the *percept* as a finished, confronted item, but on *perceiving* as an informational, responsive and adjustive activity.[10] Visual perception for instance, is not passive picturing on a photographic plate as it were. "Complex feed-forward and feed-back processes in brain direct perception."[11] Perception and even conception in the new model are believed to evolve as consequences of an organized system of action patterns which the organism possesses. These action patterns are released by a "trigger" and it is assumed that natural selection favors those patterns which let organisms act successfully in their respective environments. The triggered patterns are not merely instinctual reactions. In reacting the organisms learn from the environmental situation, and in doing so modify their own responses. The modified responses help in better adaptation enabling the organism to eke out an ecological niche, where, what does not seem to be attainable through direct, passive perception is achievable through a process of adjustive and readjustive interaction between organisms and their environment.[12]

Perhaps this can provide the skeptic with a better story of how organisms succeed in reaching out to the environing world. In situating the mechanism of perceiving in the context of biology, and in viewing the whole process of knowledge development as a direct extension of evolutionary development, it opens a new route to reality it seems. This is not to be found in the simplistic presentationalist framework of different varieties of direct realism, or even in different forms of indirect realism. It is not to be found because in both cases epistemology seems to be thwarted by the retention of a one-sided approach to the mechanism of perceiving, emphasizing either the external source of stimulus or the stimulus itself, or the mental ideas or representations. As a result the rift between the objective and the subjective, the environment and the perceiving organism tends to widen, for any one side is generally given an edge over the other. For instance, indirect realists seem to be overly preoccupied with representations, which are subjective items immediately accessible to the perceiver, items which are believed to give her an access to objects which in fact are very remote. In this they move paradoxically more and more towards their arch-enemy, the subjective idealist, who exalts ideas and representations. Direct realists on the other end of the spectrum strive desperately to march straight into the realm of objects. The effort flounders, for sense perception by itself can never justify beliefs in *objects,* as we have seen. By recasting the notion of perceiving the new approach redraws the subject-object axis, showing that the stimulus and the use made of it by the organism are equally important. The sense organs need not be taken as passive recipients of stimulus. Nor should we think that they cause forced confinement within what is passively received, namely, representations. We should focus rather on the role they have in guiding the organism in its adjustment to its environment. Is not "a fish's fin and eye . . . adapted to life in water, a bird's wing and an eye to flight and our perceptual system and hands . . . to the environment within which our ancestors developed"?[13]

Not only physiological mechanisms but also cognitive structures, according to the new approach, have arisen through the pressure of survival functions. These pressures direct the organism's perception and conception in such a way that it can cope successfully in its ecological niche. It is this adjustive ability, and the "self corrective habits" forming part of our biological endowment in Peirce's words, which must be assumed to give truthful information about the world around, and thereby explain survival. Had it not given us truthful information we would not have survived to leave progeny. In fact not only survival of organisms but also the historical reality of our ever more successful *intellectual* pursuits are to be explained, as Peirce suggested, by the power we have to correct and readjust our habits of action and expectation.

ii) It may be said however, that such a self-corrective method of inquiry cannot really be conducive to *intellectual* success. What it can testify to is its own functional effectiveness as *method* which in turn explains why it (i.e., the method) survives. It testifies to the practical utility of its adoption. But practical utility may be cognitively irrelevant. Indeed, pragmatists are always accused of equating truth with utility. There is no necessary linkage between pragmatic success and *truth,* the accuser points out. So the success-conducive character of the method can hardly prove that there are the real things of which the "externalists" seek to give the "one true and complete description." If that be the case, can the route of self-corrective inquiry lead one to the externalist terminus of such a description and allay skeptical doubts? Peirce's answer was: "If investigation cannot be regarded as proving that there are Real things, it at least does not lead to a contrary conclusion."[14]

iii) This kind of modest defence of realism may not be what the "externalists" would wish to celebrate. They would ask for weightier assurance of the ability of science to reach the "one true and complete description" of reality. And it has been said that Peirce's theory suffers from a "decisive disability" in this respect. It cannot give the weightier assurance required. For to hold that "science is destined to reach 'the truth of things' . . . one must be prepared . . . to join Peirce in *redefining* 'truth' so as to make this thesis a guaranteed fact (by reconstructing the truth in terms of the ultimate deliverences of scientific method)."[15] Then only can it give the assurance needed. This however, does not seem to me to be wholly correct, for Peirce did not subscribe to a pure consensus view. Truth is not created by the consensus ultimately destined to be reached by all inquirers. What the inquirers ultimately agree to, that is truth, is determined "by nothing human, but by some external permanency—by something upon which our thinking has no effect."[16]

This is a typical externalist claim tuned to what Putnam calls "metaphysical realisms 1 and 2." And obviously this is out of tune with the consensus interpretation foisted wrongfully upon Peirce's account. But then, the claim seems to conflict with his notion of reality as something which does not exist independently of all relation to the mind's conception of it. Moreover, it blurs the line that divides the two externalist perspectives, Peirce's own and that of Popper. The two philosophers seem to disagree on two major scores.

Firstly, Popper believes in correspondence which is what truth *is*, even though we might not have a *criterion* by applying which we feel sure about the fact that we have *attained* it.

> The correspondence theory of truth is a realistic theory; it makes the . . . realistic distinction, between a theory and the facts which the theory described: . . . (and this) . . . is the main point for the realist. The realist wants to have both a theory and the reality or the facts . . . which are different from his theory *about* these facts, and which he can somehow or other compare with the facts, in order to find out whether or not it corresponds to them.[17]

And although the comparison is extremely difficult and therefore we might not be able to *find out* whether the theory is true, this leaves "unimpaired" the legitimacy and importance of the realistic notion of truth. "The absence of *criterion* of truth could not be used as an argument against the logical legitimacy of the *notion* of truth."[18] Peirce on the contrary does not adhere to this traditional picture of "metaphysical realism$_3$," the picture that there is a fixed set of objects in a nonhuman reality having nothing to do with concepts and language, and a fixed set of terms corresponding to these objects. Of course, Peirce does not dismiss straightaway the dictionary meaning of "truth" which is "agreement with reality." But the answer he gives to the question: what does it mean for our beliefs or thoughts or ideas to agree with reality, is very different from the one suggested by the correspondence theory. The agreement is not achieved "by 'copying' facts that somehow dictate their own description."[19] "(Both) James and Peirce held that a true belief is one which, when acted upon, does not lead to unpleasant surprises."[20] It is that upon which a person is prepared to act, and by acting upon it, the subsequent experiences do not come as unpleasant surprises. This is a far cry from the "copying" metaphor by which the correspondence theorist tries to explain agreement with reality. Peirce does not sponsor "metaphysical realism$_3$," while Popper does, as stated before.

Secondly, Popper retains the opposition which is characteristic of various forms of transcendent realism or "external realism." The opposition is between a nonhuman world structured independently of concepts and language, and a world bearing the indelible mark of the structure of something human, of the nature of human species. Rorty refers to this opposition as a "seesaw." Popper holds on to the transcendent picture of the intrinsically structured nonhuman world, and believes that our cognitive enterprise is a quest for this world, that is, for the independently structured world on the other side of language. What our language and conception is to be adequate to is this nonhuman reality. But Peirce does not share the conviction concerning the picture represented by the side of the "seesaw" which Popper holds on to. He thinks that "what language, or interpretation, is expected to be adequate to is neither a nonhuman structured reality nor the essential structure of something human that is projected as an absolute."[21] In fact what prompts the seesaw analogy is the belief in the opposition, the opposition between something nonhuman and human, between the so-called intrinsically structured world and the world conditioned by human thought and language. Peirce's world-picture is a "way off" Rorty's seesaw. For he does not believe in this sharp opposition, an opposition reminiscent of the scheme and content dualism, especially of that form which speaks of something transcendent, and something we *make* or *project* or *impose*. As remarked earlier, he wants to improve on Kant's negative concept of a noumenal transcendent reality lying on the other side of human knowledge. To appreciate why Peircean "externalism," despite the notion of some "external permanency" it involves, is different from that of Popper and Kant, it is necessary to consider the two distinct strands of his thought about reality and truth. It is in the light of these two strands that one should try to appraise his optimism about the prospect of human inquiry and its progress towards the "one true conclusion" concerning reality. Moreover, the two strands throw into sharper relief the difference between Peirce's position and the "consensus" approach.

Peirce's Halfway House

Peirce's concept of truth and reality had two distinct strands, one externalist, emphasizing that truth is determined by "Reals upon which our thinking has no effect," and the other "internalist," urging that truth and reality, though not created by human inquirers have nevertheless an indissoluble connection with them and the agreement they would finally reach. This reference to humans was incorporated into the very definition of truth: "the opinion which is fated to be ultimately agreed to by all who investigate, is what we mean by truth, and the object represented in this opinion is the real."[22] This dual strain seems to represent a halfway house between "external" and "internal" realism. And this suggests, in terms of Rorty's metaphor, a third position not signified by either side of the "seesaw." There is no need to move up and down and cling on to any one of the two sides, the "nonhuman world," or "the nature of the human species" *creating* and *making* the "human world." Peirce's halfway house represents a turning point in the journey away from "external realism" to "internal realism." It retains the idea of the independent external world without which no theory can qualify as "realist," but the notion of externality retained expunges its usual accompanying idea, namely, transcendence, which is so fervently maintained by "external" or "metaphysical" realists. Peirce's realism takes a strong "internalist" stance too, but he does not capitulate to subjectivism which in its turn is usually believed to accompany "internalism." His slogan to my mind seems to be: externalism without transcendence and internalism without subjectivism. It seems so for the following reasons:

(i) Even though Peirce maintained, as noted earlier, that there are real things whose characters are *entirely independent* of *our opinions* about them,[23] and even if this seems to collide with the definition of truth as "opinion which is fated to be ultimately agreed to by all who investigate," the conflict is *apparent. Our opinions* of which the real things are said to be entirely independent refer to *present* opinions of investigators of the *finitely long run*, struggling to fix beliefs by removing doubt and settling conflict. The "opinion which is fated to be ultimately agreed to," on the contrary is the *ideal limit*, the stable knowledge which will be agreed to in the *infinitely long run* by the ultimate community of the inquirers; it is the stable knowledge, "the one true conclusion" which will not be assailed and disrupted by doubt.[24]

(ii) Moreover, Peirce holds that even in the finitely long run, there is something to compel the inquirers to a forced modification of their thinking. Their "belief, like action, must accommodate itself to that which it finds thrust upon it: that is, to the broad course of experience."[25] Peirce believes that the foundation of metaphysics as a science of reality will be better understood if its dependence on observation is borne in mind. He observes that "the ultimate analysis of all experiences is the first task to which philosophy has to apply itself."[26] However, is what we experience, the phenomenon, something that is *forced* upon our attention and stares one in the face? The Peircean answer is that every assertion involves a sign of the occasion of *compulsion*, which can be represented to the listener by compelling him to have the experience of that same occasion.[27] Apart from this belief in *compulsiveness* of experience, a typical strand in externalist thought, something else is to be noted in Peirce's answer that strengthens this strand. The compulsion is felt not only by the *individual* making the assertion, but also by the *listener* who can be compelled to have the experience of that same occasion of compulsion which this assertion involves. There is something in the occasion that can prompt and extract assertions that transcend privacy and imply sharability of experience. The experience is compulsive and *public*. Peirce rejects the widely held view that we have a direct acquaintance with the most elementary data of sense which are private contents of an individual conciousness. Our *allegedly* direct knowledge involves much more than what it seems to be at first sight . Of course if the redness of the flower is actually presented to a person with normal vision, "he certainly *sees* directly in the sense that he cannot see the flower as other than red. . . . But whether one really possesses this capacity . . ." of seeing it as red, and grouping it with red objects and not with objects of other colors, say olive-green, "is something that can only be shown by one's later actions and statements with regard to the object in question."[28] This shows that the so-called direct knowledge is something that must admit of public test, test by fetching a color chart for instance, of whose correctness different parties, the speaker saying that it is red, and her listeners also admit.

The recognition of this kind of compulsiveness of experience on the one hand, and the definition of truth as final opinion to be agreed to by the ultimate community of inquirers on the other, comprise major externalist strands of Peirce's realism.

(iii) There is nothing in this externalist strand that harks back to the transcendent approach of "metaphysical realism." Indeed the definition of truth given above can be said to epitomize the basic insight of all those who raise their voice against a totally transcendent concept of truth and reality. Peirce acknowledges his debt to Kant, but rejects Kantian transcendent realism. He sees himself as a reformed Kantian, a Kantian without the thing-in-itself. Renouncing transcendent realism is not tantamount to renouncing the minimal externalist conviction about independent existence of things. In other words renouncing transcendent realism does not amount to renouncing realism. Peirce regards for instance, the appearances of sense as signs of realities. Only the realities which these represent are not believed to be the *unknowable* cause of sensation.[29] Peircean "noumena" are intelligible, conceivable and knowable, the last products of the mental action which is set in motion by sensation. He denies that beyond the limit of inquiry there is something of which we know nothing.

(iv) Peirce's account of what he means by "real" imparts a lesson most welcome to the "internalists" too. If, as he says, the whole of our conception of an object is the conception of what effects the object has upon us, then the "real" must be conceived wholly in terms of the effects it has upon us or for us.[30] This can, and should be seen as central to (latter-day) "internal realism." It aims to eliminate the totally transcendent notion of reality. But it does not usher in subjectivism. For (a) Peirce does not mean by being *for us* a phenomenon that only *seems*. He thinks that phenomenology in the broadest sense is a study of what *seems* rather than what *appears*. He contrasts this with his own, alternative position: "phaneroscopy."[31] He does not give the status of *mere seeming* to the phenomenon, and goes on to ascertain the basic elements, which he maintains, are to be found in all phenomena alike. (b) Out of the basic elements, the three highly abstract characteristics which every experience on scrutiny would be found to exhibit according to Peirce, the second shows most prominently perhaps why the notion of "real" in terms of effects it has *upon us* or *for us,* does not slide into subjectivism. He calls this the "Second Category" which is "the conception of being relative to, the conception of reaction with, something else."[32] He gives a host of examples which show in a typical realist vein how this category holds forth the hard fact element of existence itself. Existence, Peirce writes, "is present in some experiential universe.... And this presence implies that each existing thing is in dynamical reaction with every other in that universe."[33] This involves "Secondness" because the existence of an occurence, he urges, consists in our knocking up against it. Similarly a hard fact is something "which I cannot think away, but am forced to acknowledge as an object or *second* beside myself, the subject or number one. . . . "[34] Again in our experience of physical effort and resistance, of shock, surprise and sudden change, the "Secondness" is present most conspicuously. There is in such cases a consciousness of polarity, "a double consciousness, on the one hand of an Ego which is simply the expected idea suddenly broken off, on the other hand of Non-Ego, which is the strange intruder in his abrupt entrance."[35] The duality or opposition here seems to build an *objectivity* into the very conception of the "effects" a real thing has upon us or for us.

(v) It may be argued that the category of "Second" cannot prevent the drift toward subjectivism. The categories are conceptions drawn from the logical analysis of thought and regarded as *applicable* to *being*. But this very claim can be contested. How far is it justifiable to apply conceptions of logic to metaphysics? Peirce faces Kant's problem, namely, how can categories which are general be applicable to experience which is particular? However, remember that Peirce rejected the view that sense experience is simply a direct acquaintance of an *individual* conciousness with *private* data. He insisted that even so simple a sensory experience as that of redness of a flower admits of public checks through tests which involve other objects, other statements and other persons. Kant's understanding of *sensation*, is different. Again, his understanding of concepts too does not accord with that of Peirce. The distinguishing features of Kant's pure concepts consist in just this, that they relate to their objects without borrowing anything from experience that can serve in the representation of the objects. The breeds of percepts and concepts then, in Kant, were too far apart. Peirce maintains, on the contrary, that every experience is saturated with certain basic general elements and it is the task of phenomenology to draw these to our attention. And this might refurbish his claim concerning the applicability of general categories to experience. Of course Kant also begins with a duality and then seeks to find a unity *within* the mind. But Peirce seeks this unity of percepts and concepts *outside* the mind, in an external objective world.[36] It may still be argued that Kant could save generality by having the unity inside the mind, by showing that concepts apply to objects without borrowing anything from experience in representing these objects, although this might threaten loss of touch with the external world. And it may be argued furthermore that while Peirce rightly insisted on retaining that touch through experienced effects of things outside, he must pay the price for it by giving up the claim to generality. The effects cannot give knowledge of generals, the critics will persistently point out.

(vi) The answer to this may be found in a dominant conception of Peirce's whole philosophy. The consonance between reasoning of human beings on the one hand and the logic of nature on the other is what makes scientific method possible. When we are checking our reasoning by experimentation, we are investigating the reason in nature. "Every scientific explanation of a natural phenomenon is a hypothesis that there is something in nature to which human reason is analogous."[37] The characteristics of an object in nature need not be *intrinsic* in the sense of being due entirely to that object *in itself*. And on pain of being intrinsic they need not be supposed to be features that are, or may be entirely different from how they appear to us. These may be *relational* in the sense of being characteristics that appear to us phenomenologically, but are not any less real for being relational. A real characteristic is not to be conceived (in the favoured idiom of trans-conceptual and trans-cognitive realisms) as something destined to remain hidden and ever elusive. Rather, what it has been and will be shown to be for us is built into its very being so to say, and that being, as the internalists continually remind us, need not be spilt into two aspects: the intrisincally real and apparent.

Indeed, if the "real" had not *really* been what it *appears* to be in its effects upon us, one could hardly share Peirce's optimism that in the long run science is destined to hit upon the truth. The skeptic may still look askance at such optimism, thinking that it is a dogmatic dream coming true, for apparently, she has forgotten all that Peirce says about the compulsiveness of experimental tests and the adjustive and self-corrective character of scientific inquiry. She will urge that Peirce's denial of the absolute dichotomy between the *real* and the *apparent* makes it vulnerable to the charge of being overly concerned with the cognitive values of the data of the senses, leading to an an "abnormal veneration of science."[38] But the veneration does not seem to be undue, for the evidence of our senses was not construed by Peirce in terms of *individual* sensation, as has been stressed repeatedly, but in terms of something in it that would compellingly produce *public* assent. Moreover, a rigid adherence to the alternative "externalist" account of a wholly transcendent reality is liable to the opposite charge of having an abnormal veneration for extra scientific speculation. Such an account would distance "real truth" from putative knowledge and thus fail to legitimize Peirce's hope that as science progresses over the ages the transition from error to truth is ultimately bound to be arrived at. For the pure "externalist" account requires for its implementation an anchoring of our purported knowledge in the *"terra firma* of *'the real truth,' "*[39] an anchoring which we cannot have. For we would not recognize "real truth" even if we happen to stumble upon it, especially if we remain committed to the pure "externalist" account.

Toward Internal Realism

No anchoring in the so-called "real truth" in the "externalist" sense is required according to those moving in an "internalist" direction. Even Popper, notwithstanding his firm "externalist" convictions, believed that tentatively accepted knowledge, say "knowledge 1" can rank as true knowledge, say "knowledge 2," although it cannot be effectively *recognized* as true. (This was discussed earlier in chapter 2.) Peirce never supported a transcendent view of "real truth" towards which Popper's "external realism" is inclined. He shared nevertheless the weak fallibilist thesis just referred to, namely, putative "knowledge 1" can count as "knowledge 2" although it cannot be effectively *recognized* as true. So even in the absence of a recognizable anchorage in "real truth," in whatever sense this is understood, the term "knowledge" need not be withheld from what the human inquirers claim to be the purported true description of what really is the case, in their finitely long run.

But this is only the weaker sense of the term "knowledge" as noted before. The stronger sense of the term demands not only *having* knowledge, but also *recognizing* or *knowing that* one has such knowledge. Given this stronger sense, weak fallibilism, Popperian or Peircean, is likely to collapse into strong fallibilism declaring that in the absence of knowledge of knowledge, "knowledge 2," that is, true knowledge revealing final truth, remains an unattainable *limit of inquiry*. In that case tentatively accepted "knowledge 1" can at most be said to *approximate* true knowledge or "knowledge 2." It cannot *count* as "knowledge 2."[40] Even the lesser claim about the possibility of approximation is suspect in the Popperian version of the thesis. For in it, true or objective "knowledge 2" is to be found, if at all, in the "terra firma" of "real truths" in Popper's "third world" corresponding to "reals" in the absolute sense, independently of human interpretations in the "second world." The tenuous link suggested by the insistence that the "third world" is the product of human activity is too weak to establish that cognitive acts of the "second world" can have as their content real truths of the "third world," especially since the act and the content are said to be altogether *dissimilar.*[41] Peirce's whole conception of truth as what is fated to be agreed to by human inquirers on the contrary suggest that the activity of these inquirers and the truth they would finally accept are *not dissimilar.* Something seems to be built into this very conception that makes even the ideal limit look approachable, toward which "knowledge 1" of the investigators in their finitely long run is moving steadily. Perhaps the variation in the two accounts of the nature of the ideal limit, that is, of real "knowledge 2," suggests why in one "knowledge 1" can be said to approximate "knowledge 2," while in another it cannot. It is the transcendent character of the final truth in Popper's "third world" which is independent of human interpretations in the "second world" that renders the notion of approximation problematic.

Moreover, real truths, which "knowledge 2" is fated to reveal finally, seems to be given a new locus in the firm terrain of the *effects* the "reals" have *upon us,* in numerous successful acts of scientific inquiry. They are not given a locus in the realm of objective knowledge of Popper's "third world" distant from the "second." Referring to these numerous successful acts, Peirce maintained that we can infer abductively that provisionally accepted "knowledge 1" is after all true knowledge or "knowledge 2," for that is the *best explanation* of the success we do have, when we experience the effects which we expect and predict, on the basis of such conjectured "knowledge 1." After long years, an echo of this explanationist defence of Peirce's realism is heard in the philosophy of Hilary Putnam, who "seems to have inaugurated a new era of interest in realism with his declaration that realism is the only philosophy that does not make the success of science a miracle."[42]

Strong fallibilism seems to me to be a corollary of the strong "externalist" conviction that there is a fundamental antithesis between the real-in-itself and what it appears to be to us. Peirce's pragmatic concept of truth moves beyond this antithesis and was thus an anticipation of "internal realism," the essence of which, as described by its author, is the rejection of this antithesis.

Today's Peircean

Such a view may be objected to on the ground that it tries to make truth simultaneously relative and a notion which is ideal and absolute—one which is "not relative to time, person, or circumstance. . . ."[43] If there was indeed an essential reference to a community of humans, Peirce failed, it may be claimed, to clarify the concept of truth; for saying that any truth represents a "real" upon which our thinking has no effect, and at the same time that the meaning of the "real" must be conceived wholly in terms of the effects it has upon us, is paradoxical. Despite the difference noted between Peirce's notion of the "ideal limit" and Popper's, the absolutist strain might be seen as setting up blocks in the road of inquiry. Since Putnam resonates to the Peircean view, describing truth as "an idealization of rational acceptability" and also as something that refers essentially to human observers, he too may be held guilty of making truth both absolute and relative, and consequently of blurring the line between "truth" and "warranted assertability."

But this objection misses the purport of the assertion that "to reject the idea that . . . a theory . . . is simply true "in itself," apart from all possible observers, is not to *identify* truth with rational acceptability. Truth cannot simply be rational acceptability."[44] Why this objection is unfounded has been discussed earlier (in chapter 2). Let me repeat that the two notions have been clearly distinguished. Even Davidson, who accuses Putnam of defending an epistemic concept of truth, acknowledges that Putnam does not equate truth with "justified assertability" but with "*idealized* justified assertability." He further acknowledges that Putnam is right in criticizing Dummett for confounding the two notions. If truth depends on justified assertability then truth can be lost, for justification can be lost. Putnam, on the contrary, argues that truth cannot be lost while justification can be lost.[45]

Putnam himself clarifies, in response to misgivings expressed by many, that he was "not offering a *reductive* account of truth, . . . a *reduction* of truth to epistemic notions. . . . The suggestion is simply that truth and rational acceptability are *interdependent* notions . . . (The) dependence goes both ways: whether an epistemic situation is any good or not typically depends on whether many different statements are *true*."[46] Notwithstanding this, his view is still seen as one which is infected by "the epistemological virus." The reason is not far to seek. Within the ambience of what is called a *human* kind of realism, the notion of truth as "*idealized* justified assertability" or "*idealized* rational acceptability" seems incongruous. Of course a distinction has been drawn between a fact of the matter as to what is rightly assertable for us, and a fact of the matter as to what is rightly assertable from

"God's eye view." But "one suspects that, if the conditions under which someone is ideally justified in asserting something were spelled out, it would be apparent . . . that those conditions . . . are so ideal as to make no use of the intended connection with human abilities."[47] In that event what is rightly/ideally assertable for us tends to fuse with what is rightly assertable from "God's eye view." To prevent this unwelcome consequence, the conditions might be so construed as to permit the possibility of error. But this will instantly import epistemic considerations, resulting eventually in reduction of truth to rational acceptability in contradistinction to *idealized* rational acceptability.

It does not seem to me that basically, there is something wrong about the use of regulative or limiting notions. As Putnam writes, we can "speak as if there were such things as epistemically ideal conditions, and we call a statement 'true' if it would be justified under such condition . . . (We) cannot really attain epistemically ideal conditions, or even be absolutely certain that we have come sufficiently close to them."[48] But he points out that such conditions are like "frictionless planes," which too are not attainable. Yet talk about these unattainable conditions may have "cash value." Later on he became wary. Perhaps a word of caution is called for at this juncture. Though the use of limiting notions generally speaking is unobjectionable, the particular notion used here, namely, "idealized rational acceptability" should indeed be spelled out to dispel Davidson's worry that the conditions are so ideal that they might lose the intended connection with human abilities. And Putnam has in fact tried to do so. To preserve the distinction between truth and warranted assertability, it is not incumbent he thinks, "to go back to the Peirce-James view that 'truth' (as distinct from 'warranted assertability') is to be identified with the tremendously Utopian idea of 'the final opinion,' the theory to be reached . . . at the end of the *indefinitely continued investigation.*"[49] Note that he is not dispensing with the useful and leading pragmatic idea, namely, idealization of warranted assertability. But this need not involve the Utopian fantasy of an ultimate coherent account which could only be known to God. So Davidson need not feel disconcerted perhaps.

But while one worry is driven away another may reenter. Putnam is right, it may be said, in distancing himself from the Peirce-James view of "One Complete and Consistent Theory of Everything." Nevertheless, the idea which James himself and Putnam suggest in its place is suspect on another score. The alternative idea is that if a statement can withstand all the criticism that is appropriate given its context, then that is truth enough. Success in withstanding criticism is all that is requisite here. This view, which Putnam attributes to Dummett, Nelson Goodman and himself,[50] is likely to be seen once again as one which is driven by an "epistemic engine" in Davidson's words. Other authors may have the same reservation. Has Putnam really effaced then, the line between truth and warranted assertability? Not necessarily.

The answer is to be found in a point he puts across very persuasively to remove a misconception about James's view, a misconception that gives birth to the charge that James equates "truth" with usefulness or workability. The "useful-ness of true ideas" he writes, "is the *result* of their 'agreement' with reality; their usefulness alone does not constitute that agreement. They are useful by 'leading' us to act in such a way that our subsequent experiences do not come as unpleasant surprises."[51] The warrant ultimately is issued by agreement with reality then, though this agreement is not to be understood in the way traditional correspondence theorists understood it, that is, as a representational or copying relation as noted previously. An idea agrees with fact in the sense that it works in leading us to what it purports, as Dewey said.[52] And it should be noted that the Masters of the prag-matic tradition are not suggesting that an idea agrees with fact *because* it works. Rather, it works because it agrees with fact, that is, because it is true. They are not putting an epistemic cart before the ontological horse. This may be seen as a reiteration of Peirce's claim about "abductive inference," that is, about the infer-ence to the best explanation of the success we do have in inquiry by assuming that provisionally accepted "knowledge 1" is after all to be taken as "true knowledge" or "knowledge 2" (minus the Utopian idea about the finality of such knowledge). It is an anticipation of Putnam's reassertion of Peirce's view too: realism is the only philosophy that does not make the success of science a miracle. A powerful expo-sition of this idea is given in the section on' "Survival" and "evolution" in chapter 2 of his *Reason, Truth and History,* where he argues how the fact that our beliefs are true explains survival.

The stress on the idea that "truth" resists reduction to "warranted assertability," may serve as a meeting ground where the points of view of the two Periceans, Popper and Putnam, can be seen to mesh. Both would agree that what is required over and above "warranted assertability" is an external constraint, which, in fact, issues such a warrant. Thus, while recognizing that "all knowledge . . . stems from ourselves . . . and our intellect imposes its laws . . . upon the inarticulate mass of our 'sensation,'" Popper contends that "we rarely succeed with our impositions . . . and our knowledge of the world . . . owes as much to the resisting reality as to our self-produced ideas."[53] Putnam reaffirms the idea: "Internalism does not deny that there are experiential inputs to knowledge; knowledge is not a story with no constraints except internal coherence."[54] Of course, he would not accede to the "externalist" demand that the resisting reality has an *inherent* structure by itself unrelated to human conception. What constrains, he would say, is not an *inherently* structured "nonhuman" reality, to use the expression describing one side of Rorty's seesaw. The resistance comes from the external world, but this world is one which *really is* the way it *appears* to some perspective, to some conceptual scheme.

This provokes exactly that kind of criticism against Putnam, which was seen to be mounted against Goodman (in chapter 3). If the perspective of one version is constrained and presumably corrected by that of another, then what is the second in its turn relative to? Can we talk about external constraints at all, unless we are clear as to what is external to our conceptual choices? "The answer for Putnam must be that (some) conceptual choices are relative to more conceptual choices, which constitute what is external."[55] And this is readily read as a resistance to all attempts to get outside what is internally warrantable. Putnam fails therefore, it has been argued, to reap advantage from Peirce's notion of the compulsiveness of experience, of the notion of "up againstness" so to say, of Peirce's "Second Category." I think that the objection is unfair.

Putnam is as much entitled to speak of resistances that propel thinking one way or another in different stages of inquiry as Peirce. The objection that he cannot, stems from the disavowed conviction that only *neutral* observation stripped completely of all conceptual dress is powerful enough to resist and restrain. Peirce, it should be remembered, did not believe in trans-phenomenal realities. Even in the ultimate stage of inquiry the notion of "reality" incorporates a reference to human inquirers. As for "existence" which he distinguishes from "reality," he maintained that existence is presence in some experiential universe.[56] Furthermore, this experience too is believed to be much more than a private direct encounter; it involves judgement, *publicly shared perspectives* and tests. If such data could act as constraining factors in Peirce's system, they can perform the same role in Putnam's system too. Finally, there need not be qualms about the plausibility of a view that maintains: the way things *appear* are the way they *really are* , on the ground that not *all* appearances are real. There is no need to accept an ontological egalitarianism with respect to *all* appearances and put them on a par claiming that each and every way a thing appears is built into it as its real property. One conception may be revised by another, until, through long drawn investigation by trial and error (as Peirce said), and by other evolving styles of reasoning too (as Putnam maintains), some of the ways in which things appear would be picked out as giving the true information about what really is the case. These would become entrenched and in the long run settle as facts agreed to by the community of inquirers. (Note that the "long run" is not required to lead to an Utopian end of the journey).

One may still ask of course: "If . . . an erroneous account . . . has been propagated and becomes entrenched . . . must it be *true*?"[57] One can never be sure that this erroneous account will be revised in its turn and thereby lead us eventually to truth. So in order to be sure, it has been urged, an independent criterion must be found to establish that an account fixed by investigation is not erroneous. This once again is craving for neutral data which alone are wrongly believed to be final arbiters in fixing beliefs. A reply to this has been given above. I wish to repeat that the Peirceans who optimistically hope for the long-term fixation of stable beliefs may give the following answers:

(i) The independent criterion is not to be sought for in individual sensory experience; such experience cannot differentiate appearances as true or false.

(ii) But this must not be a plea for saying that *none* of the appearances are true, for saying that *all* are erroneous is giving in to total skepticism which is incoherent.

(iii) The reason why we have to assume the truth of *some* of our beliefs then, about *some appearances* being really the case, is that we cannot give a coherent account of our beliefs if they are all false. It is this *reason*, and not a solo sensuous encounter with the real in its pristine purity, which can offer the independent criterion sought for.

The "externalist" finds the locus of this criterion in the resisting reality shorn of all conceptual dress as I said. She would not give up this contention even if we cannot satisfy the criterion, or more precisely, cannot *know that* we have satisfied it. The "internalist" finds such a transcendent notion of a resisting reality devoid of sense. This erects the wall between the two perspectives. To breach the wall one may turn to the Peircean halfway house.

"The real . . . is . . . independent of the vagaries of me and you . . . (The) conception of reality . . . essentially involves the notion of community, without definite limits, and capable of a definite increase of knowledge." The series of cognition which "the community will always continue to reaffirm" will enable us to know "the real, as it really is. There is nothing . . . to prevent our knowing outward things as they really are, and it is most likely that we do thus know them in numberless cases, although we can never be absolutely certain of doing so in any special case."[58]

If "the real as it really is" is construed as something that is wholly transcendent, independent of the way it appears, we would hardly be able to know it. Peirce perceived the need of some bond between man and nature, mind and the world, and may therefore have suggested in a "tender-minded" optimistic vein that man has an insight for divining the ways of nature. For this "substitution of the methodology of inquiry" by a "mysterious capacity of *insight* or *instinct*" he has been taken to task by "tough-minded" critics.[59] But the sympathetic reading may bring to light what lies at the heart of this optimism—a *rationale* for the whole process of inquiry to which the "tough-minded" experimenter commits himself. "Unless man has a natural bent in accordance with nature's he has no chance of understanding nature at all."[60]

It is this idea which inspires contemporary explanationist defences of realism as the best explanation of the instrumental reliability of scientific method, and also of the reliability and success of our theories about the world. To reassert the "externalist" notion of truth as wholly transcendent is to make scientific success altogether fortuitous. Peirce's hope that we may know in numberless cases the outward things as they really are, though we can never be certain of doing so in any special case, through cooperative, self-corrective, public enterprise of the community of inquirers, may guide the "externalist" towards the "externalist" ideal of a true description of reality, but only by following the "internalist" route.

Notes

A shorter version of this chapter was titled "Today's Peirceans" (paper presented at the Charles Sanders Peirce Sesquicentennial International Congress organized by Harvard University and Texas Tech University, Cambridge, Mass., September 1989). I am grateful to

Hilary Putnam who read the paper and suggested refinements.

1. Peirce drew a distinction between how things appear to *our minds* and how they will appear to the *mind of the ultimate community.* This notion of an ultimate community signifies an ideal limit. His account of "reality" is to be understood in the light of this notion. So when he speaks of the "Real" as something which must be understood in terms of the effects it has upon *us*, we should remember the distinction he drew between *us* and "our present conceptions" on the one hand and "the way things really are" on the other. And "the way things really are", to repeat, is a notion that must have a reference to the mind of the ultimate community. See Peter Skagestad, *The Road of Inquiry* (New York: Columbia University Press, 1981), 73-76.

2. Eugene Freeman and Henryk Skolimowski, "The Search for Objectivity in Peirce and Popper," in *The Philosophy of Karl Popper*, book I, vol. xiv, ed. Paul S. Schilpp (La Salle, Ill.: Open Court, 1974), 479.

3. Ian Hacking, *Representing and intervening: Introductory topics in the philosophy of natural science* (Cambridge: Cambridge University Press, 1983), 63.

4. Hilary Putnam, "A Defense of Internal Realism," in Putnam, *Realism with a Human Face*, ed. James Conant (Cambridge, Mass.: Harvard University Press, 1990), 30.

5. Putnam, "A Defense of Internal Realism,"30.

6. Putnam, "A Defense of Internal Realism," 31.

7. Charles Sanders Peirce, *The Collected Papers of Charles Sanders Peirce*, vols. 1-6, ed. Charles Hartshorne and Paul Weiss (Cambridge, Mass.: Harvard University Press, 1931-1935); vols. 7-8, ed. Arthur W. Burks (Cambridge, Mass.: Harvard University Press, 1958). Citations hereafter will be given by volume number, followed by a decimal point and paragraph number. The quotation here is from CP 5.384. CP is the abbreviation for Collected Papers.

8. Hilary Putnam with Ruth Anna Putnam, "William James's Ideas," in Putnam, *Realism with a Human Face*, 221.

9. Kai Hahlweg and C. A. Hooker, eds., *Issues in Evolutionary Epistemology* (Albany, N.Y.: State University of New York Press, 1989), 24-25.

10. R. W. Sellars's view has been briefly stated in figure 2 in chapter 4.

11. Hahlweg and Hooker, eds., *Evolutionary Epistemology*, 16.

12. Hahlweg and Hooker, eds., *Evolutionary Epistemology*, 17, 26.

13. Hahlweg and Hooker, eds., *Evolutionary Epistemology*, 28.

14. CP 5.384.

15. Nicholas Rescher, *Methodological Pragmatism* (Oxford: Basil Blackwell, 1977), 170.

16. CP 5.384.

17. Karl Popper, *Objective Knowledge: An Evolutionary Approach* (Oxford: Clarendon Press, 1972), 317.

18. Popper, *Objective Knowledge*, 320. Emphasis added.

19. Putnam with Ruth Anna Putnam, "William James's Ideas," 220.

20. Putnam with Ruth Anna Putnam, "William James's Ideas," 220.

21. Carl. R. Hausman, *Charles S. Peirce: Evolutionary Epistemology* (Cambridge: Cambridge University Press, 1993), 198.

22. CP 5.407.

23. CP 5.384.

24. Charles Sanders Peirce, "The Fixation of Belief" in Peirce, *Essays in the Philosophy of Science*, ed. Vincent Tomas (Indianapolis, Ind.: Bobbs Merrill, 1957), 11-13.

25. W. B. Gallie, *Peirce and Pragmatism* (New York: Dover Publications, 1966), 86.
26. CP 1.280.
27. James K. Feibleman, *An Introduction to the Philosophy of Charles S. Peirce* (Cambridge, Mass.: MIT Press, 1969), 131.
28. Gallie, *Peirce and Pragmatism*, 67-68.
29. CP 8.13. See also Skagestad, *The Road of Inquiry*, 73.
30. CP 5.402.
31. CP 1.284.
32. Gallie, *Peirce and Pragmatism*, 192.
33. CP 1.329.
34. CP 1.358. See also Gallie, *Peirce and Pragmatism*, 194-95.
35. CP 5.53.
36. See Feibleman, *Introduction Charles S. Peirce*, 44-45.
37. CP 1.316.
38. Justus Buchler, ed., *Philosophical Writings of Peirce* (New York: Dover Books), x.
39. Rescher, *Methodological Pragmatism*, 173-74.
40. Ilkka Niniluoto, *Is Science Progressive* (Dordrecht: D. Reidel, 1984), 42-43, 47.
41. Freeman and Skolimowski, "The Search for Objectivity in Peirce and Popper," 496.
42. Jarrett Leplin, ed. *Scientific Realism* (Berkeley: University of California Press, 1984), 1.
43. Israel Scheffler, *The Four Pragmatists* (London: Routledge, 1974), 100.
44. Hilary Putnam, *Reason, Truth and History* (Cambridge: Cambridge University Press, 1981), 55.
45. Putnam, *Reason, Truth and History*, 55. See also Putnam, *Realism and Reason, Philosophical Papers*, vol. 3 (Cambridge: Cambridge University Press, 1983), xviii, and Donald Davidson, "The Structure and Content of Truth," in *The Journal of Philosophy* LXXXVII, no.6 (June 1990), 298.
46. Hilary Putnam, *Representation and Reality* (Cambridge, Mass.: MIT Press, 1991) 115.
47. Davidson, "The Structure and Content of Truth," 307.
48. Putnam, *Reason, Truth and History*, 55.
49. Putnam with Ruth Anna Putnam, "William James's Ideas," 222-23.
50. Putnam with Ruth Anna Putnam, "William James's Ideas," 223.
51. Putnam with Ruth Anna Putnam, "William James's Ideas," 221. Emphasis added.
52. See Davidson, "The Structure and Content of Truth," 280.
53. Karl Popper, *Unended Quest: An Intellectual Autobiography* (London: Fontana, 1976), 68.
54. Putnam, *Reason, Truth and History*, 54.
55. Hausman, *Charles S. Peirce: Evolutionary Epistemology*, 214.
56. CP 1.329.
57. Scheffler, *The Four Pragmatists*, 102.
58. CP 5.311.
59. Rescher, *Methodological Pragmatism*, 164.
60. CP 6.477.

Chapter 6

Putnam's Resolution of the Realist Relativist Controversy

The "internalist" route is a route to truce and peaceful co-existence. Taking this route one may move beyond the polarization that is typically illustrated by the conflict between realism and its major opponents: subjectivism, relativism and anti-realism (of different forms).

However, even a cease-fire let alone a truce is hard to achieve, as was mentioned at the outset, as long as the dichotomy between the way the world is *in-itself* and the way it *appears in relation to us* pervades philosophical thinking. "Reality" and "appearance" are terms of seemingly irreconcilable contrasts, I said, which make it look as though the conflicting positions referred to above are the only viable alternatives. But now the tide has turned. Putnam's "internal realism" breaks away from the opposition around which the conflict revolves. My concern here is to urge once again that this new approach can be effectively applied to resolve the issue between realists (of a certain persuasion) and relativists. I wish to do so because I want to return to a point broached in chapter 1, a point that conveys the main message of "internal realism," namely, conceptual relativity is *not incompatible* with realism.

Realism versus Relativism

Realists by and large seek to perpetuate the divide between the world and us. They even consider this to be constitutive of realism, and maintain:

(1) Physical, abstract and theoretical entities, events and processes in the world exist independently of our cognitive activities. That is, they exist, if at all, whether or not we know or say anything about them.[1]

(2) They are "independent," not only in the sense of existing independently, but also in so far as they have properties intrinsically, not as objects of our experience. Since the world exists independently, it is urged, it must be described too in

117

terms that have nothing to do with humans. Unless the world is viewed in this way, it seems, one cannot make sense of its externality and independence. Hard-core realists therefore insist on drawing a sharp line between the way the world is independently of the way we take it to be and the way it is vis a vis our experience of it. This demand for preserving the line was described earlier as the "requirement of absoluteness."[2]

Putnam does not want to draw this line. Let me recapitulate the points that are central to his thesis. He thinks that externality can be maintained without endorsing (2), that is, without demanding absolute descriptions of a transcendent reality in terms of its own intrinsic properties. Relativity to thought, experience, language and conceptual schemes need not usher in constructivist irrealism. For to say that a thing really has certain properties, albeit relationally to experiencing subjects, is not to say that the subjects impose or construct these properties which the thing does not have. Saying that a thing really has properties, though relationally, is one thing. Saying that a thing is *transcendent*, having intrinsic non-relational properties which *alone* are real is another. Only the latter view tempts one to treat relational properties as unreal appearances. Putnam on the contrary has a very strong semantic thesis concerning the relation between thought/ language and the world. This relation of reference holds notwithstanding conceptual relativity. Following him many realists believe:

(3) Theories expressed in the language of science succeed in referring to real things and properties and are to be understood truth-conditionally. That is, we shall have understood the content of a theoretical claim when we understand what characteristics the real things must have to make this claim true. This may be expressed as a specific thesis characteristic of realism about natural-kind predicates. The predicates are the linguistic equivalents of the real properties of things.[3]

(4) Some realists also demand by condition (2) that only that account of the world is correct which describes it in its own terms. Further, this account is *attainable*.

The variety of realism which I choose to examine afresh in the following section is a form of what was dubbed "trans-phenomenal realism" in chapter 1. It sponsors (1) and (2) but does not accept (4), although it retains a part of (4) which considers only that account of the world as correct which describes it in its own terms. This part, one may recall, is what Putnam calls "metaphysical realism$_2$," the thesis that there is exactly one complete and true description of the world. The variety to be examined does not deny that there is an intrinsically structured world, nor that there is a unique best description of the same, but fallible humans cannot attain it. The unique description, as we have seen taking cues from Peirce and Popper, is a regulative ideal which human inquirers aspire to, but cannot achieve. What they do attain are approximations to this best description. Still, progress is possible through such approximations.

Relativists denounce this optimism. The world-as-such with intrinsic properties is beyond our reach. All descriptions arise from some conceptual scheme.

There are only world-views. And so different are these world-views, that there cannot be a cumulative enterprise converging gradually on a single privileged uniquely correct description, the description enshrining stable beliefs for instance, which Peirce's community of inquirers is ultimately fated to agree upon. There being many worlds, not one, produced by different world-views, conflicting theories cannot be adjudicated by turning to correspondence to the real "goings on" in that world, the so-called world-as-such.

I will focus on this realist/relativist controversy, particularly on Popper and Kuhn as typical exponents of the two conflicting views. I have attempted to combine what I feel is right about both, to draw up the terms of a treaty. Popper was right to stress the objectivity of observation as a basis for assessing the truth claims of rival theories, though such observation is not to be taken as a direct, neutral, infallible confrontation between an individual inquirer and what that inquirer is privately conscious of, as has been stressed repeatedly. But he was wrong insofar as he thought that such objectivity would be threatened by the rejection of the notion of real "goings on" in an inherently structured trans-phenomenal world. Kuhn, on the other hand, was right to reject the notion of a recognition-transcendent truth-condition, which obtains when there is an alleged match between the entities with which the theory populates nature and what are "really there," the so-called things-in-themselves. There is no sense in the notion of what is "really there" which is outside the scheme of concepts of any theory altogether. But he was wrong to insist that sociological factors are all that justify the choice of a theory. Putnam's novel approach holds the key to reconciliation and may help in carving out Popperian and Kuhnian zones of influence that can peacefully co-exist.

On Popper's Realism

At first glance the chances of reconciliation are remote. Those who took the "transcendental turn," following Kant, moved away from the notion of the thing itself which has to be discovered, to what we ourselves bring to the search by way of concepts, theories, etc. In fact they have gone far beyond Kant in asserting that these concepts are not universal preconditions of experience yielding an absolute vantage point from which we view the world. The concepts themselves are plunged in the flux of an ever-changing socio-historical milieu which spawns a plethora of conceptual schemes. The locus of objectivity thus is not to be found in the universal necessary structure of human knowledge. Nor is it to be sought for in a supposed tryst with the *Ding an sich*. Relativists oppose both varieties of objectivism, namely, the "transcendental" objectivism of the sort Kant envisaged, and the metaphysical or "transcendent" objectivism which he did not, in the sphere of knowledge.

Popper shares Kant's agnosticism when he interprets the "doctrine of the impossibility of *knowing* things in themselves as corresponding to the forever hypothetical character of our theories."[4] Truth is ever elusive. But this is no reason why one has to give up the "correspondence" view of truth. Popper accepts Tarski's notion of truth and thinks that it allows us to say that statements comprising a true theory *are* true because they correspond to facts even though we have no criterion to ensure that they do.[5] And scientific objectivity and progress are to be understood in terms of such a purely objectivist notion of "truth," notwithstanding its unattainability. It is hard to see, however, how these agnostic and optimist strains can mesh, or how progress can be ensured by a supposed approximation to an unrealized ideal, especially since "corroboration" is not an index of "truth-likeness." Popper's claim here is like the claim of someone who says that you must go to place X (the truth), but you cannot know of any step you take whether it takes you towards the place X or away from it. Further, you cannot know whether you have ever arrived at it even if in fact you have. But how could such an instruction be even intelligible? What sort of aim (of science) is it if one cannot know how to attain or further the aim, nor whether one has achieved it? A Popperian fallibilist may try to counter the criticism by reminding one that it is possible to know without knowing that one knows. This, as discussed previously, (in chapter 2) is the weaker sense of the term "knowledge," by admitting which the fallibilist may refuse to call her position agnostic. But we have seen how the stronger sense of the term "knowledge" demands not only *having* knowledge but *knowing that* one has such knowledge. Since knowledge in the stronger sense is unattainable, *putative* knowledge, that is, knowledge in the weaker sense can at most be said to approximate real knowledge. But even this supposed approximation to an unrealized ideal is suspect in view of what the fallibilists say about the *unattainability* of the ideal. And so I want to reiterate that the craving for objectivity may eventually lead one away from it. To insist that truth is recognition-transcendent, unattainable, is to admit its elusiveness, an idea which the skeptic will readily sieze upon as an effective weapon to be wielded against the very person who moots it. "Transcendent realism" to the realist's dismay turns out to be skeptic-friendly! Indeed, the two strains provide the matrix in which post-Popperian reflections on science are caught between the extremes of objectivity and subjectivity, realism and anti-realism.

Yet, Popper is not ready to give up optimism. It is his claim that both the objectivity of science and its convergence upon truth are entirely compatible with-

(1) the non-existence of conclusive verification;

(2) the non-existence of conclusive falsification of specific theories *if* they cannot be tested in isolation from auxiliary assumptions (the Duhem-Quine problem);[6]

(3) the necessity of conventionalism about basic statements;

(4) the theory-ladenness of all observation.

Whether Popper's claim is sustainable should be understood against the backdrop of his negative methodology. That methodology denounces the view that "truth is manifest" in some kind of basic experience. Such experience is not the basis of scientific objectivity for it can never provide conclusive evidence, as noted in (1) above. It cannot conclusively verify the hypothesis it seeks to support, no matter how many times it recurs. Still, the claim is that the absence of conclusive verification need not compel one to give up the quest for objectivity. A theory can be regarded as objective because it is falsifiable. When we decide in favor of a theory, we put forward the claim that it is a *purported* true description of some aspect of the world. That it is *about something real* is best understood when, in the course of testing it turns out to be false; when we realize that ". . . there was a reality . . . something with which it could clash."[7] Had it not been so, it could have been retained in the face of falsification. Moreover, its objectivity need not be understood in this negative way alone. For as Quine noted sympathetically, falsifying evidence can be evidence *for* and not *against*, although it is negative. It can give negative *support* to the hypothesis under test, in the absence of falsification.[8]

A theory owes its objectivity then, to falsifiability not verifiability, according to fallibilists. But can Popper's claim concerning objectivity be sustained even in the absence of conclusive falsification? "We cannot regard a false prediction as definitively falsifying a theory . . ."[9] writes Putnam, for we cannot derive predictions from theories alone. In most cases there are "auxiliary statements" (A.S.) that accompany the theory, and as Popper himself concedes "we cannot be certain whether one of them, rather than the theory under test, is responsible for any refutation."[10] This is the Duhem-Quine problem referred to in (2) above. It does not seem to me however, that non-existence of conclusive falsification jettisons the claim to objectivity after all. When Putnam argues against decisive falsification taking (2) as premise, he seems to interpret refutation or falsification rather stringently. The false prediction about the orbit of the planet Uranus could not be taken as a conclusive refutation of Newton's theory of Universal Gravitation (U.G.) he urges, because an auxiliary statement (A.S.) postulating non-gravitational forces could have been used instead, to explain why the prediction went wrong. A falsification can be conclusive, he thinks, only in case U.G. or any other theory like it could be held *singly* responsible for the wrong prediction. Popper too seems to have subscribed to the same view of conclusive falsification when he remarked that Newton's theory can be refuted without the use of A.S. in case the world "started to act in a markedly non-Newtonian way."[11] In either case U.G. is considered definitively falsifiable only when it is singly responsible for the wrong prediction. What makes me feel uneasy is not so much this stringent interpretation of definitive or conclusive falsification, but the demand that nothing short of *conclusive* falsification can give objectivity. If being sure about A.S., as Putnam says, and not using A.S., as Popper claims, is deemed a necessary condition for definitive and decisive falsification, we can hardly ever have it. Obviously we cannot have unerring knowledge concerning A.S., and scientific theories are rarely comparable to simple universal statements from which one can derive negative predictions without using A.S. But does this foreclose the possibility of attaining objectivity by subjecting theories to falsifying tests? Even if U.G. faces the tribunal of predictive success or failure together with companions like A.S., a false prediction could still be considered *decisive* in some sense, decisive in so far as it calls for revision and readjustment within the total erstwhile astronomical knowledge, if not for U.G. in isolation.

It may be said of course that it is hard to dovetail this holistic approach with a methodology which seeks in *crucial* tests a final arbiter enabling one to choose decisively a single theory and overthrow another. But this itself is a task one can hardly handle successfully for difficulties we have just considered. Popper himself is unsure, we have seen, whether one of the auxiliary statements or the theory under test is to be overthrown. Moreover, the cruciality of the tests, and decisive falsification based on it, may be questioned in view of what was noted in (3) above, namely, the necessity of accepting conventionalism in the context of the basic statements. We cannot assert unconditionally that a statement must be rejected once and for all as false, by accepting certain crucial experimental results as true. For different schools of inquiry might each have its own conventions, it has been argued, as to which "basic statements" recording these experimental results are to be accepted as true. Accordingly they reach different conclusions about whether a given theory should or should not be pronounced false in the light of such results. How then can we hope to gain objectivity by turning to falsification?

Still, I do not think that the necessity of conventionalism about basic statements is an impediment to scientific objectivity. It does not seem that this conventionality, and the inconclusive verdict of a falsifying test can frustrate efforts to falsify, and also the effort to establish objectivity on the basis of such attempted falsification. The ability to falsify is not to be denied on the plea that a falsifying test result is inconclusive, involves conventionalism, and is itself liable to falsification. An observed fact does not forfeit its claim to some sort of decisiveness or coerciveness as a falsifier simply because it cannot falsify by showing *infallibly* what is the truth about the world. No experience can yield final results—verifying or falsifying. The world retains a right to return a "no" to anything which we now decide as a "yes" or a "no" to our conjectures. But the very fact that it may be thus negated or falsified brings out the compulsiveness of facts, showing that these are in-spite-of-us. If this is not admitted, then, as noted earlier, we cannot give sense to falsification, and to the whole idea of the trial and error enterprise which Popper prizes so much in his thesis of cognitive Darwinism. The very fact that falsifying data are themselves falsifiable shows, as I have said before, that falsification has a coerciveness which verification lacks. It has a brute fact element that resists, controls and baffles our expectation showing that something has come about contrary to our wish—expectation and advocacy. It is this brute fact element, that is forced upon our attention and acknowledged as an "object or *second*, beside . . . the subject or number one . . ." as Peirce had said.[12] This lies at the heart of the realist's resistance to the relativist demand that we are free to set our norms. We are not free even if, to repeat the points (1) - (4) above,

(1) there is no conclusive supporting evidence;

(2) there is no conclusive way to show whether one of the auxiliary statements rather than the hypothesis under test is responsible for falsification;

(3) some kind of conventionalism is adopted with respect to basic propositions; and

(4) all observation is theory-laden.

In stark opposition to Popper's claim that both scientific objectivity and convergence upon the truth are compatible with all these, the *relativists* believe that (1)-(4) above are in fact incompatible with the objectivity and convergence of science. They claim that (1) and (2) above show that under-determination of theory by evidence is ubiquitous. This, coupled with the view ([3] and [4] above) that observation is theory-laden, imply that observation cannot act as a *neutral* arbitrator in theory choice. It leads to what is called the thesis of "evidence indistinguishability." Rival theories are "evidentially indistinguishable" for no neutral empirical data can ensure that any one of these rather the others gives the truer account of the way the world really is. Just as there is nothing in the lines of a Gestalt drawing to suggest that a person who sees a bird sees it better than a person who sees an antelope, there is nothing in an empirical evidence itself to show that there is a better fit between it and any of the conflicting theories, a theory on which conflicting opinions will ultimately converge. The relativists therefore would rather not embark on a so-called cumulative enterprise supposedly converging on one objective true description of one real world. They sponsor subjectivism and maintain that there are only world-views. "Different worlds" are produced by different world views, and there is no neutral empirical evidence to decide which among these is true.

On Kuhn's Relativism

Kuhn rejected the view that there is anything in *observation itself* by being checked against which a theory can be chosen as a more or less "true description of the world" as it is independently of all theories altogether. He therefore shifted emphasis from observation as a key factor in theory-choice, to "techniques of mass persuasion . . .," etc., in his earlier works, and convictions and unanimous judgements of trained specialists in later writings. In either case the new locus of scientific rationality is *sociological*.

Decades have passed since the first cries of outrage were heard against the socialization of science which exalted allegiance to some reigning paradigm as the main determinant of scientific behavior. Kuhn himself realized that there would be a total epistemological break between competing paradigms under the aegis of which the rival theories fall, if there is no external paradigm-transcendent criteria. He has emended his earlier position when he writes: "if there is no way in which the two (incommensurable theories) can be stated in a single language, then they cannot be compared, and no arguments from evidence can be relevant to the choice between them." He also admits, taking due notice of Putnam's and Davidson's criticism, that "talk about differences and comparisons presupposes that some ground is shared. And insofar as the 'incommensurability' thesis denies this, it is incoherent."[13] Yet he wanted to maintain incommensurability, though eager, at the same time, to deny irrationality and allow for communication between proponents of competing paradigms. He thought that such communication could be established not via the standard epistemic route of *common experiential evidence,* nor through *translation,* but by "the very different process of *interpretation* and language acquisition." That process, he claimed, held the clue to an understanding "not only of translation and its limitation, but also of conceptual change."[14] But I think that this purely interpretive or hermeneutic manifesto can achieve only half of what it promises. It addresses the problem of *translation,* not the problem of understanding theory change, especially change that leads to scientific progress.

Suppose one grants what Kuhn calls "local incommensurability," a theme which claims that a few inter-defined expressions in a theory resist translation, and do not have equivalents in a different theory. Suppose also that these terms are acquired not in isolation, but in a cluster as "local holism"—a second theme espoused by Kuhn enjoins. So, even when certain stray expressions of twentieth century chemistry like "oxygen enriched air" for example, are used to identify referents of out-of-date terms like "dephlogisticated air," it would be wrong to construe this process of reference-determination as *translation.*[15] If sameness of meaning and sameness of reference are the desiderata for successful translation, then "oxygen enriched air," cannot replace "dephlogisticated air." It cannot because "phlogiston" and "dephlogisticated air" (a compound formed out of the former) have non-referring occurrences too. Moreover, "phlogiston" is clustered inextricably with certain ineliminable terms like "element" and "principle," that have meanings entirely different from the ones they have in modern chemistry. So apparently Kuhn is right when he says that we cannot have a translation of the phlogistic original. But Putnam has shown that despite the *incompatibility* of two conceptual schemes, description given by one, can be translated into the language of the other, provided these descriptions are "equivalent." I will return to this later. Meanwhile, even if we concede that "local holism" shows failure of translation, it hardly explains how *interpretation* succeeds where *translation* fails. That is to say, it fails to explain how the two schemes can be compared and a communication be forged between their proponents by interpretation.

Kuhn says that circumstances encountered in our attempt to understand out-of-date scientific texts are comparable to situations where "there need be no English description coreferential with the native term 'gavagai.'"[16] Terms like "phlogiston" are similar to such irreducibly native expressions. Interpreting therefore, in this context, is like learning a new language—just describing the ways in which alien terms were understood by native speakers. But this means we can understand only how they understood these terms. And since it is implausible that these should change meaning when transferred to a new theory without infecting the other terms transferred with them, we also understand that our understanding differs from theirs not merely in respect of what they said about substances denoted by expressions like "phlogiston" considered in *isolation.* It means that the *whole* way they structured the chemical world is different from the way we structure it. But if all we understand is that *their* understanding is drastically different from *ours*, then the upshot of comparison is that the two world-views should be deemed *incomparable*. Can this provide a satisfactory answer to those who wanted to know how incommensurability does not lead to incomparability? I do not suggest that one has to exercise excessive "charity" to make sense of comparability of outmoded and extant theories, and claim there really was such a thing as phlogiston. Still, however different the whole network of beliefs of the Phlogistinians be, there were areas which suggested avenues of exploration in the right direction. Some beliefs go totally astray and are replaced. Some others like the ones that groped for something to explain why the atmosphere is enriched, supports life, or aids combustion, show how *continuity* underlies change. The story of conversion in science is a "story of continuous change of belief, not . . . a story of successive meaning changes."[17] If this continuity is ignored, Kuhn's new response in defence of "incommensurability" would fail to rebut the old criticism that incommensurability leads to incomparability and incomparability to irrationality. It may stress the need for some other way of understanding conceptual change that is different from translation. But simply describing a language or culture hermeneutically is not answering why science changes and changes for the better. To understand change we must be able to compare and see the difference between what changes and what has come about after change. And this is not possible unless some ground is shared between changing perspectives. This is presupposed by the talk about differences and comparisons as Kuhn himself remarked. Again, to understand how science changes for the *better*, we cannot simply *describe* different cultures and their respective conceptual schemes and leave the matter at that. An *assessment* is called for. And even if their worth is assessed by norms internal to these cultures, there must be room for further assessment, as we shall presently see, in the light of paradigm-transcendent criteria which are not peculiar to this or that culture. To desist from efforts to make cross-paradigm comparison and evaluation is to leave unexplained why one view adapts itself to, converges on, or is even overthrown by another. Without such efforts one hardly comprehends how change can be progressive.

Kuhn of course offers an alternative sociological account of progress in terms of commitment to a particular culture. But the acceptance of the finality of local principles internal to that culture may explain progress and justify "normal" choice *within* a paradigm. It does not explain progress that survives paradigm change. It does not explain why extraordinary choice which paradigm-change involves, is also rational. A dual commitment to two different notions of rationality seems unavoidable—one to paradigm-bound rationality rooted in the "living law" of day-to-day practice of a concrete tradition, the other to a "transcendent" view of rationality that gets its sanction from certain abstract overarching values. Kuhn himself stressed the need for invoking such values. He reiterates his faith in standard methodological canons like "accuracy," "consistency," etc.[18]

Still this does not allay misgivings about theory-choice being reduced to a matter of taste. For what ultimately decides the fate of the theory chosen is not "accuracy," or some other methodological canon. Kuhn maintained on the contrary the ultimacy of *decision* of individual scientists. For instance, when one theory matches experience better in one area, while the other in another, what prevails in the end, is the *decision* of the scientist as to which was the area where accuracy was more significant. So even if the scientist belongs to a community which is more like a "body of lawyers" than a "revolutionary mob," the ultimate decisive factor is not an abstract paramount value like "accuracy," or "unanimity as such" as to how much weight should be attached to "accuracy." Rather it is "unanimity of *one particular group*" which the individual scientist's decision reflects.[19] The swing in the direction of "living laws" governing a concrete research tradition is patent, and this rehabilitates the sociological account of rationality. It inspires one to hold: "when I say something is true, I mean that it is correct according to the norms of my culture." But then, one cannot consistently take a transcendent stance and make a similar utterance about someone else. One cannot say: "When Karl says 'Schnee ist weiss,' what Karl means . . . is that, snow is white as determined by the norms of his own culture." For this utterance itself, when made by, say, an American would be true according to the norms of American culture. A consistent relativist would thus be driven into saying: what Karl says is true, as determined by the norms of German culture, is true according to the norms of American culture. If truth is equated with warranted assertability and warranted assertability is given a consensus definition, the consensus being that of one's own cultural peers, then so-called relativist norms would collapse into crypto-absolutist ones.[20]

The internal realist who is also a conceptual relativist celebrates plurality, but she will not succumb to crypto-absolutist standards which tend to treat the "schemes" as hermetically sealed. Even incompatible schemes are comparable, and the comparison may bring to light their "equivalence," a notion explained below, which seeks to show that conceptual relativity does not lead to incommensurability and incommensurability to constructivist irrealism.

Putnam's Internal Realism: Resolving the Issue

If the use and worth of methodological canons depend ultimately on the scientist's decision, and this decision on her submission to a particular paradigm, then such canons really seem to be non-cognitive and hence incapable of rational appraisal. In that case problems pertaining to "incommensurability" of different paradigms are bound to arise. Kuhn now concedes however, as his thesis of "local incommensurability" implies that only a few high-level terms like "element" and "principle" of the phlogiston theory are incommensurable with the terms of modern chemistry while observations in different schemes frequently correspond. This is a key concession which shows how Putnam's resolution of the problem of appraisal of rival paradigms works. It shows how descriptions in *different* schemes can still be regarded as "empirically equivalent" (in a sense discussed subsequently). This indeed is a step towards solving the puzzle of how conceptual relativity does not slip into incomparability and incomparability into an ultra-subjectivist "different worlds" thesis.

Kuhn realized that incommensurability makes sense only against the background of commensurability. So he would probably agree that a "sunrise" as described by a Copernican astronomer at a given time and place, would correspond to a "sunrise" as described by a Ptolemaic astronomer at the same time and place. The descriptions used by astronomers in their ordinary meaning are uncommitted to any particular theory. But though a welcome move, the concession that observational descriptions are commensurable, has not been used by Kuhn himself to show how "apparently incompatible bodies of theory turn out to be equivalent" in the sense that they *refer to,* and *explain* the *same* events.[21] Common observation by itself cannot ensure that referring expressions of one scheme match co-referential expressions in another. They cannot, even if it is possible to identify the putative referents of terms like "phlogiston" for instance, by ordinary observational expressions like "unfit to breathe." For though this expression describes one of the ways in which the referent of the term "phlogiston" might have been picked out, there are a number of *other* inter-related expressions too like "element" and "principle" which fix its reference. "Phlogiston" and these inter-related expressions must be "acquired together, as a whole," and the taxonomy given by these expressions, must be retained if referring expressions of one scheme are to be mapped on to co-referential expressions of the other.[22] Since the taxonomy of the two schemes are rarely commensurable, the expressions used therein cannot generally be shown to be co-referential. And if not, the descriptions in these incompatible schemes cannot be regarded as translations of each other, and therefore not as "equivalent" either, to be which translation must be possible. Stray observational descriptions, though able to pick out referents of old terms like phlogiston, can hardly succeed in showing that the phlogistinians were referring to the *same* things which twentieth-century chemists were referring to. And so, observations though shared, cannot provide the path for journeying from one scheme to another. What can be said at most is that two or more observers would give the same description of an event provided they observe it from the *same* point of view. This does not explain how *incompatible* descriptions can be "equivalent" by virtue of referring to, and explaining the same events, though from *different* points of view. Indeed, given Kuhn's thesis that *intension* determines *extension,* different descriptions from different points of view must be construed as descriptions of *different* events. Putnam wants to avoid this "different worlds" thesis. He wants to show how descriptions given from *different* points of view can still be *equivalent* notwithstanding their incompatibility.

To understand this, one may consider the special relativistic descriptions of two events: an explosion on the Moon, and an explosion on Mars, abbreviated as

X and Y respectively, which Putnam cites, to explicate his notion of "equivalence."
If X and Y are described in *neutral* observational terms then, in two different
frames, say, the earth and a rocket-ship moving almost at the speed of light compared
to earth, there would be two incompatible descriptions. For example, if the word
"simultaneous" used for describing the events is construed observationally in
neutral terms, say, in terms of light signals received in each frame, then, the description
given by the observers on the earth would say "X and Y happened simultaneously,"
while the one given by those in the rocket-ship would say "X happened before Y."
But "how can two such flatly contradictory accounts both be true?"[23] Both can be
true according to Putnam, notwithstanding the glaring incompatibility of the two
descriptions: (A) "X and Y happened simultaneously" and (B) "X and Y did not
happen simultaneously". For even if the incompatible descriptions A and B given
by observers on the earth and the rocket-ship respectively, do not agree on the
temporal distance between the events, they may agree on an "invariant quantity"
namely, the *space-time distance* between any two events. This implies of course, a
relativity underpinning ascriptions of simultaneity, and brings out the theory-laden
character of the observational terms. But if terms like "simultaneous," "distance,"
etc., are incompatible given a neutral observational definition, then such terms may
be avoided, or be interpreted theoretically. If they are avoided, the events in question can be described in the language of "invariants." And since each of the frame-
bound descriptions can be recovered from this invariant description, namely, "the
space-time distance," when we are given the coordinate systems associated with
the frames, the two frame-bound descriptions A and B can be said to be *equivalent*
notwithstanding their incompatibility. The invariant description is the basis on
which the terms figuring in description A can be translated into the language of
description B. For given the space-time distance between the events, and given
that the earth moves with a velocity, v, much less than the speed of light, c, the
observers on the earth can determine the coordinates of an event in the rocket-ship
from the coordinates in the frame which they presently occupy (the earth). They
may therefore be able to make correct predictions about what they would observe
in case they were transported to the rocket-ship. And if they can do so, then, the
observation sentences they use in describing X and Y by A, can be mapped on to
corresponding observation sentences used by observers in the rocket-ship. This is
another way of saying that the observers on the earth would be able to identify the
events they describe by A, as referents of B, though B alters the description A.
They can legitimately claim that the events they describe, namely X and Y, are the
same as the events countenanced by observers in the rocket-ship. Special Relativistic descriptions of the explosions on the Moon and Mars by observers in relative
motion are *equivalent descriptions* in this sense, and enable us to account for the
most salient cases of conceptual relativity in science.

Putnam accepts conceptual relativity but would not endorse Kuhn's "different
worlds" thesis premised wrongly on conceptual relativity. Kuhn thought that the
incompatible descriptions given by different conceptual schemes, were "eviden-

tially indistinguishable," since no observation, however "accurate," could determine which among them was the true story about the world. To have a true story, he seems to have assumed, we need *neutral* observation. Since we cannot have it, Kuhn concluded that observation could be suitably interpreted to fit any of the different schemes. And since the stories told by these schemes were incompatible, they could not be stories about the *same* world. The different stories were thus thought to lead ineluctably to constructivism, preaching that different world-views create "different worlds." Moreover, the choice of one out of these warring world-views, being guided by a suitable *interpretation* of observation, and not by any interpretation-independent hard fact of the matter, the "accuracy" testified to by observation could only *influence* choice, not *determine* it. Hence the move to treat "accuracy" as a "value" and not as something which determines choice by showing how well interpretation independent hard experiential data match the chosen theory. Kuhn sociologised theory-choice thinking choice cannot be *determined* without objective observations, and observations cannot be objective without being neutral. Putnam points out that observations can be objective even if they are not neutral in the classical empiricist sense.[24] It is at this point that he may hail Popper's correct insistence that observation blocks facile sociologism. It may still be argued that this cannot be blocked, for observation is indecisive and parasitic upon theoretical assumptions. For instance, the fact that observations on the earth can be correlated with observations in the rocket-ship, depends on the *assumption* that the invariant description of the "space-time distance" is a *complete* account of what is really going on. If anyone does not abide by the *decision* to take the invariant description as *complete,* and also refuses to accept the ontological implications of theoretical assumptions, then observations would lose presumably, their claim to objectivity. To take a different example, the measurement of temperature by the rise of mercury in a thermometer, or by electrical resistance in a platinum wire, depend on the theoretical assumption that the length of bodies, and also electrical resistance vary with temperature. But if someone insists that the dependence of instrumentation on this assumption has no ontological implication, then can observations constrain our choice as to what should be considered the true account of the world? Apparently not, and the choice of a theory is thus left by relativists to be settled by institutional norms. But this does not answer the simple question: why do *these* assumptions, rather than some others, seem to be the best explanation of experimental success, and so claim to have a privileged epistemic status over the others? The fact that they explain so well would be a miracle, and the choice of instrumental procedures they guide, would have no rationale, if the data-theory link was as tenuous as relativists suppose. Long-ranging experimental and observational information compellingly supports the reasoned assumption that realism about the *theoretical assumptions* involved in such observations is the best explanation of experimental success. Popper was right to stress the objectivity of observations and regard it as one of the main pillars of scientific realism.

To say this however is not to endorse the claim of a "hard-core" realist that the invariant space-time distance is a property, which the world possesses *intrinsically*, not vis-a-vis the choice of a conceptual scheme. The claim is not tenable for it is devoid of sense. It is devoid of sense because saying that the world has properties unrelated to conceptions and points of view, is like saying that a body has the property of a certain *degree* of temperature, *measurable* by the rise of mercury in the thermometer, by itself, unrelated to the measuring device. The body really has the degree of temperature which the thermometer or the electrical resistance in the platinum wire shows, just as it *really* feels warm to the hand that touches it. But it does not make sense to say that it has such and such a degree of temperature unrelated to the device measuring the degree, or has the warmth unrelated to the touching hand. This may be dismissed as a garden variety of subjectivism and relativism by "hard-core" realists. One cannot be a realist, they would urge, unless one maintains the external existence of the world (dubbed as thesis [1] at the outset), and one cannot make sense of this externality, unless the world that exists independently is also *described* in terms that have nothing to do with humans and their ways of viewing it (dubbed as thesis [2] in the first section). To be a realist therefore, one must believe that the world has *intrinsic* properties apart from contributions made by language and the mind. How else, these realists would further contend, can we make sense of *external* control and criticism of thought, so much stressed by both Popper and Putnam? How else can reason regulate thought, if not by checking against something that is independent of thought? The mind-world polarity according to hard-core realists, is the very essence of "realism" properly so-called, enshrining its absolutely compelling contention that there was, is and will be a world whether or not any mind knows it, in whatever way or ways. In denying this dichotomy the self-styled "internal realist" is virtually presiding over the liquidation of "realism" and not carving out a zone of influence!

But which world does the "hard-core" realist characterize as absolutely independent?

(i) Surely it is not absolutely transcendent, eluding conceptual characterization altogether?

(ii) Is it then the world behind the veil of perceptual experience, with intrinsic primary properties that are accessible only to science? "Scientific realists" wedded to the science of the Galilean style would answer affirmatively, and relegate the lived world of everyday experience to the inferior status of a merely subjective phenomenon. But even if this is considered a local victory for the "hard-core" realist, he wins it at the cost of skepticism about the plain man's (allegedly) invincible territory of ordinary objects like sticks and stones, and tables and chairs.

(iii) Alternatively, the lived world itself can be said to be truly independent and real, where we have a face-to-face encounter, so to say, with what is intrinsically the case in contradistinction to what the theories project or impose. In exalting the "phenomenal" as real, and denouncing the "theoretical" as "deceitful," realism of this variety would claim reality for what is tangible, concrete and readily available, and direct skepticism at what lay behind the perceptual veil.

The "internal realist" on the contrary would regard both the "theoretical" and the "perceptual" as real. She need not surrender to any form of local skepticism into which the heroic "hard-core" realists are likely to be ensnared. The "hard-core" realists committed to the mind-world split, pick out some aspects of the world as real and intrinsic, and label others as mere "appearances." But why should there be any ontological preference for something which is wholly transcendent, for something "we know not what" (as in [i] above)? Why again should there be an ontological preference for something, which the scientists say are the intrinsic hard facts of the matter, the swarm of molecules for example, contrasted with perceptual appearances (as claimed in [ii] above)? Can science claim to have a priori knowledge about *noumenal* realities behind the veil of perception, and say on extra-scientific grounds that the story of molecules alone qualifies as the true story of the *noumenal* world? Moreover to say "yes" is to reserve reality for molecules while denying it to tables and chairs, and thus deprive realism of the most legitimate appeal it has. The plain man's preserve of stable perceptions then, should perhaps be ontologically preferred, and the "theoretical entities" be construed as mere "instruments" (as in [iii] above)? For nothing seems more convincing than the claim that there is an immediate foundational experience which alone can anchor our beliefs, and sentences expressing the same, to the world outside. But Davidson has persuasively argued that sensations can *cause* beliefs about the world, they cannot *justify* the beliefs which they cause. To take them as "justifiers" is to make room for *skepticism* not realism. For "sensations justify belief in sensation, we do not see how they justify belief in external objects."[25]

Saying that Davidson's contention takes away our warrant for believing in an external world, is raising a false alarm. And saying that the only way to leap out of the mind to the world outside is through sense experience, is to give a false answer to the skeptic who raises this false alarm. Even if we grant a la Quine that patterns of sensory stimulation serve as *evidence* connecting beliefs to the objects outside, we cannot have what the hard-core realists want, namely, a perfect match between what we perceive and what the case *intrinsically* is, independent of interpretations. There are many ways in which the case *really* is, vis-a-vis different perspectives. And the ways it *actually* is, do not become "appearances" simply because they are perspectival. Nor need any *one* of these be preferred ontologically to the exclusion of the others, to qualify as something that is *intrinsically* the case.

It may still be argued that Putnam's ontological egalitarianism can at most put all "*appearances*" on a par. It cannot establish the thesis central to realism, that there is an external world with these appearances built into it as *real* properties. Even with respect to the single, most convincing way it appears in *perception,* there is no knowing whether what appears is *really* the case, according to the skeptic, not to speak of the other ways it is supposed to be—"theoretical," "artistic," etc. For the *real* tree which is seen by a normal waking individual may be placed ontologically on a par with a tree *image* seen by a "brain in a vat" switched on to a super-computer having exactly the same sensory experience as that of the waking individual. There being nothing in the experience itself to differentiate real trees from tree images, the skeptic would urge, we can never know whether there are real trees or external things. All that we believe to be real may merely be mental images and conceptual constructions.

Putnam's answer, we have seen, is that the skeptic cannot state her own position coherently and intelligibly, without assuming the truth of the beliefs which she controverts. Saying that we can never know whether there are real trees, and can only know tree images, is tantamount to saying "we *all* are hallucinating, and are therefore like the brains in a vat." But to say this truthfully and coherently it must be ensured that we are *not* hallucinating when we claim: "We all are hallucinating like the 'brains in a vat.'"[26] At least some of our beliefs about the real world must not be hallucinatory. The *reason* why we have to assume their truth is that we cannot give a coherent account of our beliefs if they are *all* false. The sanction of our belief in *externality* then, is not to be sought for in sensory stimulation. It is *reason which justifies* our belief in the world outside, not the impossible venture of having a tryst with the real-in-itself through a neutral perceptual encounter. And the "internal realist" does not have to harbour false hopes of abandoning *all* points of view to reach out to the real, shorn *entirely* of its conceptual dress through such an encounter, in order to be a bona fide realist. She can make sense of *externality* even when she unlinks thesis (1) and (2) as stated in the first section.

Popper was right, then, to regard objectivity of observational tests as a basis of scientific realism. But he was wrong in supposing that objectivity would be threatened by the rejection of the notion of the *Ding an sich*. Observation, even if it is falsifying, is objective not in the sense of deriving its objectivity from correspondence to a noumenal reality in its pristine purity. It is objective in the sense that methodical and long-ranging observations do lead to *stable* beliefs, when the community of inquirers can *publicly* ascertain how objects behave, and react to experimental handling, and thereby achieve a coherent and generally accepted idea of what the objects are. Uniform experimental results showing that things do behave in ways predicted extract *general* assent as it were, from the inquirers, and yield the only kind of objectivity we can attain. This objectivity is not intelligible apart from reference to *coherent beliefs* held by *human inquirers,* i.e., apart from reference to subjects. This coherence and common acceptance in their turn would not be intelligible unless what we commonly accept *is really the case.* The case is not something wholly transcendent, but something which *really* is the way it *appears.* Unless we *assume* this we cannot answer and explain why our beliefs *do cohere.* A *full* answer to the question "what makes scientific objectivity possible?" must await an investigation of many other aspects of the growth of science. My concern here has been to urge that what is right in Popper, namely, the doctrine of the objectivity of observation, does not require metaphysical realism; and that what is right in Kuhn, namely, the insistence that observation without points of view is impossible, does not require his thesis that sociological factors are all that really determine our choice of theories, and that different theories *create* "different worlds." Combining these insights, realists and relativists can have their zones of influence and peacefully co-exist.

Notes

This chapter is an expanded version of my paper: "Putnam's Resolution of the Popper Kuhn Controversy" published in *The Philosophical Quarterly* 43, no.172 (July 1993), 319-34. I am grateful to the referees of *The Philosophical Quarterly* for comments, and to Hilary Putnam for the suggestions I received during the course of writing this paper.

1. This is the minimal realist contention. Internal realists maintain additionally that independently existing realities can be intelligibly talked about only when construed as thinkable, describable and knowable. Things which fallible humans may or may not know exist independently, but this need not imply that these are "trans-conceptual," "trans-cognitive" and "trans-phenomenal" in senses discussed in chapters 1 and 2.

2. This expression is Bernard Williams's. His notion of the "absolute conception of the world" in which this requirement is rooted, is discussed in chapter 1.

3. In fact Putnam's semantic thesis concerning the relation between natural-kind words and substances they refer to is even stronger than what is suggested here. Although he now rejects Kripke's notion of "metaphysical necessity," he embraces nevertheless some kind modal realism. He believes that to decide whether some substance in a hypothetical situation is really the chemically pure water of scientists, for instance, one has to assume that it has the same microstructure and obeys the same laws which chemically pure water obeys. And he believes that "physical law" is characterized by an objective nonlogical modality. See Hilary Putnam, "Is Water Necessarily H_2O?" in Putnam, *Realism with a Human Face*, ed. James Conant (Cambridge Mass: Harvard University Press, 1990), 68-70.

4. Karl Popper, *Unended Quest: an Intellectual Autobiography* (London: Fontana, 1976), 82. Emphasis added.

5. Karl Popper, *Objective Knowledge: An Evolutionary Approach* (Oxford: Clarendon, 1972) 40, 46, 317.

6. See Hilary Putnam, "The Corroboration of Theories," in *The Philosophy of Karl Popper*, book 1, ed. P. A. Schilpp (La Salle, Ill.: Open Court, 1974), 228.

7. Karl Popper, "Three Views Concerning Human Knowledge," in Popper, *Conjectures and Refutations: The Growth of Scientific Knowledge* (London: Routledge, 1963), 116.

8. W. V. O. Quine, "On Popper's Negative Methodology," in Schilpp, *The Philosophy of Karl Popper*, book 1, 218.

9. Putnam, "The Corroboration of Theories," 228.

10. Karl Popper, "Replies to Critics," in Schilpp, *The Philosophy of Karl Popper*, book 2, 998.

11. Popper, "Replies to Critics," 998. See also Putnam, "The Corroboration of Theories," 226-28.

12. Charles S. Peirce, CP 1.358. CP is the abbreviation for *The Collected Papers of Charles Sanders Peirce*; 1 is the volume number and 358 the paragraph number. See also W. B. Gallie, *Peirce and Pragmatism* (New York: Dover Publications, 1966), 194-95

13. Thomas S. Kuhn, "Commensurability, Comparability, Communicability," *PSA* 1982, vol. 2 (East Lansing, Mich.: published by Philosophy of Science Association, 1983). I am grateful to Professor Kuhn who had given me a copy of this paper.

14. Kuhn, "Commensurability, Comparability, Communicability," section 1.

15. See Philip Kitcher, "Theories, Theorists and Theoretical Change," *Philosophical Review* lxxxvii, no. 4 (October 1978), 519-47.

16. Kuhn, "Commensurability, Comparability, Communicability," section 2.

17. Hilary Putnam, "Meaning and Our Mental Life" (a paper privately circulated during a course given by Professor Putnam on Philosophy of Language at Harvard in 1985).

18. Thomas S. Kuhn, "Objectivity, Value Judgement and Theory Choice," in Kuhn, *The Essential Tension* (Chicago: University of Chicago Press, 1977), 323.

19. See M. D. King, "Reason, Tradition and the Progressiveness in Science," in *Paradigms and Revolutions*, ed. G. Gutting (Notre Dame: University of Notre Dame Press, 1980),113.

20. Hilary Putnam, "Why Reason Can't be Naturalized," *Synthese* 52, no. 1 (July 1982), 11. Reprinted in Putnam, *Realism and Reason: Philosophical Papers, vol. 3* (Cambridge: Cambridge University Press, 1983).

21. See Hilary Putnam, "Equivalence," in Putnam, *Realism and Reason: Philosophical Papers*, vol. 3, 39, 41.

22. Kuhn, "Commensurability, Comparability, Communicability," sections 3 and 4.

23. Putnam, "Equivalence," 34.

24. Putnam, as we have seen acknowledge the role of what he describes as "experiential inputs" and "contribution of the environment." Such inputs are objective constraints on our thoughts. But the role which experienced data play is different from what classical empiricists believe about it, according to him. As pointed out in the last section of chapter 1, neutral data *by themselves do not get hooked to things outside and thereby justify* beliefs in such things. Nevertheless they are objective constraints. To realize this one has to focus not simply on data, but on the ability and practice of the experiencing agents who relate the data appropriately and coherently in the right situation in coping with things outside. The right coherent use of data by these agents strengthens the realist's belief in external realities. The role which observation plays in securing objectivity as an adjustive, self-corrective activity, guiding the experiencing agents and other organisms in acting successfully, is also discussed in the first section of chapter 5

25. Donald Davidson, "A Coherence Theory of Truth and Knowledge," in *Kant oder Hegel* (Stuttgart: Klett-Cotta, 1983), 428, 430. Reprinted in *Truth and Interpretation: Perspectives on the Philosophy of Donald Davidson*, ed. E. Lepore (Oxford: Basil Blackwell, 1986).

26. See Hilary Putnam, *Reason, Truth and History* (Cambridge: Cambridge University Press, 1981), 12, 15

Postscript

Is Internal Realism a Variety of Constructive Realism?

Many in the realm of metaphysics limit their ontological options to certain dichotomies that polarize philosophical viewpoints. It is pointless, according to them, to make any reconciliatory effort to evolve a kind of fusion philosophy which would combine elements of conflicting positions. My main concern in this book on the contrary has been to move away from this polarization in search of a reconciliatory ontology that seeks to syncretise opposed perspectives.

Years have passed since the book was first published, but the debate has not ended. There are thinkers who would urge that "realism" and "constructivism," standardly seen as contrast positions, can never come to terms. Others move in exactly the opposite direction which I have tried to follow. In his excellent book *Limits of Rightness*[1] Michael Krausz collects under the irenic heading of what he calls "Constructivism Realism" certain reconciliatory ontologies which try to synthesise two rival viewpoints: constructivist and realist. He provides a rich and absorbing overview of such ontologies which are resonant with "internal realist" ideas.

Many philosophers might have misgivings about the viability of this pacifist venture. But Krausz appears to have an answer for them. The rival views may peacefully co-exist, he seems to suggest, if each is allowed to retain its own core conviction even after entering into an alliance with its philosophical "other," that is, if realism cleaves typically to the idea of "objects" or "properties" or "powers" which are *representation-independent*, and constructivism continues to regard everything as *representation or interpretation-dependent* construing interpretation as *imputation*.

Toward a Non-Imputationist Version of Constructive Realism

Krausz regards Putnam's "internal realism" (IR for short) as a variety of "constructive realism" (abbreviated henceforward as CR). I agree that CR is imbued with internal realist ideas in a very basic sense. Insofar as IR has a reconciliatory aim, Krausz is justified in including it in his inventory of irenic ontologies. It does not seem to me however that the modality he suggests of keeping intact the core contentions of the dichotomous views can be effectively used for moving beyond the dichotomy. In what follows, I wish to show that both the dichotomous views, stated above, are problematic, and may frustrate the reconciliatory exercise. To succeed in this exercise proponents of both views need to compromise. A realist should give up the notion of a *transcendent, interpretation-independent reality*, and a constructivist should abandon the *imputationist view of interpretation*. This is the line of thinking pursued by "internal realism."

To understand how IR can syncretize its realism with a kind of constructivism, few points which have been emphasized in the book may be reiterated.

(1) Since IR drops the notion of a pre-systematic transcendent reality, it tends to coalesce with constructivism. Even if there is something beneath the object as represented to us, that something too is intentionalized.

(2) But this does not collide with realism. Things and their features exist independently. Even if we cannot "view" them "from nowhere" and can only do so from within some conceptual scheme, they are not our own making. They are not projections of our cognitive and conceptual resources, and are in this sense *non-epistemic*. Insofar as IR stresses the *independence-condition*, it qualifies as realism.

(3) However, contrary to the standard construal of realism, IR maintains additionally that no meaningful discourse is possible about anything, unless it is an object, at least a putative object of some belief, conception or knowledge. The *intelligibility-condition* is built into the notion of an object in such a way that it can be meaningfully talked about only when construed as thinkable, knowable and describable. This strengthens the tie with constructivism.

(4) Once again this is no threat to realism. Things and their features are *relational*, an internal realist insists, but are not unreal for being relational. The way things appear are the way they are. To say that things have features which are relational is not to say that these features are imputed or projected on to these things which do not have them. Relativization need not imply *construction* in the sense of *imputation* or *projection*. The idea of a relatively real world is different from that of a world constructed. If the term "construction" carries with it the idea of imputation or projection, it would be hard to find a place for it within realism. A non-imputationist version of CR however can reverberate "internal realist" ideas. The kind of "constructive realism" which can be properly called irenic perhaps is a

realism minus absolutism and a constructivism minus projectivism. So if IR is to be brought under the banner of CR at all, then the constructivism which CR incorporates must be *non-imputationist*.

Yet, one may have doubts about the prospect of this pacifist project and ask: is it not futile to try to combine realism with constructivism, be it imputationist or non-imputationist, given the standard construal of the two opposed positions?

Realism and Constructivism

The difference between the two positions seems to be too sharp to make possible peaceful co-existence. The points of contrast usually noted are the following:

(1) "The basic idea of realism is that the kinds of thing which exist, and what they are like, are *independent* of us and the way in which we find out about them; ... how many planets there are in the solar system (for instance) does not depend on how many *we think* there are. . . ."[2]

(1`) Constructivism, endorsing the anti-realist denial of this, holds on the contrary that things and their features do depend on us. Primarily regarded as a sociological view of scientific knowledge it even goes to the extent of believing that "scientists literally make the world."[3]

(2) Realism, in one of its epistemological versions, is characterized in terms of limits of knowledge, inasmuch as it believes in facts which are "recognition-transcendent." This seems to suggest a slant towards skepticism. Indeed, if the way something is, is *utterly independent* of the way we are, and the way we think about it, then what could rule out the possibility of there being facts which are beyond the reach of our cognitive powers?

(2`) Constructivism maintains that knowledge, more specifically "scientific knowledge is 'produced' by scientists. . .," and is determined minimally (if at all) by the independent world.[4] It maintains further that the object of such knowledge is a "construct" too. And so, contra the realist's skeptical stance, it would argue: if the nature of what we know is due to the way we "construct" it through our experience and investigation, then how could there be anything about it that our cognitive faculties cannot recover?

(3) The object which knowledge aims to discover according to realists is a reality existing independently of knowledge. "Knowledge is of what there is anyway."[5] This conception of the object of knowledge has been called the "absolute conception of reality."[6] The conception, widely held by realists, may be interpreted in two ways. It may signify only whatever it is that our representations of it represent. This needless to add, is an empty notion. Or, it could suggest a fuller and more determinate notion of the world as it *really* is, understood in terms of its *own intrinsic* primary qualities, in contrast to what merely *seems to us*. It is this world, standing apart from the peculiarities of observers, which the scientists wish to explore, according to realists.

(3`) Constructivists reject both these notions. The *object of knowledge* can never stand apart from *representations*. The only access to the world which we may have is via representations. The object of knowledge is what can be called "object-as-represented."

(4) Realists think of truth in terms of correspondence to facts which exist independently of how anyone thinks about them.

(4`) Constructivists, who subscribe to the sociological view of knowledge, claim that the truth or falsehood of beliefs, derives not from their relation to the world but from social interests and practice of inquirers. "Truth and falsity of scientific beliefs can be established independently of any evidence from the real world."[7]

If so glaring is the difference on such major issues, then how can the debating parties show tolerance to each other and formulate the kind of mixed ontology which Krausz wants to develop? Krausz himself seems to have given an answer as I pointed out at the outset. He has discerned a common strategy which most of the "irenic ontologies" he considers, appear to have adopted. The strategy seems to be that each party is allowed to retain its own partyline even though it is entering into a coalition, so to say, with its philosophical "other." Thus "constructive realism" has space for both "realism" as it is standardly interpreted, and "constructivism."

An Imputationist Variety of Constructive Realism

The variety of "constructive realism" which Krausz first discusses is the one advanced by Paul Thom. Thom seems to remain committed to the typical realist party position when he posits a "representation-independent" object that precedes our interpretive activity. His position may be perceived as one which reiterates the basic idea of realism noted above, namely, real things are independent of what we *take* them to be. He calls such an independent object the "further object."

Yet Thom embraces constructivism also. Despite the conviction he has concerning the interpretation-independent "further object," he believes nevertheless in imputational interpretations which *construct*, on *another level*, various "objects-as-represented," or what Krausz calls "objects-of-interpretation."[8] Thom's advocacy of this kind of constructivism seems to stem from a loss of faith in the foundationalist picture of a pure uninterpreted factual reality on the one hand, and an attraction for perspectivism on the other. These two traits are distinctive marks of what Krausz has described elsewhere as the "interpretive turn" of our age.[9] The turn signals the replacement of the absolute conception of realities with fixed and independent identities by dynamic and competing interpretations of facts, which do not merely describe these facts but also *shape* or *create* them. Thom's constructivism celebrates this "interpretive turn" and subscribes to an "*imputationist* view of interpretation."[10]

In what way however can the strategy of keeping intact two radically opposed viewpoints within a composite ontology succeed in maintaining peace? Does not the notion of an interpretation-independent "further-object" collide head-on with that of an "object-as-interpreted"? Thom and Krausz think that there would be no such collision as long as we recognize the distinction which Thom draws between the level of the "further object" and the level of the "object-of-interpretation." This can be understood by considering the well-known example of face-vase configuration (reminiscent of Thomas Kuhn's "duck-rabbit"). A line drawing, which is a presented configuration, is the single "further-object" which can be seen or interpreted differently—either as two facing heads or as a vase, by imputing "salience to certain features of the presented configuration." If "there are different saliences there are different intentional objects" or different *constructed* objects-as-represented.[11] So like Thom, one can be a realist with respect to the "further object" on one level, and still be a constructivist as well on another level with respect to the "object-as-represented." If anyone asks why a realist should posit the "further object," even after taking the "interpretive turn," the answer will be:

(i) interpretation is "not spun out of nothing";

(ii) there must be something—a "further object" which is "that which is interpreted"; and

(iii) imputation of salience to certain features of the presented configuration or the "further object" would confirm the *propriety* of interpreting it in one way or the other.

Yet, no matter what rationale is offered for the admission of the "further object," the notion seems to be contentious. It is likely to create an inner dissension between the partisan views which Krausz wants to harmonize. One might have problems about this notion because:

(a) The representation-independent "further-object" seems to mirror Kant's noumenon if it is construed as an empty notion, i.e., as something which is simply "that which is interpreted" (as stated in [ii] above), or which is simply "whatever the representations represent" (as in the first sense of the absolute conception of reality" noted in point 3 of the previous section). Given this empty notion it would be hard to understand the passage from the representation-independent "further-object" to the "objects-as-represented," as in the case of noumena and phenomena in view of the schism that divides them.

Of course Thom would vehemently oppose this reading of his notion of the "further object." When he speaks of the "features of the presented configuration" or the "further object" to which saliences are imputed, he is surely not suggesting an empty notion of something which is featureless in relation to our cognition, like Kant's noumenon. In fact when Krausz calls him an "external constructive realist," he resists this characterization on the ground that the "external object . . . does not have to be independent of all representation."[12] So, when he says that objects-of-interpretation are representations of *something prior* the "something prior" in all likelihood is not intended to mean anything which is simply there. Rather, it should be taken to mean an *individuated existent*.[13] But then, switching a fuller notion of an individuated "further object" in place of a bare "thereness" may generate a fresh problem.

(b) One may agree that the object-as-represented is not "spun out of nothing." But if the "further object" out of which it is spun is an individuated object, a presented configuration with definite features, and if interpretation involves *selecting* some of these *presented* features, then where is the room for *construction*? *Selection* does not amount to *construction*. It only *represents* what is already *presented*, and so the object-as-represented might tend to collapse into the "further object." Krausz acknowledges the point. One could hold, he writes, that "there is no need to introduce a separate . . . object-as-represented—to account for the fact that people see the pertinent configuration differently." "There is only the (further) object seen one way or another."[14] Still he takes sides with Thom and argues that when certain properties of the "further object" are singled out as salient, then such properties are not predicated of the "further object" *as such*. They are predicated of objects-as-represented. The imputed properties like face or vase, for example, are part of the objects-as-represented, but they are no part of the "further object."[15]

(c) This however is a point that raises further questions. Even if one agrees that certain *imputed* properties are brought into being by some favored interpretation, it would be wrong to suggest that they are *no part* of the "further object." For the newly imputed emergent properties are the selected features of the presented configuration as well, to which salience is assigned by various interpretive concerns. One may concede that the features of the "further object" by themselves are not the *sufficient condition* of the emergence of the imputed properties, but they are *necessary* nevertheless. One cannot rule out the rootedness of the emergent or constructed properties in properties that are part of the "further object." To say they are *no part* of the "further object" is to suggest that the emergent properties are *created* by the interpreter and her interpretation *alone*. And this account does not seem to coincide with Dewey's view of art works, as Krausz claims. For even though Dewey's "art product" finds a parallel in Thom's "further object," and his "work of art" is an analogue of Thom's "object-as-represented," "Dewey defines a work of art as a complex, *co-created* by the experiencing viewer and the art product."[16] To insist therefore that "there is *nothing in the further object* as such that recommends that it should be seen this way or that" is to go against Dewey's insight about the *co-creation* of the work of art by *both* the viewer and the art product.[17] Moreover, it leaves unexplained how certain features of the "further object," selected as salient, would confirm the *propriety* of interpreting it in one way or the other.

A break between the parties which wished to stay together then seems imminent. If the "further object" is *interpretation-independent*, and an interpretation is just a matter of *selection* of its *given* features, then this might be seen as a threat to constructivism. If on the other hand there is nothing in the "further object" that recommends an interpretation, and it is the "object-as-represented" on the contrary that transfers its interpretative elements to the "further object," then the latter will tend to collapse into the former. This obviously would be a blow to realism, and would pave the path for *pan constructivism* or a *"constructivist-reductio,"* as Krausz says.

Krausz on Constructive Realism

Thom's ideas find resonance in Krausz's account of realism and constructivism *vis-a-vis* an intriguing example. Krausz had seen a dead baby floating in river Ganges at Benaras, and was told that the baby was *honored* by being returned to the river which was a hallowed place according to Hindu tradition. Later on, he read about a parallel case of a newborn being *dumped* in the shallow waters of Cobbs Creek in Philadelphia. Applying Thom's distinction one could say that the *baby* in both cases is an *object as such*—a "further object" which is a *given* fact of the matter, autonomous, and independent of interpretive practice. The "baby honored" in the Ganges river case, and the "baby dumped" in Cobbs Creek, on the other hand, are "objects-as-represented" *taken* in certain ways—as "honored" and "dumped"—within their respective cultural settings. The realists hold that however represented, there is a baby *as such*, and whatever properties are imputed to objects-as-represented, viz., the "baby honored" and the "baby dumped," they are no part of the "baby-as-such." In contrast to this, the constructivists maintain that objects are never *given* but are always *taken*. There is no point in talking about the "baby-as-such." "Even minimally, as a baby, the object is always represented somehow. No object is presented independent of some representation of it."[18]

The problems noted in Thom's ontology seem to reappear.

(a) If the "object-as-such" is an empty notion signifying a bare "thereness," then one may wonder whether it is fit to play any role at all in interpretation—even that of an interpretendum. Krausz is aware of the problem and observes poignantly that "objects-as-such" cannot be fixed independently of their representations, not even by *ostention*, as Wittgenstein showed. One needs a supplementing story, he reminds us, for *identifying* the things pointed at.[19]

(b) But if the realist replaces this problematic notion by that of an individuated object-as-such (or "further object") and makes interpretation a matter of selection, as previously noted, then this would jeopardize the imputationist thesis of constructivists. Will not this imperil the alliance between realists and constructivists?

(c) The constructivists nevertheless would urge, as Krausz points out, that *just* the baby in both examples can never be made intelligible without being nested in some symbol-system, though not the symbol-system of Hindu tradition and that of the North Americans. We simply cannot make sense of an interpretation-independent "object-as-such."

(d) A possible realist retort to this is anticipated by Nelson Goodman himself, a constructivist par excellence. "How can there be no fact, no content, but only alternative ways of describing nothing?"[20] Still, the constructivists believe that there is no reason to posit an interpretation-independent object-as-such that interpretations or "versions" are *about*. Krausz articulates the constructivist's answer succinctly: "It is not the case that there was *nothing* that had been intentionalized. There was an intentional *something* that was further intentionalized."[21] The realists remain unconvinced. When intentionality is fully minimized, there must be an object-as-such at the limit.

Despite this growing dissension between the two views however, Krausz rightly continues his reconciliatory exercise. But to minimize discord and strengthen the reconciliatory tie, the strategy of leaving intact the standard construals of realism and constructivism needs to be altered. Krausz considers several versions of "constructive realism" other than Thom's and his own. In none of these versions however, there has been a shift from the standard construal of realism and constructivism. The versions considered keep intact the typical realist belief in *representation-independent* objects and properties and powers, and also the typical constructivist claim that *representation-dependent* things and properties are *made*, rather than *found*.

Krausz refers to three "piecemeal views" with respect to "objects," "properties" and "levels of discourse," and calls them:

(i) constructive realism (abbreviated as CR) with respect to *objects*.

(ii) CR with respect to *properties*; and

(iii) CR with respect to *levels of discourse*, respectively.[22]

The piecemeal views are so labelled because they try to reach an accord by demarcating and reserving one domain for the realists, where some "objects" and "properties" declared to be *representation-independent* would answer to realism, and another for constructivists, where some other objects and properties which are *representation-dependent* would answer to constructivism. But the accord will not last. For, as indicated in the figure below, which encapsulates the main contentions of these three "piecemeal views," the line of control demarcating realist and constructivist territories might be challenged, especially by the constructivists. Indeed, though he does not take the "constructivist reductio" to be decisive, Krausz himself is aware that it might "tend toward the conclusion that constructivism must be global and that realism cannot be injected in a piecemeal way."[23]

Figure 1

Piecemeal Constructive Realism

Piecemeal CR with respect to objects. There are representation-independent middle sized objects with respect to which this version vindicates realism. But it subscribes to constructivism with respect to cultural objects which are representation-dependent. Yet this version may be vulnerable to the constructivist's *reductio*, for even sticks and stones seem to be nested in some symbol-system.

Piecemeal CR with respect to properties. Some properties, like an electron's mass must be understood realistically, but some other properties like position and momentum which electrons do not possess simultaneously are to be given a constructivist treatment. Still even this version can be vulnerable to constructivist reduction, if such properties of an electron as charge and mass can be given a constructivist construal.

Piecemeal CR with respect to levels of discourse. Both realists and constructivists agree that there is at the first order a distinction between objects and properties which are representation-independent and those that are representation-dependent. But a second-order realist holds that this distinction is *found* while a second-order constructivist thinks that the distinction is *made*. However, if this very distinction is constructed, then the first order distinction too should be between objects which are constructed in different ways. Here too there would be a slide towards global constructivism.

Krausz discusses yet another version of constructive realism with respect to "real objects." The constructivist and realist partners in such a version try to maintain the status quo of their coalition by agreeing that what they call "real objects" can be said to be *constructed, if* of course the realist is allowed to posit "*something* (not yet ordained as real)" beyond any symbol system. The "real objects" which are internal to some symbol system, are not identified with that "something" which is *presystematically posited* to be there. But to the question, "Where do the 'real objects' come from?" the realist answer could be: from a presystematic "materia."[24] This time, the reconciliation between the coalition partners is sought to be achieved by giving a leeway to the realists. The status quo however is bound to be disturbed. The appeal to anything that precedes all representing systems will not be accepted by the constructivist faction within the coalition. Indeed the disruption which this might cause will end in a feud between the partners. Krausz characterizes the two groups as "external constructive realists" and "internal constructive realists."[25] The partners agree that "real objects" are internal to some representation system, and may therefore be regarded as intra-systematic and constructed. So far their CR is constructivist. But their agreement ends with respect to the notion of a pre-systematic external reality which is variously described as "materia," "power" or "environment." The points of difference between the two groups are briefly noted in the figure given below:

Figure 2

Constructive Realism vis-a-vis "Real Objects"

External Constructive Realism posits that there is something outside the symbol-systems—the "materia" from which "real objects" are constituted. Harre, a vigorous exponent of this version, contends that this external reality beyond symbol-systems is *power*. What there is has the power to produce phenomena. Other exponents of a different type of this version are Harrison and Hanna. Paul Thom and Putnam, also are "external constructive realists" according to Krausz. Fritz G. Wallner defends another version. The "real," on Wallner's view, is constructed. But there is an order beyond this "real" and that is the "environment." The reference to something beyond qualifies Wallner's view as external constructive realist.

Internal Constructive Realism, sponsored by Margolis, denies that what is out there can be spoken of in terms of powers to afford phenomena, as Harre maintains, or to deliver true or false judgements about constructed objects and features, as Harrison and Hanna argue in their version of external constructive realism.

All the versions of CR noted in the two figures then, seem to be committed to the core contentions of realism and constructivism as they are standardly construed. Realism cleaves to the idea of things, properties, levels of discourse, "materia" and "power" which are *interpretation-independent*. Constructivism considers nearly everything to be *constructed* or *made* by interpretation. To avert tension stemming from such dichotomous contentions, a realist may give up the notion of a *transcendent, interpretation-independent* reality, and a constructivist may cease to accept an *imputationist* view of interpretation. This precisely seems to be the line of thinking which Putnam pursues.

Internal Realism: a Non-Imputationist Version of Constructive Realism

The notion of an interpretation-independent reality is a legacy of Kant's "thing-in-itself" or "noumenal objects" or the "noumenal world" as it is collectively called. Putnam's "internal realism" (IR) is indeed an endeavor to ". . . reassess and appropriate Kant's philosophical legacy,"[26] but this does not amount to an acceptance of Kant's notion of a *transcendent* noumenal reality. We "can form no real conception of . . . noumenal things"; Putnam writes, "even the notion of a noumenal world is a kind of limit of thought rather than a clear concept." And even if he concedes that "we can't help thinking that there is *somehow* a mind-independent 'ground' for our experience . . ." he adds that "attempts to talk about it lead . . . to nonsense."[27]

Still, one may contend that Putnam has not given up the notion of "noumenon" altogether. For when anyone makes a judgement about an external object, say a chair, he points out, a *power* is ascribed to *something* on Kant's view,—a power which makes it look like a chair to the person making the judgement. So, one could ask whether this something was a noumenal object. Of course neither Putnam, nor Kant to whom this view is ascribed, maintain that this *something* is a *noumenal* chair to which the chair as it *appears* corresponds. There is no one to one correspondence between noumenal and phenomenal objects. But on Kant's view, any judgement about external or internal objects is to be interpreted nevertheless as saying that the noumenal world as a whole is such that this is the judgement which beings like ourselves would make. "Power is ascribed to *the whole noumenal world*."[28] However, does Putnam himself endorse this view? If he too posited a whole noumenal world which is supposed to provide the interpretation-independent "materia" for the construction of "real objects," then he might be called, in Krausz's words: "an external constructive realist," a realist who does not abandon the notion of a noumenon-like reality altogether. On the basis of what Putnam says about the constructions of objects from "experiential inputs," Krausz describes him as an "external constructive realist."[29]

I wonder however whether this label can be applied, if the "external constructive realist" is one who holds that some *presystematic* materia must be admitted. Since the "very *inputs* upon which our knowledge is based are conceptually contaminated . . ."[30] according to Putnam, I do not know how it can be said that "his view allows the minimal claim that there is *presystematic materia* upon which our knowledge is based."[31] It seems to me that Putnam's IR cannot be placed on a par with those versions of CR in the figures, which remain committed to the notion of a *presystematic interpretation-independent* reality—a notion that harks back to Kant's "thing-in-itself."

Krausz himself has clearly expressed the central tenet of IR, namely, "all things and their features should be understood in *relational* terms as expressed in (Putnam's) idea of *conceptual relativism.*"[32] This idea is not incompatible with realism. On the contrary it is an integral part of his "internal realism" or "relative realism" as it might be aptly called. And this realism can be introduced "without helping itself to the notion of the thing in itself."[33]

At this point IR seems to coalesce with constructivism. Any notion of a presystemic transcendent reality is dropped. There even seems to be a slide towards global "property constructivism," for neither the properties of middle-sized objects, nor the microstructural features of elements can escape the sweep of intentionality. But does this not amount to a "constructivist reductio" of realism as Krausz says? How can IR syncretise constructivism with its professed realism?

The points stated at the outset and stressed repeatedly in the book may be noted once again to understand how this syncreticism could be possible.

(1) Things and their features do exist independently notwithstanding their perspectival nature. Even if we cannot "view" them "from nowhere," they are *not our own making*, the internal realists maintain like all realists. They are not projections and reifications of our own conceptual and cognitive nature, and are in this sense *non-epistemic*. This minimal sense of the *independence condition* can be adapted to the basic idea of realism noted before. Indeed the existence of planets does not depend on us. However, contrary to the standard construal of realism, IR maintains that "how many planets there are in the solar system" is a question which cannot be answered *intelligibly* without referring *to us* and *our counting systems*. The independence condition, in its minimal sense does not mandate transcendence. This brings IR close to constructivism.

(2) Krausz sums up the dual claim of IR very clearly. (a) Real things and their features are not anyone's making.(This is welcome to realism though it is denied by constructivism.) But at the same time, IR maintains additionally that (b) the *condition of intelligibility* is built into the notion of an object (or reality) such that it can be intelligibly talked about only when construed as thinkable, knowable and describable.[34] (This is welcome to constructivism.) No meaningful discourse is possible about anything, including its most fundamental features, unless it is an object, at least a putative object of some belief, conception or knowledge. To stress *relativity* of things and their features to thought in this way however, is not to deny that things exist whether or not we know or say anything about them. Relativity here

means that things which we may or may not know, are *not transcendent*, that is, they are not trans-conceptual, trans-cognitive and trans-phenomenal.

(3) "External" or "transcendent" realists are opposed to this very idea of relativization. They may grudgingly admit at most that an idea of secondary quality like warmth can be *relativized*. Surely there is no sense in saying that an object itself is warm apart from the touching hand. But this according to them is only an *appearance*, something we *project* upon the thing which it really does not have. IR by contrast holds that the object *really* has warmth, though *relationally* and this feature is not a projection. The object may certainly have a subvisible structure and causal power, but this does not mean that it does not have warmth. *All* features, primary and secondary, are *relational*, but are *not unreal* for being relational. The way things *appear* are the way they *are*.

(4) To appreciate how relativity is compatible with reality, one may follow Putnam by invoking a distinction between two kinds of nonepistemicity. In one sense, *not acceptable to IR*, things and their features are *radically non-epistemic*. This means things and their features are entirely independent of us. This is another way of saying that all our beliefs and conceptions may remain just as they are and yet reality and truth about reality may be entirely different from *all* our beliefs and conceptions held true by us at several stages of our cognitive enterprise. The "radically non-epistemic" is something *transcendent*, something that can transcend *all* states of knowledge. The kind of nonepistemicity which IR accepts by contrast is *non-epistemicity simpliciter*. In this sense the nonepistemic is *knowable*, though not a *projection* of the knowing mind. Things and their features are non-epistemic in the sense that they are not our own making. The features are *not projected* on to something which does not have them.

(5) Projection means imposing something upon something else which does not have what we impose upon it. When a thing is believed to have some property, even microstructural property, no realist, and also no internal realist would say that this was a projection of the knowing mind, or of a certain theory which the knowing mind conceives at a certain stage of inquiry. The knowing mind or the theory it conceives does not *impart* the microstructural property to a stuff any more than the touching hand *imparts* warmth to a body which does not have it. Of course the claim that the stuff really has the property which a theory conceives it to have is a defeasible claim. Some other theory may conceive it to have a different property. The fact remains that the stuff must be said to have the composition which *some* theory conceives it to have. We cannot meaningfully talk about anything that is *totally unrelated* to *all* our beliefs and conceptions.

If the term "construction" carries with it the idea of imputation—projection or ascription, it would be hard to find a place for it within realism, both "external" and "internal." A non-imputationist version of constructive realism however is resonant with internal realist ideas. The kind of "constructive realism" which can properly be called irenic seems to be a realism minus absolutism and a constructivism minus projectivism.

Notes

1. Michael Krausz, *Limits of Rightness* (Lanham, Md.: Rowman & Littlefield, 2000).

2. Edward Craig, "Realism and Antirealism," in *Routledge Encyclopedia of Philosophy*, vol. 8, ed. Edward Craig (London: Routledge, 1998), 115.

3. Stephen M. Downes, "Constructivism," in *Routledge Encyclopedia of Philosophy*, vol. 2, 625.

4. Downes, "Constructivism," 625.

5. Bernard Williams, *Descartes: The Project of Pure Enquiry* (Harmondsworth, Middlesex: Harvester Press, 1978), 64.

6. Williams, *Descartes: The Project of Pure Enquiry*, 64-66, 236-46.

7. Downes, "Constructivism," 625.

8. Krausz, *Limits*, 26-27.

9. Michael Krausz and Richard Shusterman, ed., *Interpretation, Relativism, and the Metaphysics of Culture: Themes in the Philosophy of Joseph Margolis* (Amherst, N.Y.: Humanity Books, 1999), 8.

10. See Krausz, *Limits*, 25. Emphasis added.

11. Krausz, *Limits*, 27.

12. Krausz, *Limits*, 31. The line is quoted by Krausz from Paul Thom, "Rightness and Success in Interpretation," in *"Is There a Single Right Interpretation?* ed. Michael Krausz (University Park: Pennsylvania State University Press, 2001).

13. Krausz, *Limits*, 31.

14. Krausz, *Limits*, 26.

15. Krausz, *Limits*, 26.

16. Krausz, *Limits*, 30. Emphasis added.

17. Krausz, *Limits*, 27.

18. Krausz, *Limits*, 42. See also 37-38.

19. Krausz, *Limits*, 42.

20. Krausz, *Limits*, 44. The line quoted by Krausz from Nelson Goodman, "Just the Facts Ma'am," in *Relativism: Interpretation and Confrontation*, ed. Michael Krausz (Notre Dame: Notre Dame University Press, 1989).

21. Krausz, *Limits*, 45.

22. Krausz, *Limits*, 51-56.

23. Krausz, *Limits*, 52.

24. Krausz, *Limits*, 56.

25. Krausz, *Limits*, 57.

26. See Introduction by James Conant in Hilary Putnam, *Realism with a Human Face*, ed. James Conant (Cambridge Mass.: Harvard University Press, 1990), xxiii.

27. Hilary Putnam, *Reason, Truth and History* (Cambridge: Cambridge University Press, 1981), 61-62.

28. Putnam, *Reason, Truth*, 63.

29. Krausz, *Limits*, 77.

30. Putnam, *Reason, Truth*, 54.

31. Krausz, *Limits*, 77. Emphasis added.

32. Krausz, *Limits*, 77.

33. Hilary Putnam, *The Many Faces of Realism* (La Salle, Ill.: Open Court, 1987), 17.

34. Krausz, *Limits*, 83.

Bibliography

Bennet, Jonathan. *Kant's Analytic*. Cambridge: Cambridge University Press, 1966.

Broad, C. D. *Kant: An Introduction*. Ed. C. Lewy. Cambridge: Cambridge University Press, 1978.

Buchdahl, Gerd. "Kant: From Metaphysics to Transcendental Logic." In *Metaphysics and the Philosophy of Science*. Oxford: Basil, Blackwell, 1969.

Buchler, Justus, ed. *Philosophical Writings of Peirce*. New York: Dover Books.

Chattopadhyaya, D. P. *Anthropology and Historiography of Science*. Athens, Ohio: Ohio University Press, 1990.

————. *Induction, Probability and Skepticism*. Albany, N.Y.: State University of New York Press, 1991.

Craig, Edward. "Realism and Antirealism." In Edward Craig, ed. *Routledge Encyclopedia of Philosophy*. Vol. 8. London: Routledge, 1998.

Davidson, Donald. "A Coherence Theory of Truth and Knowledge." In Henrich Dieter, ed. *Kant oder Hegel*. Stuttgart: Klett-Cotta, 1983. Reprinted in Ernest Lepore, ed. *Truth and Interpretation: Perspectives on the Philosophy of Donald Davidson*. Oxford: Basil Blackwell, 1986.

————. "On the Very Idea of a Conceptual Scheme." In *Inquiries into Truth and Interpretation*. Oxford: Clarendon, 1984.

————. "The Structure and Content of Truth." *The Journal of Philosophy* LXXXVII, no. 6 (June 1990).

Delaney, C. F. "Presidential Address: Beyond Realism and Antirealism." In *Proceedings of the American Catholic Philosophical Association* (1985).

Devitt, Michael. *Realism and Truth*. Oxford: Basil Blackwell, 1984 (Princeton: Princeton University Press, 1984).

————. "Meanings just ain't in the head." In George Boolos, ed. *Meaning and Method: Essays in Honour of Hilary Putnam*. New York: Cambridge University Press, 1990.

Donnellan, Keith. "Reference and Definite Descriptions." In Stephen Schwartz, ed. *Naming, Necessity and Natural Kinds*. Ithaca, N.Y.: Cornell University Press,

1977.

Downes, Stephen M. "Constructivism." In Edward Craig, ed. *Routledge Encyclo-pedia of Philosophy*. Vol. 2. London: Routledge, 1998.

Dummett, Michael. "Realism." In *Truth and Other Enigmas*.London: Duckworth, 1978.

Feibleman, James K. *An Introduction to the Philosophy of Charles S. Peirce*. Cam-bridge, Mass.: MIT Press, 1969.

Freeman, Eugene, and Henryk Skolimowski. "The Search for Objectivity in Peirce and Popper." In Paul S. Schilpp, ed. *The Philosophy of Karl Popper*, Book 1. La Salle, Ill.: Open Court, 1974.

Gallie, W. B. *Peirce and Pragmatism*. New York: Dover Publications, 1966.

Goodman, Nelson. *Problems and Projects*. Indianapolis, Ind.: Bobbs Merrill, 1972.

———. "The Way the World Is." In *Problems and Projects*. 1972.

———. "A World of Individuals." In *Problems amd Projects*. 1972.

Goodman, Nelson with W. V. O. Quine. "Steps toward a Constructive Nominalism." In *Problems and Projects*. 1972.

———. *The Structure of Appearance*. 3d ed. Dordrecht: Reidl, 1977.

———. *Ways of Worldmaking*. Indianapolis, Ind.: Hackett, 1978.

———. "Just the Facts Ma'am." In Michael Krausz, ed. *Relativism: Interpretation and Confrontation*. Notre Dame: Notre Dame University Press, 1989.

Gupta, Chhanda. "Putnam's Resolution of the Popper-Kuhn Contoversy." *The Philosophical Quarterly* 43, no. 172 (July 1993).

Gutting, Gary, ed. *Paradigms and Revolutions: Appraisals and Applications of Thomas Kuhn's Philosophy of Science*. Notre Dame: Notre Dame University Press, 1980.

Hacking, Ian. *Representing and Intervening: Introductory topics in the philoso-phy of natural science*. Cambridge: Cambridge University Press, 1983.

Hahlweg, Kai, and C. A. Hooker, eds. *Issues in Evolutionary Epistemology*. Al-bany, N.Y.: State University of New York Press, 1989.

Hausman, Carl R. *Charles S. Peirce: Evolutionary Epistemiology*. Cambridge: Cam-bridge University Press, 1993.

Horwich, Paul. "Three Forms of Realism." *Synthese* 51, no. 2 (1982).

Hume, David. *Enquiry Concerning Human Understanding*. Ed. L. A. Selby Bigge. London: Oxford University Press, 1902.

Kant, Immanuel. *Critique of Pure Reason*. Trans. Norman Kemp Smith. London: Macmillan, 1933.

King, M. D. "Reason, Tradition and the Progressiveness in Science." In Gary Gutting, ed. *Paradigms and Revolutions*. Notre Dame: Notre Dame University Press, 1980.

Kitcher, Philip. "Theories, Theorists and Theoretical Change." *Philosophical Re-view* lxxxvii, no. 4 (October 1978).

Krausz, Michael and Richard Shusterman, eds. *Interpretation, Relativism and the Metaphysics of Culture: Themes in the Philosophy of Joseph Margolis*.

Amherst, N.Y.: Humanity Books, 1999.

Krausz, Michael. *Limits of Rightness*. Lanham, Md.: Rowman and Littlefield, 2000.

Kripke, Saul. "Naming and Necessity." In Donald Davidson and Gilbert Harman, eds. *Semantics of Natural Language*. Dordrecht: Reidel, 1972.

Kuhn, Thomas S. "Objectivity, Value Judgement and Theory Choice." In *The Essential Tension*. Chicago: University of Chicago Press, 1977.

———. "Commensurability, Comparability, Communicability." *PSA 1982*. Vol. 2. East Lansing, Mich.: Philosophy of Science Association, 1983.

Leplin, Jarrett, ed. *Scientific Realism*. Berkeley: University of California Press, 1984.

Mackie, J. L. *Problems from Locke*. Oxford: Clarendon, 1976.

Musgrave, Alan. *Common Sense, Science and Skepticism: A historical introduction to the theory of knowledge*. Cambridge: Cambridge University Press, 1993.

Niniluoto, Ilkka. *Is Science Progressive*. Dordrecht: Reidel, 1984.

Peirce, Charles Sanders. *The Collected Papers of Charles Sanders Peirce*. Eds. Charles Hartshorne and Paul Weiss. Vols. 1-6. Cambridge, Mass.: Harvard University Press, 1931-1935.

———*The Collected Papers of Charles Sanders Peirce*. Ed. Arthur W. Burks. Vols. 7-8. Cambridge: Cambridge University Press, 1958.

———. "The Fixation of Belief." In *Essays in the Philosophy of Science*. Ed. Vincent Tomas. Indianapolis, Ind.: Bobbs Merrill, 1957.

Plantinga, Alvin. "How to be an Anti-realist." *Proceedings of the American Philosophical Association*, 56 (1982).

Popper, Karl R. *Conjectures and Refutations: The Growth of Scientific Knowledge*. London: Routledge, 1963.

———. "Three Views Concerning Human Knowledge." In *Conjectures and Refutations: The Growth of Scientific Knowledge*. 1963.

———. *Objective Knowledge: An Evolutionary Approach*. Oxford: Clarendon, 1972.

———. "Replies to Critics." In P. A. Schilpp, ed. *The Philosophy of Karl Popper*. Book 2. La Salle, Ill. Open Court, 1974.

———. *Undended Quest: An Intellectual Autobiography*. London: Fontana, 1976.

Putnam, Hilary. "The Corroboration of Theories." In P. A. Schilpp, ed. *The Philosophy of Karl Popper*. Book 1, La Salle, Ill.: Open Court, 1974.

———. "The Meaning of 'Meaning.'" In *Mind, Language and Reality, Philosophical Papers*. Vol. 2. Cambridge: Cambridge University Press. 1975.

———. *Reason, Truth and History*. Cambridge: Cambridge University Press, 1981.

———. *Realism and Reason, Philosophical Papers*. Vol. 3. Cambridge: Cambridge University Press, 1983.

———. "Reflections on Goodman's Ways of Worldmaking." In *Realism and Reason, Philosophical Papers*. Vol. 3. 1983.

———. "Why Reason Can't be Naturalized." *Synthese* 52, no. 1 (July 1982). Reprinted in *Realism and Reason, Philosophical Papers*. Vol. 3. 1983.

————. "Equivalence." In *Realism and Reason, Philosophical Papers*. Vol. 3. 1983.

————. *The Many Faces of Realism*. La Salle, Ill.: Open Court, 1987.

————. *Representation and Reality*. Cambridge, Mass.: MIT Press, 1988.

————. *Realism with a Human Face*. Ed. James Conant. Cambridge, Mass.: Harvard University Press, 1990.

————. "A Defense of Internal Realism." In *Realism with a Human Face*. 1990.

————. "The Way the World Is." In *Realism with a Human Face*. 1990.

————. "Truth and Convention." In *Realism with a Human Face*. 1990.

————. "Is Water Necessarily H$_2$O." In *Realism with a Human Face*. 1990.

Putnam, Hilary with Ruth Anna Putnam. "William James's Ideas." In *Realism with a Human Face*. 1990.

Putnam, Hilary. "A Comparison of Something with Something Else." *New Literary History* xvii, 1985. Reprinted in *Words and Life*. Ed. James Conant. Cambridge, Mass.: Harvard University Press, 1994.

Quine, W. V. O. *From a Logical Point of View*. Cambridge, Mass.: Harvard University Press, 1953.

————. "On What There Is." In *From a Logical Point of View*. 1953.

————. "Logic and the Reification of Universals." In *From a Logical Point of View*. 1953.

————. "Two Dogmas of Empiricism." In *From a Logical Point of View*. 1953.

————. "Identity, Ostension and Hypostasis." In *From a Logical Point of View*. 1953.

————. "Ontic Decision." In *Word and Object*. Cambridge, Mass.: MIT Press, 1960.

————. "Carnap and Logical Truth." In P. A. Schilpp, ed. *The Philosophy of Rudolf Carnap*. La Salle, Ill.: Open Court, 1963.

————. "Epistemiology Naturalized." In *Ontological Relativity and Other Essays*. New York: Columbia University Press, 1969.

————. "On Popper's Negative Methodology." In P. A. Schilpp, ed. *The Philosophy of Karl Popper*. Book 1. La Salle, Ill.: Open Court, 1974.

————. "On Empirically Equivalent Systems of the World." *Erkenntnis* 9, 1975.

————. "The Nature of Natural Knowledge." In S. Guttenplan, ed. *Mind and Language*. Oxford: Clarendon, 1975.

————. *Theories and Things*. Cambridge, Mass.: Belknap Press of Harvard University Press, 1981.

————. "Goodman's Ways of Worldmaking." In *Theories and Things*. 1981.

————. "On the Very Idea of a Third Dogma." In *Theories and Things*. 1981.

————. *Pursuit of Truth*. Cambridge, Mass.: Harvard University Press, 1990.

Rescher, Nicholas. *Methodological Pragmatism*. Oxford: Basil Blackwell, 1977.

Rorty, Richard. *Consequences of Pragmatism*. Brighton, U.K.: Harvester Press, 1982.

————. "Pragmatism, Davidson and Truth." In Ernest Lepore, ed. *Truth and Interpretation: Perspectives on the Philosophy of Donald Davidson*. Oxford: Basil Blackwell, 1986.

————."Putnam and the Relativist Menace." *The Journal of Philosophy* XC, no. 9 (September 1993).

Russell, Bertrand. *The Problems of Philosophy*. Oxford: Oxford University Press, 1912.

Sandberg, Eric C. " Thinking Things-in-Themselves." In Gerhard Funke and Thomas M. Seebohm, eds. *Current Continental Research 603, Proceedings of the Sixth International Kant Congress*. Vol. 11/2 (1989). Lanham, Md.: Center of Advanced Research in Phenomenology and University Press of America, 1989.

Scheffler, Israel. *The Four Pragmatists*. London: Routledge, 1974.

Sen, Pranab Kumar. *Reference and Truth*. New Delhi: Indian Council of Philosophical Research in association with Allied Publishers, 1991.

Skagestad, Peter. *The Road of Inquiry*. New York: Columbia University Press, 1981.

Strawson, P. F. *The Bounds of Sense*. London: Methuen, 1966.

————. *Skepticism and Naturalism: Some Varieties*. New York: Columbia University Press, 1985.

Stroud, Barry. *The Significance of Philosophical Scepticism*. Oxford: Clarendon, 1984.

Thom, Paul. "Rightness and Success in Interpretation." In Michael Krausz, ed. *Is There a Single Right Interpretation?* University Park: Pennsylvania State University Press, 2001.

Van Cleve, Jim. "Incongruent Counterparts and Things In Themselves." In Gerhard Funke and Thomas M. Seebohm, eds. *Current Continental Research, 603, Proceedings of the Sixth International Kant Congress*. Vol 11/2. Lanham, Md.: Center for Advanced Research in Phenomenology and University Press of America, 1989.

Veatch, Henry B. "Is Quine a Metaphysician?" *the review of metaphysics* (March 1978).

Whorf, Benjamin Lee. *Language Thought and Reality: Selected Writings of Benjamin Lee Whorf*. Ed. John B. Carroll. Cambridge, Mass.: MIT Press, 1956.

Williams, Bernard. *Descartes: The Project of Pure Enquiry*. Harmondsworth, Middlesex: Harvester Press, 1978.

Woozley, A. D. "Universals." In Paul Edwards, ed. *Encyclopedia of Philosophy*. Vol. 8. New York: Macmillan and Free Press, 1967.

Index

version of constructive, 140;
naive, 87, 89; new, 87, 89;
versus nominalism, 53-78;
non-fallibilistic, 87, 88, 89;
non-imputationist version of
constructive, 138, 139;
perspective, 87, 89;
piecemeal constructivist,145;
relative, 148; versus relativism, 119-
121; scientific, 5, 131, 132, 134;
semantic, 85, 86, 87, 95;
transcendent, 5-6, 7, 12, 16, 20, 23-
26, 33, 61, 85, 90, 92, 108, 149;
transcendental, 24; trans-
cognitive, 5-7, 16, 18, 20, 24,
25, 26, 85, 90, 92, 93; trans-
conceptual, 5, 16, 20, 25, 26, 85, 90,
92; trans-phenomenal, 5, 6, 7, 9, 16,
18, 20, 25, 26, 85, 90, 120
reality, 1, 2, 3, 25, 55, 62, 96;
absolute conception of, 139,
141; interpretation-
independent, 148
reductionism, 30
reference, 8, 10-12, 14-17, 60, 61, 64, 70,
75, 76, 77, 78, 81, 82; as a social
phenonmenon, 16, 17; causal
theory of, 15-17; interpretation-
independent, 77; objective, 34, 35
relativism, 1, 2, 60, 61, 75, 120, 121, 125,
128, 131, 132; conceptual, 148;
ontological, 60, 61; radical, 75;
about truth, 46
relativity, 74, 120, 148, 149;
conceptual, 12, 17, 20, 23,
25, 28, 29, 35, 41, 47, 48, 49,
129, 130; ontological, 60, 61,
74, 75, 82, 128, 129, 130; to
version, 75
relativization, 75, 77, 149
Rorty, Richard, 33, 106
Russell, Bertrand, 36, 56

Sapir, Edward, 64
scheme, 30, 43, 62, 63, 65, 72, 78, 82, 83,
129, 131
scheme-content dualism, 20, 29, 30, 31,
32, 33, 34, 36, 41-42, 106
Sellars, R. W., 103
Sextus, 90, 91
skeptic/ skepticism, 19, 37, 38, 40, 47,
84, 90, 91, 92, 93, 95, 96;
academic, 90; Cartesian, 91, 92;
about physical objects, 37, 38;
against realisms, 81-96
subjective, 1, 2-3
subjectivism, 2, 108, 109, 125

Tarski, Alfred, 75
theory, underdetermination of, 83, 125
Thom, Paul, 140, 141, 142, 143, 146
transcendental arguement, 19
translation, 82, 126; indeterminacy of,
64, 83
true/truth, 37, 40, 45, 46, 47, 48, 63, 64,
75, 83, 84, 99, 100, 104, 105, 106,
107, 108, 110, 112, 114, 116, 122,
128; absolute, 112; -claim, 45;
-conditions, 37, 40, 46, 64, 121; in
its context, 47, 48; externalist, 116;
as idealization of rational
acceptability, 112, 113; as idealized
justified assertability, 46, 112;
radically non-epistemic, 48;
relative, 112; and warrantability,
112, 113

universals, 53, 54, 55, 56, 57, 58, 67, 71,
77; as common property, 54, 55,
56; as entity, 53, 54, 55, 58;
mind-independent, 56; relational,
56

version-relative worlds, 61

About the Author

Chhanda Gupta (Ph.D., 1971) is professor of philosophy at Jadavpur University, Calcutta, and the author of *Realism versus Realism*, the first edition of which was published by Jadavpur University and Allied Publishers in 1995. She has published many articles in different philosophical journals and anthologies including *The Philosophical Quarterly*, *Philosophy East and West* and *Journal of Indian Council of Philosophical Research*, and has co-edited three books: *Essays in Social and Political Philosophy* (1989), *Philosophy of Science* (1992) and *Cultural Otherness and Beyond* (1998). She was a Fellow of the Indian Council of Philosophical Research (1985-86) and a Fulbright Research Fellow at Harvard University in 1985 and 1995.